MW00816909

HISTORIC
𝔊erman 𝔑ewspapers
ONLINE
Second Edition

Compiled by
Ernest Thode

Genealogical Publishing Company
Baltimore, Maryland

Published by Genealogical Publishing Company
Baltimore, Maryland, 2018

Library of Congress Catalog Card Number 2018961889
ISBN 9780806320922

Contents

Introduction

This book is an attempt to discover all digitally available German-language newspapers of an arbitrary age (50 years or older), list them by location and title, and narrow down the dates for which they are available online. These newspapers are useful to genealogists, family historians, demographers, migration researchers, and social historians. One tenet of genealogical research is that it is not complete until you have performed a thorough search of all the resources available. To me, that includes newspapers. And in the case of German-Americans or Germans, it includes German-language newspapers.

To be sure, many American German-language newspapers are only available at libraries in hard copies or microform; for a survey, see *The German Language Press of the Americas*, by Karl J. R. Arndt and May Olson, and https://chroniclingamerica.loc.gov/newspapers/. For European papers, check the holdings of the International Newspaper Museum in Aachen (international, first editions, final editions, famous events), the German Newspaper Museum in Dortmund (more comprehensive), and the German Press Research Institute in Bremen (very early papers, propaganda papers). This book is limited to online historic newspapers.

This second edition of *Historic German Newspapers Online* is greatly enlarged, as more and more historic German newspapers have been digitized since the first edition was published. Nearly all are accessible on free sites of universities, libraries, institutions, and museums, though a few are found only on subscription services. As a rule, I listed daily or weekly newspapers and not monthly publications, but I arbitrarily included some one-time, seasonal, or yearly publications for their genealogical significance—for example, wartime casualty lists, spa visitor lists, and a sampling of annual school reports that generally include pupils' ages, names and occupations of parents, and residence. To find school reports for other areas, use a search engine with the German name of the place, the word *Bericht* or *Jahresbericht*, and a word such as *Schule* or *Gymnasium*.

Certain websites are particularly useful because of improved OCR technology that works with the Fraktur typeface, has full-text search capability, and covers multiple newspapers. For example, ANNO (http://anno.onb.ac.at/) covers hundreds of titles from the entire Austro-Hungarian Empire, with 20 million newspaper pages and an every-word search capability; Bavarica (https://www.bsb-muenchen.de/en/collections/bavarica/) does much the same for Bavaria, including the Palatinate; and the Europeana project (https://www.europeana.eu/portal/en) has coverage throughout Europe. Check each of these sites for your ancestors and their home village, as the every-name overall index to these three sites might include your ancestor's name.

One of the most productive types of paper for genealogical purposes is the official governmental gazette that published official items such as applications to emigrate, forced auctions, governmental appointments, government payments to fire and disaster victims, and sometimes births, marriages, and deaths. Typical titles are *Allgemeiner Anzeiger, Amtsblatt, Intelligenzblatt,* and *Regierungsblatt.* Sometimes a *Beilage* or supplement is the section that contains the emigration requests and auctions. Typically there will be fairly long runs of these papers online, as they document official acts.

General newspapers have a wide variety of names. *Abend-, Morgen-, Tages-* are prefixes for dailies, *Wochen-* for weeklies. *Arbeiter-* or *Volks-* are tipoffs for a labor or socialist paper. A few of the most common newspaper titles are *Anzeiger, Beilage* or *Beylage, Beobachter, Blatt, Bote, Herold, Journal, Korrespondenz, Kurier, Nachrichten, Post, Presse, Rundschau,* and *Zeitung.*

To use this book, first go to the **Places** section, look up your locality of interest or the largest nearby city, and note the title of the paper and the years covered. In non-German countries, look for large cities or capital cities. Next, go to the **Titles** section, noting the abbreviation for the URL (website) where it is located. Then click on the **Key to URLs** section and go to the website corresponding to the abbreviation you found. As of August 2018 all URLs were valid, but navigation within websites varies; most home pages are portals and you have to look deeper. Look for words like *elektronisch, digital,* or *Digitalisat.*

This book's coverage is quite literally worldwide. Of course, by far the largest number are from Germany, followed by Austria, then present-day Poland, etc. But astonishingly, all the following places from A to Z published German-language newspapers, which are all available online and are listed in this book: **A**pia, Samoa; **B**runico (Bruneck), Italy; **B**altiysk (Pillau), Russia; **C**airo (Kairo), Egypt; **C**uritiba, Brazil; **D**aressalaam (Dar es Salaam), Tanzania; **E**ast Kildonan, Manitoba, Canada; **E**gg Harbor, New Jersey, USA; **F**ernheim, Paraguay; **G**uebwiller (Gebweiler), France; **H**ollerich, Luxembourg; **I**stanbul (Konstantinopel), Turkey; **J**elgava, Latvia; **K**ošice (Kaschau), Slovakia; **L**emberg (Lviv), Ukraine; **M**exico City, Mexico; **N**ovisad, Serbia; **O**slo, Norway; **P**tuj (Pettau), Slovenia; **Q**ingdao (Tsingtau), China; **R**eval (Talinn), Estonia; **St**. Vith, Belgium; **T**anunda, Australia; **T**iflis, Georgia (country); **U**ničov (Mährisch Neustadt), Czech Republic; **V**ilnius (Wilna), Lithuania; **W**ałbrzych (Waldenburg), Poland; **X**anten, Germany; **Y**bbs an der Donau, Austria; and **Z**ürich, Switzerland.

Enjoy!

Key	Site	URL
Aargau	Canton Aargau Library	www.ag.ch/kantonsbibliothek
Aargau Dig	Aargau Digital	http://kbaargau.visual-library.de/
AAS	Austrian Academy of Science	www.oeaw.ac.at
Abendblatt	Hamburger Abendblatt	https://www.abendblatt.de/archiv/
A-Bib	Anarchistische Bibliothek	www.a-bibliothek.org
ABLIT	Abenteuerliteratur	www.abenteuer-literatur.de
ALO	Austrian Literature Online	www.literature.at
Altenburg	Kreisarchiv Altenburg	www.altenburg.eu
Amberg	Staatsarchiv Amberg	www.gda.bayern.de/archive/amberg/
Anarch	Anarchismus.at	www.anarchismus.at
Ancestry	Ancestry.com	www.ancestry.com
ANL	Austrian National Library	www.onb.ac.at/en/
ANNO	AustriaN Newspapers Online	http://anno.onb.ac.at
ArbZ	Arbeiter-Zeitung	www.arbeiter-zeitung.at
Archivaria	Archivaria	www.archivaria.com
ArchOrg	Archive.org	www.archive.org
Baden	Badische Landesbibliothek	www.blb-karlsruhe.de
Baeck	Leo Baeck Institute	www.lbi.org
Bavarica	Bavarica	http://bavarica.digitale-sammlungen.de

Key	Site	URL
BBC	Baltycka Biblioteka Cyfrowa	http://bibliotekacyfrowa.eu
BBF	Library of Educational Research	http://bbf.dipf.de
Belg Arch	National Archives of Belgium	http://arch.arch.be
Belg Lib	Royal Library of Belgium	www.kbr.be
Berlin Lib	Berlin State Library	http://staatsbibliothek-berlin.de/en/
Bethel	Bethel College (Mennonite)	https://mla.bethelks.edu/gmsources/newspapers/
BF	Burgenländische Freiheit	http://bf-archiv.at
Bio	Biodiversity Library	www.biodiversitylibrary.org
Blank	Albrecht Blank	www/albrecht-blank.eu
Boxer	Boxeraufstand	www.boxeraufstand.com/1901/pekinger_deutsche_zeitung_060101.jpg
Brazil	Brazilian National Library	https://bndigital.bn.gov.br/hemeroteca-digital
Breslau	Wroclaw University Library (Breslau)	www.bibliotekacyfrowa.pl/dlibra/
BritLib	British Library	www.bl.uk
BSL	Bayerische Landesbibliothek	www.bayerische-landesbibliothek-online.de
CH	Swiss Confederation	www.admin.ch
Chron	Chronicling America	http://chroniclingamerica.loc.gov/newspapers/
Cieszyn	Cieszyn Library	http://biblioteka.cieszyn.pl
Colo	Colorado Historic Newspapers	www.coloradohistoricnewspapers.org

8

Key	Site	URL
CompMem	Compact Memory (Jewish)	http://compactmemory.de
CRL	Center for Research Libraries	www.crl.edu
Croatia	Croatian Historic Newspapers	http://dnc.nsk.hr/newspapers/English.aspx
Dach	Dachau Municipal Archive	http://archiv.dachau.de
DeGruy	De Gruyter	https://www.degruyter.com/view/db/vosso
DiFMOE	Digitales Forum Mittel- und Osteuropa	www.difmoe.eu
DigiBern	DigiBern	https://www.digibern.ch/ueberblick/medien?tid=27
DigiBib	Gen-Wiki Digitale Bibliothek	http://wiki-de.genealogy.net/Portal:DigiBib
DigiPress	DigiPress	http://digipress.digitale-sammlungen.de
Dilibri	Digital Library Rheinland-Pfalz	www.dilibri.de
Dithm	Dithmarschen Wiki	www.dithmarschen-wiki.de
DLS	Digital Library of Slovenia	www.dlib.si
DSL	Saxon State Library Dresden	www.slub-dresden.de
Elbing	Elbing Library	http://dlibra.bibliotekaelblaska.pl/dlibra/
E-Lib	Swiss Electronic Library	www.e-rara.ch
Est	Estonian National Library	http://dea.digar.ee
Estonia	National Archives of Estonia	http://ra.ee/
Eur	Europeana	www.europeana.eu
Eusk	Kreisarchiv Euskirchen	www.kreis-euskirchen.de/kreishaus/kreisarchiv/unterhaltungsblatt.php

Key	Site	URL
Eutin	Eutin State Library	www.lb-eutin.de/
FES	Friedrich Ebert Foundation	www.fes.de
France	French National Library	www.bnf.fr/en/tools/a.welcome_to_the_bnf.html
Gale	Cengage	www.gale.cengage.com
GateBay	Gateway Bayern (Bavaria)	www.gateway-bayern.de
GB	GenealogyBank	www.genealogybank.com
Geneanet	Geneanet	www.geneanet.org
GHM	German Historical Museum	www.dhm.de
GNL	German National Library	www.dnb.de/EN/Kataloge/kataloge_node.html
Goo	Google Books	http://books.google.de
Goo News	Google Historic Newspaper Archive	http://news.google.com/newspapers
Hathi	HathiTrust	www.hathitrust.org
Hennef	Hennef City Library	http://da.stadt-hennef.de
HIgnst	Heiligenstadt City Archive	http://heilbad-heiligenstadt.de/stadtinformation/stadtarchiv.html
Humb	Humboldt University Berlin	www.hu-berlin.de/suche/
Hungary	Electronic Periodical Archive Hungary	http://epa.Oszk.hu
IHS	Indiana Historical Society	www.indianahistory.org
Jag	Jagellionian Digital Library	http://jbc.bj.uj.edu.pl/dlibra/
Jelenia	Jelenia Gora Library	http://jbc.jelenia-gora.pl/

Key	Site	URL
Jud Allg	Juedische Allgemeine Zeitung	www.juedische-allgemeine.de
KDL	Kentucky Digital Library	http://kdl.kyvl.org
Kosz	Koszalin State Archive	www.koszalin.ap.gov.pl
Kram	Kramerius	http://kramerius.nkp.cz
Kuja	Kujawsko-Pomorska Digital Library	http://kpbc.umk.pl/dlibra/
Latvia	Latvian National Library	www.lnb.lv/en
Leipzig	Leipzig City Museum	www.stadtgeschichtliches-museum-leipzig.de/index_en.php
Liecht	Eliechtensteinensia	www.eliechtensteinensia.li
Lippe	Lippe Library Detmold	www.llb-detmold.de/
Lpzg	Leipzig City Museum	www.stadtgeschichtliches-museum-leipzig.de/index_en.php
Lux	Luxemburgensia	www.luxemburgensia.bnl.lu
Meck	Mecklenburg-Vorpommern State Library	www.digitale-bibliothek-mv.de
Memel	Memeler Dampfboot	http://memel.klavb.lt/
MICHAEL	Multilingual Inventory Cultural Heritage	www.michael-culture.eu/
NAUSA	North American Emigration Center	www.nausa.uni-oldenburg.de/pionier/frame.html
NewsArch	Newspaper Archives	www.genealogybank.com/gbnk/newspapers/
Newsbank	Newsbank	www.newsbank.com
Newspapers	America's Historic Newspapers	www.newsbank.com
NRW	Zeitpunkt NRW	https://zeitpunkt.nrw/

Key	Site	URL
NRWLib	North Rhine-Westphalia Library	www.hbz-nrw.de/recherche/
NWZ	Nordwestzeitung Oldenburg	https://epaper.nwzonline.de/archiv/
NZ	PapersPast	https://paperspast.natlib.govt.nz
NZZ	Neue Zürcher Zeitung	www.nzz.ch
Ohio Mem	Ohio Memory Project	www.ohiomemory.org
OKHist	Oklahoma History	www.okhistory.org/research/newspapers
OPACP	OPAC Plus	https://openlibrary.org
Ostfr	Ostfriesen	http://ostfriesen.advantage-preservation.com/
PNP	Passauer Neue Presse	www.pnp.de/service/verlag/historisches_zeitungsarchiv/
Poland	Polish National Library	www.bn.org.pl/en/digital-resources/polona/
Polona	Polish Digital Library	https://polona.pl
Pom	Pomeranian Digital Library	http://pbc.gda.pl/
Poznan	Greater Poland Digital Library	www.wbc.poznan.pl/dlibra/
Raether	Raether Buch	www.raether-buch.de/
Rendsbg	Rendsburg Municipal Archive	www.rendsburg.de/tourismus-freizeit-kultur/museen-archive.html
RERO	REseau ROmand (western Switzerland)	https://www.e-newspaperarchives.ch/?l=en
RheinM	Rhine-Main Library in Wiesbaden	www.hs-rm.de/bibliothek
Sandusky	Sandusky Public Library (Ohio)	http://sanduskyhistory.blogspot.com/2007/11/
SBgZ	Siebenbürgische Zeitung	www.siebenbuerger.de/zeitung/

Key	Site	URL
Schaffh	Schaffhauser Nachrichten	www.shn.ch
SFU	Simon Fraser University (Canada)	http://newspapers.lib.sfu.ca
Silesia	Silesian Digital Library	www.sbc.org.pl/dlibra
Simplic	Simplicissimus	www.simplicissimus.info
Spiegel	Der Spiegel	www.spiegel.de
SPO	Scripta Paedagogica Online	http://bbf.dipf.de/scripta-paedagogica-online
Swarth	Swarthmore College Library	www.swarthmore.edu
Sweden	Royal Library of Sweden	www.kb.se/english/
Switz	Swiss National Library	www.nb.admin.ch
TCO	Texas Cultures Online	http://texashistory.unt.edu/explore/collections/TCO/
Tessmann	Tessmann Library	www.tessmann.it
Trove	Trove (Australia)	https://trove.nla.gov.au/newspaper
TX	Portal to Texas History	http://texashistory.unt.edu/explore/collections/TDNP/
UAUGS	University and State Library of Augsburg	www.bibliothek.uni-augsburg.de/
UBERN	University of Bern (Switzerland)	www.ub.unibe.ch
UBIEL	University of Bielefeld	http://ds.ub.uni-bielefeld.de/viewer/
UBONN	University of Bonn	http://s2w.hbz-nrw.de/ulbbn
UBREM	University of Bremen	http://brema.suub.uni-bremen.de
UBRUN	Technical University of Braunschweig	www.biblio.tu-bs.de/benutzung/flyer/digibib-bs2.pdf

Key	Site	URL
UCLAU	Technical University of Clausthal	www.ub.tu-clausthal.de/en/literatur-suchen/ezb/
UCOTT	Technical University of Cottbus	www.b-tu.de/b-tu/
UDARM	Technical University of Darmstadt	www.tu-darmstadt.de/index.en.jsp
UDRES	State and University Library of Dresden	www.slub-dresden.de/en/home/
UDUS	University of Düsseldorf	http://digital.ub.uni-duesseldorf.de/
UFBRG	University of Freiburg (Baden)	www.ub.uni-freiburg.de/?id=fz
UFFM	University of Frankfurt am Main	http://sammlungen.ub.uni-frankfurt.de/
UFRIB	University of Fribourg (Switzerland)	http://www2.fr.ch/bcuf/
UFULD	Fulda Technical Institute	https://fuldig.hs-fulda.de/viewer/zeitungen-und-zeitschriften/
UGDA	Gdańsk Polytechnic Institute	https://pg.edu.pl/
UGOT	University of Göttingen	http://gdz.sub.uni-goettingen.de/gdz/
UGRF	University of Greifswald	https://ub.uni-greifswald.de/
UHAL	University of Halle-Wittenberg	http://digitale.bibliothek.uni-halle.de/zd
UHBG	University of Hamburg	https://digitalisate.sub.uni-hamburg.de/zeitungen.html
UHEID	University of Heidelberg	www.ub.uni-heidelberg.de/helios/
UJENA	Technical University of Jena (Thuringia)	www.digitalesthueringen.de
UKASL	University of Kassel (Hesse)	www.uni-kassel.de/ub/index.php
UKIEL	University of Kiel	https://dibiki.ub.uni-kiel.de/

Key	Site	URL
UKLN	University of Cologne (Köln)	www.ub.uni-koeln.de/digital/digitsam/index_ger.html
UMST	University of Münster	www.ulb.uni-muenster.de/recherche/digibib/
UMUN	University of Munich (München)	www.ub.uni-muenchen.de/en/electronic-media/
UOLD	University of Oldenburg	www.bis.uni-oldenburg.de/startseite/
UpAust	Upper Austria State Library	www.landesbibliothek.at/
UPULA	University of Pola (Pula) (Croatia)	http://library.foi.hr/metelgrad/
UREG	University of Regensburg	http://rzblx1.uni-regensburg.de/ezeit/
UROS	University of Rostock	www.ub.uni-rostock.de/ub/xdlib/dlib_xde.shtml
USTR	University of Strasbourg (France)	www.bnu.fr/numistral/collections-numeriques
UTARTU	University of Tartu (Estonia)	https://utlib.ut.ee/en
UTUEB	University of Tübingen	https://tue.ibs-bw.de/
UZRCH	Technical University of Zürich	www.library.ethz.ch/en/Resources/Journals-newspapers
WarPr	wartimepress.com	www.wartimepress.com
WikiComm	Wikimedia Commons	http://commons.wikimedia.org/wiki/Main_Page
WikiS	WikiSource	http://de.wikisource.org
Worms	Stadtarchiv Worms	www.worms.de/de/kultur/stadtarchiv/aktuelles/WK-I/WK-I-WZ.php
ZEFYS	ZEFYS Zeitungsinformationssystem	http://zefys.staatsbibliothek-berlin.de/en/
Zeit	Die Zeit	www.zeit.de

Key	Site	URL
ZielG	University of Zielona Góra	http://zbc.uz.zgora.pl/dlibra
ZLB	Zentral- und Landesbibliothek Berlin	https://digital.zlb.de/viewer/.
ZVDD	Central List of Digitized Publications	www.zvdd.de/startseite/

Country	Published at	Title	Notes
Argentina	Buenos Aires	Argentinisches Wochenblatt	Argentina
Argentina	Buenos Aires	Hüben und drüben	Argentina
Australia	Adelaide	Adelaider Deutsche Zeitung	South Australia
Australia	Adelaide	Südaustralische Zeitung	South Australia
Australia	Tanunda and Adelaide	Süd Australische Zeitung	South Australia
Austria	Amstetten	Der Front-Kamerad	WW II paper
Austria	Aussee	Cur- und Fremden-Liste des Badeortes Aussee	spa visitors
Austria	Baden	Badener Bezirks-Blatt	Lower Austria
Austria	Baden	Badener Zeitungen	Lower Austria
Austria	Bludenz	Anzeiger für die Bezirke Bludenz und Montafon	Vorarlberg
Austria	Bludenz	Bludenzer Anzeiger	Vorarlberg
Austria	Braunau am Inn	Neue Warte am Inn	Upper Austria
Austria	Bregenz	Bregenzer Wochenblatt	Vorarlberg
Austria	Bregenz	Bregenzer/Vorarlberger Tagblatt	Vorarlberg
Austria	Bregenz	Der Vorarlberger	Vorarlberg
Austria	Bregenz	Der Vorarlberger Volksbote	Vorarlberg
Austria	Bregenz	Vorarlberger Landes-Zeitung	Vorarlberg
Austria	Bregenz	Vorarlberger Volksblatt	Vorarlberg
Austria	Bürs	Neueste Bürser Funken-Zeitung	Vorarlberg dialect

Country	Published at	Title	Notes
Austria	Dornbirn	Der Vorarlberger Volksfreund	Vorarlberg
Austria	Dornbirn	Vorarlberger Wacht	Vorarlberg
Austria	Feldkirch	Feldkircher Anzeiger	Vorarlberg
Austria	Feldkirch	Feldkircher Wochenblatt	Vorarlberg
Austria	Floridsdorf (Wien)	Floridsdorfer Zeitung	Vienna
Austria	Grätz	Grätzer Zeitung	Styria
Austria	Graz	Akademische Frauenblätter	academic women's paper
Austria	Graz	Allgemeine Eisenbahn-Zeitung	railroad paper
Austria	Graz	Arbeiterwille	labor paper
Austria	Graz	Die Tagespost	Styria
Austria	Graz	Frauenblätter	women's paper
Austria	Graz	Grazer Mittags-Zeitung	Styria
Austria	Graz	Grazer Tagblatt	Styria
Austria	Graz	Grazer Volksblatt	Styria
Austria	Graz	Grazer Zeitung	Styria
Austria	Graz	Iris	women's paper
Austria	Graz	SA im Feldgrau	WW II paper
Austria	Graz	Steirerland	WW II paper
Austria	Graz	Steyermärkische Intelligenz-Blätter der Grätzer Zeitung	Styria
Austria	Güssing/Köszeg	Günser Zeitung	Burgenland

Country	Published at	Title	Notes
Austria	Güssing/Kőszeg	Güssinger Zeitung	Burgenland
Austria	Hainburg an der Donau	Niederösterreichischer Grenzbote	Lower Austria
Austria	Hallein	Der Halleiner Bothe	
Austria	Hollabrunn	Amtsblatt der Bezirkshauptmannschaft Hollabrunn	Lower Austria
Austria	Innsbruck	Allgemeiner Tiroler Anzeiger	Alpine paper
Austria	Innsbruck	Andreas Hofer Wochenblatt	Alpine paper
Austria	Innsbruck	Der Alpenfreund	Alpine paper
Austria	Innsbruck	Der Bote für Tirol	Tirol
Austria	Innsbruck	Der Weckruf	Tirol
Austria	Innsbruck	Innsbrucker Nachrichten	Tirol
Austria	Innsbruck	Innsbrucker Zeitung	Tirol
Austria	Innsbruck	Innzeitung	Tirol
Austria	Innsbruck	Kaiserlich-Königlich privilegirter Bothe von und für Tirol und Vorarlberg	Tirol & Vorarlberg
Austria	Innsbruck	Neue Tiroler Stimmen	Tirol
Austria	Innsbruck	Südtiroler Heimat	South Tirol
Austria	Innsbruck	Südtiroler Ruf	regional paper
Austria	Innsbruck	Tiroler Bauern-Zeitung	Tirol agricultural
Austria	Innsbruck	Tiroler Schützenzeitung	Tirol
Austria	Innsbruck	Tiroler Zeitung	Catholic

Country	Published at	Title	Notes
Austria	Innsbruck	Ynnsbruckische Mittwochige Ordinari-Zeitung	Tirol
Austria	Ischl/Bad Ischl	Ischler Bade-Liste	spa visitors
Austria	Ischl/Bad Ischl	Ischler Fremden-Salon	resort paper
Austria	Klagenfurt	Alpenländische Rundschau	Alpine paper
Austria	Klagenfurt	Carinthia II	Carinthia
Austria	Klagenfurt	Carinthia. Zeitschrift für Vaterlandskunde, Belehrung und Unterlahtung	Carinthia
Austria	Klagenfurt	Freie Stimmen	labor paper
Austria	Klagenfurt	Kärntner Nachrichten	Carinthia
Austria	Klagenfurt	Kirchliches Verordnungsblatt für die Diözese Gurk	church paper
Austria	Klagenfurt	Klagenfurter Zeitung	Carinthia
Austria	Klosterneuburg	Erkenntnis und Befreiung	anarchist paper
Austria	Klosterneuburg	Jahresbericht des N. ö. Landes-Realgymnasiums in Klosterneuburg	annual school report
Austria	Krems an der Donau	Jahresbericht über die nied. Österr. Landes-Oberrealschule in Krems	annual school report
Austria	Krems an der Donau	Kremser Wochenblatt	Lower Austria
Austria	Krems an der Donau	Österreichische Land-Zeitung	agricultural
Austria	Leoben	Die G. K. B. Zeitung für Eisenbahn und Bergbau	railroad and mine paper
Austria	Lienz	Lienzer Zeitung	Tirol

Country	Published at	Title	Notes
Austria	Linz	Amtliche Linzer Zeitung	Upper Austria
Austria	Linz	Der Arbeitersturm	National Socialist
Austria	Linz	Die Alpenländische Morgen-Zeitung	Upper Austria
Austria	Linz	Die Oberösterreichischen Nachrichten	Upper Austria
Austria	Linz	Linzer Abendbote	Upper Austria
Austria	Linz	Linzer Tagespost	Upper Austria
Austria	Linz	Linzer Volksblatt	Upper Austria
Austria	Linz	Linzer Zeitung	Upper Austria
Austria	Linz	Oberdonau-Zeitung	Upper Austria, National Socialist
Austria	Linz	Oesterreichisches Bürgerblatt	Upper Austria
Austria	Linz	Unsere Zeitung	Austrian veterans paper
Austria	Linz; Krumau	Böhmerwald-Volksbote	political paper
Austria	Mödling	Allgemeine Schutzhütten-Zeitung für die Ostalpen	Alpine paper
Austria	Neulengbach	Neulengbacher Zeitung (Wienerwald-Bote)	Lower Austria
Austria	Oberwart	Oberwarther Sonntags-Zeitung	Burgenland, National Socialist
Austria	Pottenstein	Triestingtaler und Priestingtaler Wochenblatt	Lower Austria
Austria	Radkersburg	Steirische Grenzwacht	Styria, National Socialist
Austria	Ried	Innviertler Heimatblatt	Upper Austria
Austria	Salzburg	Amts- und Intelligenz-Blatt von Salzburg	Salzburg

Country	Published at	Title	Notes
Austria	Salzburg	Berichte und Informationen des österreicchischen Forschungsinstituts für Wirtschaft und Politik	Austrian economic and political research
Austria	Salzburg	Betrieb und Front	wartime paper
Austria	Salzburg	Das Salzburger Sportblatt	Salzburg
Austria	Salzburg	Die Volksblätter aus Salzburg	Salzburg
Austria	Salzburg	Intelligenzblatt von Salzburg	Salzburg
Austria	Salzburg	Königlich baierisches Intelligenzblatt des Salzach-Kreises	Bavaria at that time
Austria	Salzburg	Königlich baierisches Salzach-Blatt-Kreis	Bavaria at that time
Austria	Salzburg	Landes-Regierungsblatt für das Herzogthum Salz burg	Salzburg
Austria	Salzburg	Medicinisch-chirurgische Zeitung	surgical paper
Austria	Salzburg	Neue Salzburger Zeitung	Salzburg
Austria	Salzburg	Oberdeutsche Staatszeitung	Salzburg
Austria	Salzburg	Polizei-Blatt für das Herzogthum Salzburg	Salzburg
Austria	Salzburg	Salzburger Chronik	Salzburg
Austria	Salzburg	Salzburger Constitutionelle Zeitung	Salzburg
Austria	Salzburg	Salzburger Intelligenzblatt	Salzburg
Austria	Salzburg	Salzburger Morgen-Zeitung	Salzburg
Austria	Salzburg	Salzburger Tagblatt	Salzburg
Austria	Salzburg	Salzburger Volksblatt	Salzburg
Austria	Salzburg	Salzburger Wacht	Salzburg

Country	Published at	Title	Notes
Austria	Salzburg	Salzburger Zeitung	Salzburg
Austria	Salzburg	Wochenblatt der Bauernschaft für Salzburg	Salzburg
Austria	Schwechat	Die Volkspost	Lower Austria
Austria	St. Pölten	Der St. Pöltner Bote	Lower Austria
Austria	St. Pölten	Eggenburger Zeitung	Lower Austria
Austria	St. Pölten	Sankt Pöltener Diözesanblatt	Catholic diocesan paper
Austria	Steyr	Die Judenfrage	500 years U Heidelberg
Austria	Tulln	Brand Aus	Lower Austria firemen's paper
Austria	war theatre	Feldpostbrief Niederdonau	wartime paper
Austria	Wels	Landpost	National Socialist agricultural
Austria	Wien/Vienna	12 Uhr Blatt	daily
Austria	Wien/Vienna	84er Zeitung	veteran paper for 84th Regiment
Austria	Wien/Vienna	Agrarische Post	agricultural paper
Austria	Wien/Vienna	Allgemeine Automobil-Zeitung	automobile paper
Austria	Wien/Vienna	Allgemeine Bau-Zeitung	construction paper
Austria	Wien/Vienna	Allgemeine Land- und forstwirthschaftliche Zeitung	agricultural and forest paper
Austria	Wien/Vienna	Allgemeine Literatur-Zeitung zunächst für das katholische Deutschland	literature paper
Austria	Wien/Vienna	Allgemeine musikalische Zeitung	music paper

Country	Published at	Title	Notes
Austria	Wien/Vienna	Allgemeine Österreichische Gerichts-Zeitung	judicial newspaper
Austria	Wien/Vienna	Allgemeine Österreichische Zeitschrift für den Landwirth, Forstmann und Gaertner	agricultural and forest paper
Austria	Wien/Vienna	Allgemeine Radio-Zeitung	radio paper
Austria	Wien/Vienna	Allgemeine Sport-Zeitung	sports paper
Austria	Wien/Vienna	Allgemeine Theaterzeitung	theater paper
Austria	Wien/Vienna	Allgemeine Theaterzeitung und Unterhaltungsblatt	theater paper
Austria	Wien/Vienna	Allgemeine Wiener medizinische Zeitung	medical paper
Austria	Wien/Vienna	Allgemeines Reichs-Gesetz- und Regierungsblatt für das Kaiserthum Oesterreich	laws for Austrian Empire
Austria	Wien/Vienna	Alphabetisches Verzeichnis der Verlustlisten	Austro-Hungary casualty index
Austria	Wien/Vienna	An der schönen blauen Donau	music paper
Austria	Wien/Vienna	Arbeiter Schachzeitung	chess paper
Austria	Wien/Vienna	Arbeiterinnen-Zeitung	women's political paper
Austria	Wien/Vienna	Arbeiter-Zeitung	Austrian labor paper
Austria	Wien/Vienna	Arbeiter-Zeitung	political paper
Austria	Wien/Vienna	Armeeblatt	Austrian army paper
Austria	Wien/Vienna	Austria: Tagblatt für Handel und Gewerbe	business and industry paper
Austria	Wien/Vienna	Auszug aus der Tagespresse	WW I press reports
Austria	Wien/Vienna	Bade- und Reise-Journal	travel guide

Country	Published at	Title	Notes
Austria	Wien/Vienna	Beilage zur politischen Chronik	parliamentary news
Austria	Wien/Vienna	Belehrendes und Unterhaltendes	cultural paper
Austria	Wien/Vienna	Blätter für Theater, Musik und Kunst	fine arts paper
Austria	Wien/Vienna	Centralblatt für Eisenbahnen und Dampfschiffahrt in Oesterreich	railroad and steamship paper
Austria	Wien/Vienna	Christlich-soziale Arbeiter-Zeitung	political paper
Austria	Wien/Vienna	Cook's-Welt-Reise-Zeitung	travel paper
Austria	Wien/Vienna	Cur-Liste Bad Ischl	lists guests at spa
Austria	Wien/Vienna	Danzers Armee-Zeitung	military paper
Austria	Wien/Vienna	Das deutsche Echo	National Socialist
Austria	Wien/Vienna	Das Fremden-Blatt	tourist paper
Austria	Wien/Vienna	Das Interessante Blatt	Austria
Austria	Wien/Vienna	Das Kleine Blatt	Austria
Austria	Wien/Vienna	Das kleine Volksblatt	Austria
Austria	Wien/Vienna	Das Motorrad	motorcycle paper
Austria	Wien/Vienna	Das neue Wiener Tagblatt	Austria
Austria	Wien/Vienna	Das Panier des Fortschrittes	Austria
Austria	Wien/Vienna	Das Vaterland	Austrian monarchy paper
Austria	Wien/Vienna	Das Wienerblättchen	Austria

Country	Published at	Title	Notes
Austria	Wien/Vienna	Das Wort der Frau	women
Austria	Wien/Vienna	Das Zelt	Jewish
Austria	Wien/Vienna	Deborah	Jewish
Austria	Wien/Vienna	Der Adler	Austria
Austria	Wien/Vienna	Der Alpenfreund	Alpine paper
Austria	Wien/Vienna	Der Architekt	architect's paper
Austria	Wien/Vienna	Der Bauernbündler	Lower Austria farm paper
Austria	Wien/Vienna	Der Bautechniker	construction paper
Austria	Wien/Vienna	Der deutsch-österreichische Photograph	photography paper
Austria	Wien/Vienna	Der gute Film	motion pictures
Austria	Wien/Vienna	Der Hausbesitzer/Hausherren Zeitung	homeowner paper
Austria	Wien/Vienna	Der Humorist	humor
Austria	Wien/Vienna	Der jüdische Arbeiter	Jewish political
Austria	Wien/Vienna	Der Kinobesitzer	movie theater paper
Austria	Wien/Vienna	Der Krüppel	paper for handicapped
Austria	Wien/Vienna	Der Kuckuck	illustrated news
Austria	Wien/Vienna	Der Landbote	Austria
Austria	Wien/Vienna	Der Montag	Austria
Austria	Wien/Vienna	Der Morgen, Wiener Montagblatt	Austria

Country	Published at	Title	Notes
Austria	Wien/Vienna	Der neue Mahnruf	Austria
Austria	Wien/Vienna	Der Omnibus	Austria
Austria	Wien/Vienna	Der österreichische Zuschauer	Austria
Austria	Wien/Vienna	Der Radikale	radical
Austria	Wien/Vienna	Der Reporter	Austria
Austria	Wien/Vienna	Der Schnee	seasonal Alpine paper
Austria	Wien/Vienna	Der Telegraph	Austria
Austria	Wien/Vienna	Der Unpartheyische	independent political
Austria	Wien/Vienna	Der Wähler	political paper
Austria	Wien/Vienna	Der Wanderer	travel paper
Austria	Wien/Vienna	Deutsche Musik-Zeitung	music paper
Austria	Wien/Vienna	Deutsches Volksblatt	Austria
Austria	Wien/Vienna	Deutsches Wochenblatt	Austria
Austria	Wien/Vienna	Die Alpenländische Morgen-Zeitung	Austria
Austria	Wien/Vienna	Die Arbeit	labor paper
Austria	Wien/Vienna	Die Arbeit	labor paper
Austria	Wien/Vienna	Die Arbeiterin	women's labor paper
Austria	Wien/Vienna	Die Arbeiterinnen	women's labor paper
Austria	Wien/Vienna	Die Bombe	fashion paper

Country	Published at	Title	Notes
Austria	Wien/Vienna	Die Bühne	theater paper
Austria	Wien/Vienna	Die Debatte und Wiener Lloyd	Austria
Austria	Wien/Vienna	Die Drogisten-Zeitung	pharmacist paper
Austria	Wien/Vienna	Die Fackel	society members
Austria	Wien/Vienna	Die Film-Welt	movie paper
Austria	Wien/Vienna	Die Geissel, Tagblatt aller Tagblätter	daily
Austria	Wien/Vienna	Die Gerechtigkeit	anti-racism paper
Austria	Wien/Vienna	Die Kino-Woche	movie paper
Austria	Wien/Vienna	Die Lokomotive	locomotive industry
Austria	Wien/Vienna	Die Muskete	humor
Austria	Wien/Vienna	Die Neue Feie Presse	Austria
Austria	Wien/Vienna	Die Neue Illustrirte Zeitung	Austria
Austria	Wien/Vienna	Die neue Welt	Jewish
Austria	Wien/Vienna	Die neue Zeitung	Austria
Austria	Wien/Vienna	Die Neuzeit	Austria
Austria	Wien/Vienna	Die Österreichische Volksstimme	Communist paper
Austria	Wien/Vienna	Die Presse	press
Austria	Wien/Vienna	Die rote Fahne	Communist party paper
Austria	Wien/Vienna	Die Stimme [Alte Folge]	Jewish

Country	Published at	Title	Notes
Austria	Wien/Vienna	Die Stimme [Neue Folge]	Jewish
Austria	Wien/Vienna	Die Vedette	military paper
Austria	Wien/Vienna	Die Wählerin	women's political paper
Austria	Wien/Vienna	Die Wahrheit	Jewish
Austria	Wien/Vienna	Die Welt	Jewish
Austria	Wien/Vienna	Die Weltpresse	British, German-language
Austria	Wien/Vienna	Die Zeit	Austria
Austria	Wien/Vienna	Die Zukunft	Socialist paper
Austria	Wien/Vienna	Dr. Blochs Österreichische Wochenschrift	Jewish
Austria	Wien/Vienna	Drey wahrhafftige erbärmliche newe Zeitungen	early paper
Austria	Wien/Vienna	Erdöl-Zeitung	petroleum paper
Austria	Wien/Vienna	Erste Allgemeine Nachrichten	Austria
Austria	Wien/Vienna	Erste allgemeine öster. Hebammen-Zeitung	midwife paper
Austria	Wien/Vienna	Esra	Jewish academic paper
Austria	Wien/Vienna	Freie Tribüne	Jewish political
Austria	Wien/Vienna	Freiheit!	Austria
Austria	Wien/Vienna	Fremden-Blatt	tourist paper
Austria	Wien/Vienna	Fussball-Zeitung	soccer
Austria	Wien/Vienna	Gambrinus, Brauerei- und Hopfen-Zeitung	brewery paper

Country	Published at	Title	Notes
Austria	Wien/Vienna	Gemeinde-Zeitung: unabhängiges politisches Journal	political paper
Austria	Wien/Vienna	Gerichts-Halle	court paper
Austria	Wien/Vienna	Götz von Berlichingen	satire
Austria	Wien/Vienna	Hebammen-Zeitung	midwife paper
Austria	Wien/Vienna	Heimat	Austria
Austria	Wien/Vienna	Helios	electrotechnology
Austria	Wien/Vienna	Illustrierte Wiener Kronen-Zeitung	Austria
Austria	Wien/Vienna	Illustriertes Familienblatt	Austria
Austria	Wien/Vienna	Illustriertes Wiener Extrablatt	Austria
Austria	Wien/Vienna	Illustrirte Monatshefte	Jewish
Austria	Wien/Vienna	Jagd-Zeitung	hunting paper
Austria	Wien/Vienna	Jahresbericht der Schulen des Frauenerwerb-Vereins	annual school report
Austria	Wien/Vienna	Jahresbericht des Mädchen-Lyzeums am Kohlmarkt	annual school report
Austria	Wien/Vienna	Jahresbericht des Vereins für erweiterte Frauenbildung in Wien	annual school report
Austria	Wien/Vienna	Jahresbericht. Josephstädter Obergymnasium	annual school report
Austria	Wien/Vienna	Jüdische Korrespondenz	Jewish
Austria	Wien/Vienna	Jüdische Volksstimme	Jewish
Austria	Wien/Vienna	Jüdische Zeitung	Jewish

Country	Published at	Title	Notes
Austria	Wien/Vienna	Jüdisches Volksblatt	Jewish
Austria	Wien/Vienna	Kalender und Jahrbuch für Israeliten	Jewish
Austria	Wien/Vienna	Kalender und Jahrbuch für Israeliten [II. Folge]	Jewish
Austria	Wien/Vienna	Kalender und Jahrbuch für Israeliten [III. Folge]	Jewish
Austria	Wien/Vienna	Kikirikij	humor
Austria	Wien/Vienna	Kinematographische Rundschau	cinematography
Austria	Wien/Vienna	Kino-Journal	film paper
Austria	Wien/Vienna	Kleine Volks-Zeitung	Austria
Austria	Wien/Vienna	Kleine Wiener Kriegszeitung	wartime paper
Austria	Wien/Vienna	Konstitutonelle Volks-Zeitung	Austria
Austria	Wien/Vienna	Mein Film	film paper
Austria	Wien/Vienna	Menorah	Jewish multilingual
Austria	Wien/Vienna	Militär-Zeitung	military paper
Austria	Wien/Vienna	Montags-Zeitung	Austria
Austria	Wien/Vienna	Morgenpost	daily
Austria	Wien/Vienna	Musikalisches Wochenblatt	music paper
Austria	Wien/Vienna	Nationalzeitung	Jewish
Austria	Wien/Vienna	Neu-ankommender Currier Auß Wienn	Austria
Austria	Wien/Vienna	Neue Allgemeine Wiener Handlungs- und Industrie-Zeitung	business and industry paper

Country	Published at	Title	Notes
Austria	Wien/Vienna	Neue Folge der Gesundheits-Zeitung	health paper
Austria	Wien/Vienna	Neue Freie Presse	Austria
Austria	Wien/Vienna	Neue Illustrirte Zeitung	Austria
Austria	Wien/Vienna	Neue Kino Rundschau	movie paper
Austria	Wien/Vienna	Neue Nationalzeitung	Jewish
Austria	Wien/Vienna	Neue Zeitung	Jewish
Austria	Wien/Vienna	Neues 8-Uhr Blatt	daily
Austria	Wien/Vienna	Neues Fremdenblatt	tourist paper
Austria	Wien/Vienna	Neues Österreich	Austria
Austria	Wien/Vienna	Neues Wiener Journal	Austria
Austria	Wien/Vienna	Neues Wiener Tagblatt	daily
Austria	Wien/Vienna	NS-Telegraf	National Socialist paper
Austria	Wien/Vienna	Oesterreichische Jugend-Zeitschrift	youth paper
Austria	Wien/Vienna	Österreichische Auto-Rundschau	automobile paper
Austria	Wien/Vienna	Österreichische Buchhändler-Korrespondenz	bookseller paper
Austria	Wien/Vienna	Österreichische Fahrrad- und Automobil-Zeitung	bicycle and automobile paper
Austria	Wien/Vienna	Österreichische Illustrirte Zeitung	illustrated news
Austria	Wien/Vienna	Österreichische Lehrerinnen-Zeitung	female teachers

Country	Published at	Title	Notes
Austria	Wien/Vienna	Österreichische Nähmaschinen- und Fahrrad-Zeitung	sewing machine paper
Austria	Wien/Vienna	Österreichischer Beobachter	Austria
Austria	Wien/Vienna	Österreichisches Abendblatt	political paper
Austria	Wien/Vienna	Österreichisches entomologisches Wochenblatt	entomology paper
Austria	Wien/Vienna	Österreichisches pädagogisches Wochenblatt	teachers
Austria	Wien/Vienna	Österreichisch-ungarisches Cantoren-Zeitung	Jewish cantor publication
Austria	Wien/Vienna	Politische Frauen-Zeitung	women's supplement
Austria	Wien/Vienna	Populäre österreichische Gesundheits-Zeitung	health paper
Austria	Wien/Vienna	Punch	humor
Austria	Wien/Vienna	Ranglisten der k. k. Landwehr und der k. k. Gendarmerie	muster rolls of Austro-Hungarian militia and gendarmes in World War I
Austria	Wien/Vienna	Ranglisten des kaiserlichen und königlichen Heeres	muster rolls of Austro-Hungarian army in World War I
Austria	Wien/Vienna	Reichs-Gesetz-Blatt für das Kaiserthum Österreich	Austrian law paper
Austria	Wien/Vienna	Reichspost	Austria
Austria	Wien/Vienna	Rohö Zeitung	women
Austria	Wien/Vienna	Rote Frauenpost	Communist women
Austria	Wien/Vienna	Ruhestands Schematismus der Österreich-Unagrischen Armee	Austro-Hungarian military retirees

Country	Published at	Title	Notes
Austria	Wien/Vienna	Schematismus der k. k. Armee	Austro-Hungarian army members
Austria	Wien/Vienna	Schematismus der k. k. Landwehr und der k. k. Gendermarie	Austro-Hungarian militia and gendarmes
Austria	Wien/Vienna	Schematismus der Oesterreich-Kaiserlichen Armee	Austro-Hungarian army members
Austria	Wien/Vienna	Schematismus für das kaiserliche und königliche Heer und die kaiserliche und königliche Kriegs-Marine	Austro-Hungarian army and navy members
Austria	Wien/Vienna	Schild und Schwert	Austria
Austria	Wien/Vienna	Selbst-Emancipation	Jewish
Austria	Wien/Vienna	Social-politische Frauen-Zeitung	women's political paper
Austria	Wien/Vienna	Sonntagsblätter	religious
Austria	Wien/Vienna	Sport im Bild	sports paper
Austria	Wien/Vienna	Sportblatt	sports paper
Austria	Wien/Vienna	Stenographische Protokolle der Verhandlungen der Zionisten-Kongresse	Jewish
Austria	Wien/Vienna	Union	insurance trade paper
Austria	Wien/Vienna	Unsere Tribüne	Jewish political
Austria	Wien/Vienna	Vaterländische Blätter für den österreichischen Kaiserstaat	Imperial paper
Austria	Wien/Vienna	Verlustliste	Austro-Hungary casualties
Austria	Wien/Vienna	Verlustliste Alphabetisches Verzeichnis	Austro-Hungary casualty index

Country	Published at	Title	Notes
Austria	Wien/Vienna	Völkischer Beobachter	Austrian National Socialist paper
Austria	Wien/Vienna	Volkswirtschaftliche Wochenschrift	economic paper
Austria	Wien/Vienna	Volks-Zeitung	
Austria	Wien/Vienna	Vom Nordkap bis nach Afrika	WW II paper
Austria	Wien/Vienna	Vorwärts. Organ der Gewerkschaft Druck und Papier.	printers union paper
Austria	Wien/Vienna	Warhafftige neue Zeitung des Sendtbrieffs	early paper
Austria	Wien/Vienna	Warhafftige newe zeidtung wie die Türken dem Siebenbürger	early paper
Austria	Wien/Vienna	Wele-Neuigkeitsblatt	Austria
Austria	Wien/Vienna	Werkzeitung Wien Staatsdruckerei	Vienna printer paper
Austria	Wien/Vienna	Wiener Allgemeine Zeitung	500 years U Heidelberg
Austria	Wien/Vienna	Wiener Allgemeine Zeitung	general paper
Austria	Wien/Vienna	Wiener Bilder	pictorial
Austria	Wien/Vienna	Wiener Caricaturen	caricatures
Austria	Wien/Vienna	Wiener Diözesanblatt	Catholic diocesan paper
Austria	Wien/Vienna	Wiener entomologische Zeitung	entomology
Austria	Wien/Vienna	Wiener Feuerwehrzeitung	fireman paper
Austria	Wien/Vienna	Wiener Film	film paper
Austria	Wien/Vienna	Wiener Gassen-Zeitung	revolutionary paper

Country	Published at	Title	Notes
Austria	Wien/Vienna	Wiener illustrierte Frauen-Zeitung	women's paper
Austria	Wien/Vienna	Wiener illustrirte Garten-Zeitung	garden paper
Austria	Wien/Vienna	Wiener Kirchenzeitung für Glauben, Wissen, Freiheit und Gesetz	Vienna church paper
Austria	Wien/Vienna	Wiener Medizinische Wchenschrift	medical paper
Austria	Wien/Vienna	Wiener Montagsjournal	Austria
Austria	Wien/Vienna	Wiener Morgenzeitung	Jewish
Austria	Wien/Vienna	Wiener neueste Nachrichten	Austria
Austria	Wien/Vienna	Wiener Theater-Zeitung	theater paper
Austria	Wien/Vienna	Wiener Zeitung	Austria
Austria	Wien/Vienna	Wienerische Kirchenzeitung	Vienna church paper
Austria	Wien/Vienna	Wienerisches Diarium	Austria
Austria	Wien/Vienna	Wochenschrift der K.K. Gesellschaft der Ärzte	physicians
Austria	Wien/Vienna	Wochenschrift des ö. Ingenieur- und Architekten-Vereins	construction paper
Austria	Wien/Vienna	Wohlstand für Alle	anarchist paper
Austria	Wien/Vienna	Zeitschrift des Österreichischen Ingenieur-und Architekten-Vereins	construction paper
Austria	Wien/Vienna	Zeitschrift des österreichischen Ingenieur-Vereins	construction paper

Country	Published at	Title	Notes
Austria	Wien/Vienna	Zeitung für Landwirtschaft	agricultural paper
Austria	Wien/Vienna	Zollämter- und Finanzwacht-Zeitung	customs and finance paper
Austria	Wien/Vienna	Zwischen-Akt	theater paper
Austria	Wien/Vienna; Preßburg/Bratislava	Jüdische Presse	Jewish
Austria	Wien/Viennaü	Süddeutscher Geschäftsanzeiger	business paper
Austria	Wiener Neustadt	Front-Zeitung Wiener-Neustadt	wartime field paper
Austria	Wiener Neustadt	Jahresbericht der Niederösterreichischen Ober-Realschule	annual school report
Austria	Wolfsberg	Lavanttaler Bote	Carinthia
Austria	Wolfsberg	Unterkärntnerische Nachrichten	Carinthia
Austria	Ybbs an der Donau	Ybbser Zeitung	Lower Austria
Austria	Znaim/Znojmo	Jahresbericht des Mädchen-Lyzeums der Stadt Znaim	annual school report
Belgium	Aalst	Der Landsturm	soldier paper WW I
Belgium	Arel/Arles	Areler Zeitung	wartime paper
Belgium	Brüssel/Brussels	Deutsche Brüsseler Zeitung	for German community in Belgium
Belgium	Brüssel/Brussels	Deutsche Soldatenpost	wartime paper
Belgium	Malmédy	La semaine	mostly French; German ads
Belgium	Malmédy	Organe de Malmédy	mostly French; German ads
Belgium	Menin/Menen	Kriegs-Zeitung für das XV. Armee-Korps	wartime field paper

Country	Published at	Title	Notes
Belgium	Mons	Unser Landsturm im Hennegau	wartime field paper
Belgium	St. Vith	Kreisblatt für den Kreis Malmedy	Belgium
Belgium	St. Vith	Malmedy–St. Vither Volkszeitung	Belgium
Belgium	St. Vith	St. Vither Volkszeitung	Belgium
Belgium	St. Vith	Wochenblatt für den Kreis Malmedy	Belgium
Belgium	Tongres/Tongeren	Scharfschützen-Warte	wartime field paper
Brazil	Curitiba	Der Beobachter	Brazil
Brazil	Curitiba	Deutsche Post	Brazil
Brazil	Curitiba	Deutsche Volkszeitung	Brazil
Brazil	Curitiba	Deutsche Zeitung	Brazil
Brazil	Curitiba	Deutsches Wochenblatt	Brazil
Brazil	Porto Alegre	Deusches Volksblatt	Brazil
Brazil	Porto Alegre	Deutsche Zeitung	Brazil
Brazil	Porto Alegre	Illustrirtes Sonntagsblatt	Brazil
Brazil	Rio de Janeiro	Allgemeine deutsche Zeitung	Brazil
Brazil	Rio de Janeiro	Deutsches Tageblatt	Brazil
Brazil	Rio Negro	Rio Negrische Zeitung	Brazil
Brazil	São Leopoldo	Deutsche Post	Brazil

Country	Published at	Title	Notes
Canada	East Kildonan, Manitoba	Mennonitische Volkswarte	Mennonite
Canada	East Kildonan, Manitoba	Mennonitische Warte	Mennonite
Canada	Herndon, Manitoba	Mennonitische Welt	Mennonite
Canada	Kitchener, Ontario	Berliner Journal	Ontario
Canada	North Kildonan, Manitoba	Warte Jahrbuch	Mennonite
China	Peking/Beijing	Pekinger Deutsche Zeitung	Boxer rebellion
China	Shanghai	Shanghai Echo	China
China	Tsientsin/Tianjin	Deutsch-chinesische Nachrichten	China
China	Tsientsin/Tianjin	Deutsche Zeitung in Nordchina	China
China	Tsingtau/Qingdao	Tsingtauer neueste Nachrichten	China
Crimea	Simferopol	Deutsche Zeitung für die Krim und Taurien	wartime paper
Croatia	Abbazia	Curliste von Abbazia	guests at spa
Croatia	Agram/Zagreb	Agramer Zeitung	Croatia
Croatia	Agram/Zagreb	Der Kroatische Korrespondent	Croatia
Croatia	Agram/Zagreb	Kroatischer Korrespondent	Croatia
Croatia	Brioni/Brijuni	Brioni Insel-Zeitung	Croatia
Croatia	Pola/Pula	Pola	southern Austria
Croatia	Pola/Pula	Polaer Tagblatt	southern Austria
Croatia	Pola/Pula	Südösterreichische Nachrichten	southern Austria

Country	Published at	Title	Notes
Czech Republic	Brünn/Brno	Brünner Hebammen-Zeitung	midwife paper
Czech Republic	Brünn/Brno	Brünner Tagesbote	Moravia
Czech Republic	Brünn/Brno	Brünner Zeitung der k.-k. priv. mähr. Lehenbank	banking
Czech Republic	Brünn/Brno	Deutsches Südmährisches Blatt	southern Moravia
Czech Republic	Brünn/Brno	Hebammenzeitschrift	midwife paper
Czech Republic	Brünn/Brno	Mährischer Correspondent	Moravia
Czech Republic	Brünn/Brno	Neuigkeiten	Moravia
Czech Republic	Brünn/Brno	Regierungsblatt für das Markgrafthum Mähren	Moravia; bilingual
Czech Republic	Brünn/Brno	Tagesbote	Moravia
Czech Republic	Brünn/Brno	Zeitschrift für die Geschichte der Juden in der Tschechoslowakei	Jewish Czech
Czech Republic	Budweis/České Budějovice	Südböhmische Volkszeitung	Bohemia
Czech Republic	Chomutov/Komotau	Allgemeine Feuerwehr-Zeitung	firemen's paper
Czech Republic	Eger/Cheb	Egerer Anzeiger	Bohemia
Czech Republic	Eger/Cheb	Egerer Zeitung	Bohemia
Czech Republic	Eger/Cheb	Unser Egerland	Bohemia
Czech Republic	Franzensbad/ Františkovy Lázně	Franzensbader Curliste	Bohemia
Czech Republic	Freiwaldau/Jesenik	Die Mährisch-Schlesische Presse	Moravia and Silesia
Czech Republic	Hohenelbe/Vrchlabi	Das Riesengebirge in Wort und Bild	travel publication

Country	Published at	Title	Notes
Czech Republic	Krumau/Český Krumlov	Böhmerwald Volksbote	political paper
Czech Republic	Leitmeritz/Litoměřice	Leitmeritzer Zeitung	Bohemia
Czech Republic	Mährisch Neustadt/Uničov	Nordmährische Rundschau	Moravia
Czech Republic	Mährisch Ostrau/Ostrava	Local-Anzeiger für Mähr.-Ostrau und Umgebung	Moravia
Czech Republic	Neuhaus/Jindřichův Hradec	Neuhauser Allgemeiner Anzeiger	Bohemia
Czech Republic	Neuhaus/Jindřichův Hradec	Neuhauser Wochenblatt	Bohemia
Czech Republic	Neuhaus/Jindřichův Hradec	Neuhauser Wochenpost	Bohemia
Czech Republic	Nikolsburg/Mikulov	Frontzeitung	military paper
Czech Republic	Nikolsburg/Mikulov	Nikolsburger Kreisblatt	Moravia
Czech Republic	Nikolsburg/Mikulov	Nikolsburger Wochenschrift	Moravia
Czech Republic	Nikolsburg/Mikulov	Nikolsburger Wochenschrift für landwirtschaftliche, gemeinnützige Interessen und Unterhaltung	Moravia
Czech Republic	Olmütz/Olomouc	Deutsches Nordmährerblatt	Moravia
Czech Republic	Olmütz/Olomouc	Mährisches Tagblatt	Moravia
Czech Republic	Pilsen/Plzeň	Die Pilsner Abendpost	Bohemia
Czech Republic	Pilsen/Plzeň	Echo aus Pilsen und Westböhmen	Bohemia
Czech Republic	Pilsen/Plzeň	Jahresbericht des K. K. Gymnasiums zu Pilsen	annual school report

Country	Published at	Title	Notes
Czech Republic	Pilsen/Plzeň	Pilsener Zeitung	Bohemia
Czech Republic	Pilsen/Plzeň	Pilsner Fremdenblatt	Bohemia
Czech Republic	Pilsen/Plzeň	Pilsner Tagblatt	Bohemia
Czech Republic	Pilsen/Plzeň	Unterhaltungs-Blatt zum Pilsner Fremdenblatt	Bohemia
Czech Republic	Prag/Prague	Aerztliche Correspondenz-Blatt für Böhmen	Bohemia medical
Czech Republic	Prag/Prague	Bohemia	Bohemia
Czech Republic	Prag/Prague	Bohemia, ein Unterhaltungsblatt	literary
Czech Republic	Prag/Prague	Bohemia, oder Unterhaltungsblätter für gebildete Stände	literary
Czech Republic	Prag/Prague	Centralblatt der Land- und Forstwirthschaft in Böhmen	Bohemia agricultural paper
Czech Republic	Prag/Prague	Correspondenz	Bohemia
Czech Republic	Prag/Prague	Das Abendland	Jewish
Czech Republic	Prag/Prague	Der böhmische Bierbrauer	Bohemia beer brewing
Czech Republic	Prag/Prague	Der Tagesbote aus Böhmen	Bohemia
Czech Republic	Prag/Prague	Deutsche Volks-Zeitung	Bohemia
Czech Republic	Prag/Prague	Deutsche Zeitung Bohemia	Bohemia
Czech Republic	Prag/Prague	Die Wahrheit	Jewish
Czech Republic	Prag/Prague	Erschreckende Zeitunge von Zwayen Mördern	early paper
Czech Republic	Prag/Prague	Israelitische Gemeinde-Zeitung	Jewish
Czech Republic	Prag/Prague	Israelitischer Lehrerbote	Jewish teachers

Country	Published at	Title	Notes
Czech Republic	Prag/Prague	Jahrbuch der Gesellschaft der Geschichte der Juden in der Čechoslowakischen Republik	Jewish in Czech area
Czech Republic	Prag/Prague	Jüdisches Gefühl	Jewish youth publication
Czech Republic	Prag/Prague	Jung–Juda	Jewish youth publication
Czech Republic	Prag/Prague	Kais. Kön. Privilegiertes Prager Intelligenzblatt	Bohemia
Czech Republic	Prag/Prague	Landes-Gesetzblatt für das Königreich Böhmen	Bohemia; bilingual
Czech Republic	Prag/Prague	Landes-Regierungsblatt für das Königreich Böhmen	Bohemia; bilingual
Czech Republic	Prag/Prague	Lochner's Geschäfts-Zeitung über diverse Fabrikate und Waaren	agricultural paper
Czech Republic	Prag/Prague	Ost und West, Blätter für Kunst, Literatur und geselliges Leben	art and literary paper
Czech Republic	Prag/Prague	Prager Abendblatt	daily
Czech Republic	Prag/Prague	Prager land- und volkswirthschaftliches Wochenblatt	agricultural paper
Czech Republic	Prag/Prague	Selbstwehr	Jewish
Czech Republic	Prag/Prague	Unterhaltungsblätter	Bohemia
Czech Republic	Prag/Prague	Warnsdorfer Volkszeitung	early paper
Czech Republic	Preßburg/Bratislava	Intelligenzblatt für Ungarn	for Hungary
Czech Republic	Preßburg/Bratislava	Judaica	Jewish literary publication
Czech Republic	Preßburg/Bratislava	Pannonia	Slovakia
Czech Republic	Preßburg/Bratislava	Preßburger jüdische Zeitung	Jewish

Country	Published at	Title	Notes
Czech Republic	Preßburg/Bratislava	Preßburger Zeitung	Slovakia
Czech Republic	Preßburg/Bratislava	Preßburgisches Wochenblatt	Slovakia
Czech Republic	Preßburg/Bratislava	Schrattenthals Frauenzeitung	women's paper
Czech Republic	Prossnitz/Prostĕjov	Prossnitzer Wochenblatt	Moravia
Czech Republic	Reichenberg/Liberec	Front und Heinat	World War II paper for Sudetenland
Czech Republic	Reichenberg/Liberec	Reichenberger Zeitung	Bohemia
Czech Republic	Rumburg/Rumburk	Nordböhmischer Gebirgsbote	northern Bohemia
Czech Republic	Teplitz-Schönau/Teplice-Šanov	Cur-Liste von Teplitz und Schönau	spa paper
Czech Republic	Teplitz-Schönau/Teplice-Šanov	Teplitz-Schönauer Anzeiger	Bohemia
Czech Republic	Troppau/Opava	Kais. Königl. Schlesische Troppauer Zeitung	Silesia
Czech Republic	Warnsdorf/Varnsdorf	Nordböhmisches Volksblatt	Bohemia
Czech Republic	Warnsdorf/Varnsdorf	Österreichische Volkszeitung	Bohemia
Czech Republic	Warnsdorf/Varnsdorf	Warnsdorfer Volkszeitung	Bohemia
Czech Republic	Znaim/Znojmo	Der Lehrerbote	teacher paper
Czech Republic	Znaim/Znojmo	Znaimer Tagblatt	Moravia
Czech Republic	Znaim/Znojmo	Znaimer Wochenblatt	Moravia
Egypt	Cairo	Aegyptische Nachrichten	Egypt

Country	Published at	Title	Notes
England	London	Die Autonomie	anarchist paper
England	London (etc)	Europe Speaks	exile papers; multilingual
Estonia	Dorpat/Tartu	Das Inland	Baltic region
Estonia	Dorpat/Tartu	Dörptsche Zeitung	Baltic region
Estonia	Fellin/Viljand	Kreis-Blatt der Kreisverwaltung Fellin	Estonia
Estonia	Pernau/Pärnu	Pernausches Wochenblatt	Estonia
Estonia	Tallinn/Reval	Revalsche Post-Zeitung	Estonia
France	war theatre	Armee-Zeitung der 2. Armee	wartime field paper
France	war theatre	Badener Lazarett-Zeitung	wartime field paper
France	war theatre	Daheim	wartime field paper
France	war theatre	Der Champagne-Kamerad	wartime field paper
France	war theatre	Die Mauer	wartime field paper
France	war theatre	Die Somme-Wacht	wartime field paper
France	war theatre	Die Wacht im Osten	wartime field paper
France	war theatre	Die Wacht im Westen	wartime field paper
France	war theatre	Düna-Zeitung	wartime field paper
France	war theatre	Gazette des Ardennes	wartime field paper
France	war theatre	Kriegs-Zeitung der Elften Armee	wartime field paper
France	war theatre	Kriegs-Zeitung für das XV. Armee-Korps	wartime field paper

Country	Published at	Title	Notes
France	war theatre	Landsturm	wartime field paper
France	war theatre	Landsturm's Krieg's Bote	wartime field paper
France	war theatre	Liller Kriegszeitung	wartime field paper
France	war theatre	Meldereiter im Sundgau	wartime field paper
France	war theatre	Seille-Bote	wartime field paper
France	war theatre	Unser Landsturm im Hennegau	wartime field paper
France	war theatre	Zwischen Maas und Mosel	wartime field paper
France	10th Army	Zeitung der 10. Armee	wartime field paper
France	14th Bayr. Armierungsbataillon	Der Armierer	wartime field paper
France	19th Res. Inf. Regt.	Die Sappe	wartime field paper
France	1st Bayr. Ersatz-Inf.-Regt.	Im Schützengraben in den Vogesen	wartime field paper
France	2nd Bayr. L. Esk.	Die Patrulle	wartime field paper
France	2nd Bayr. Landwehr-Inf.-Regt.	Der bayerische Landwehrmann	wartime field paper
France	2nd Bayr. Landwehr-Inf.-Regt.	Die bayerische Landwehr	wartime field paper
France	3rd Bayr. Landwehr-Inf.-Regt.	Der Drahtverhau	wartime field paper
France	6th Bayr. Landwehr-Division	Vogesenwacht	wartime field paper

Country	Published at	Title	Notes
France	7th Army	Kriegszeitung der 7. Armee	wartime field paper
France	8. Reserve-Korps	Chamlagne-Kriegs-Zeitung	wartime field paper
France	8th Bayr. Res. Div.	Schützengrabenzeitung	wartime field paper
France	Bapaume	Bapaumer Zeitung am Mittag	wartime field paper
France	Bapaume	Der Schützengruber	wartime field paper
France	Briey	Der Landsturm-Bote von Briey	wartime field paper
France	Champagne	Champagner Kriegs-Zeitung	wartime field paper
France	Charleville	Der Champagner-Zeitung	wartime field paper
France	Gaede Abteilung, Logelbach	Bacillus verus	wartime field paper
France	Guebwiller/Gebweiler	Gebweilerer Wochenblatt	wartime; bilingual
France	Hagenau/Haguenau	Hagenauer Zeitung	Alsace
France	Hagenau/Haguenau	Unterländer Kurier	Alsace
France	Kolmar/Colmar	Der Drahtverhau	wartime field paper
France	Kolmar/Colmar	Die bayerische Landwehr	wartime field paper
France	Kolmar/Colmar	Die Sappe	wartime field paper
France	Kolmar/Colmar	Elsässer Kurier	Alsace
France	Kolmar/Colmar	Elsässer Tagblatt	Alsace
France	Kolmar/Colmar	Schützengrabenzeitung	wartime field paper

Country	Published at	Title	Notes
France	Kolmar/Colmar	Vogesenwacht	wartime field paper
France	Logelbach	Bacillus verus	wartime field paper
France	Metz	Der Orientfrontkaempfer	military paper
France	Metz	Zwischen Maas und Mosel	wartime field paper
France	Mülhausen/Mulhouse	Mülhauser Frauenzeitung	Alsace
France	Mülhausen/Mulhouse	Mülhauser Tagblatt	Alsace
France	Mülhausen/Mulhouse	Neue Mülhauser Zeitung	Alsace
France	Mülhausen/Mulhouse	Oberelsässische Landes-Zeitung	Alsace
France	Paris	Der Internationale Klassenkampf	Communist party paper
France	Schlettstadt/Sélestat	Schlettstadter Tageblatt	Alsace
France	St. Ludwig/Saint-Louis, France	Ober-Elsäßischer Volksfreund: Anzeiger für Hüningen, Sierenz und die angrenzenden Kantone	Sundgau Upper Alsace
France	St. Quentin	Armee-Zeitung der 2. Armee	wartime field paper
France	Strasburg/Strasbourg	Central- und Bezirks-Amtsblatt für Elsass-Lothringen	Alsace-Lorraine
France	Strasburg/Strasbourg	Elsäss-Lothringisches Schulblatt	teacher paper
France	Strasburg/Strasbourg	Freie Presse für Elsaß-Lothringen	Alsace-Lorraine; Social Democrat
France	Strasburg/Strasbourg	La Tribune Juive (multilingual)	Jewish paper
France	Strasburg/Strasbourg	Le Juif (bilingual)	Jewish paper
France	Strasburg/Strasbourg	Niederrheinischer Kurier	

Country	Published at	Title	Notes
France	Strasburg/Strasbourg	Relation aller Fuernemmen und gedenckwuerdigen Historien	oldest newspaper in the world
France	Strasburg/Strasbourg	Strassburger Bürger-Zeitung	
France	Strasburg/Strasbourg	Strassburger Diözesanblatt	diocesan paper
France	Strasburg/Strasbourg	Straßburger Handelsblatt	business paper
France	Strasburg/Strasbourg	Strassburger neueste Nachrichten: General-Anzeiger für Strassburg und Elsass-Lothringen	Alsace-Lorraine
France	Strasburg/Strasbourg	Strassburger Post	Alsace-Lorraine
France	Strasburg/Strasbourg	Strassburger privilegierte Zeitung	Alsace-Lorraine
France	Strasburg/Strasbourg	Strassburgisches Wochenblatt	weekly; bilingual
France	Strasburg/Strasbourg	Weltbote	
France	Strasburg/Strasbourg	Zentral- und Bezirks Amtsblatt für Elsaß-Lothringen	Alsace-Lorraine
France	Strasburg/Strasbourg	Zentral- und Bezirks Amtsblatt für Elsaß-Lothringen	Alsace-Lorraine
France	Strasburg/Strasbourg	Zentral- und Bezirks Amtsblatt für Elsaß-Lothringen	Alsace-Lorraine
France	Vouziers	Landsturm	wartime field paper
Georgia	Tiflis	Kaukasische Post	Georgia; Caucasus
Germany	Aachen/Aix-la-Chapelle	Aachener allgemeine Zeitung	Rhineland
Germany	Aachen/Aix-la-Chapelle	Aachener Rundschau	Rhineland
Germany	Aachen/Aix-la-Chapelle	Aachener Wahrheits-Freund	Rhineland
Germany	Aachen/Aix-la-Chapelle	Amtsblatt der Regierung zu Aachen	Rhineland

Country	Published at	Title	Notes
Germany	Aachen/Aix-la-Chapelle	Echo der Gegenwart	500 years U Heidelberg
Germany	Aachen/Aix-la-Chapelle	Journal des Nieder- und Mittelrheins	Rhineland
Germany	Aachen; Düren	Dürener Zeitung	Rhineland
Germany	Adenau	Adenauer Kreis- und Wochenblatt	Rhineland
Germany	Adenau	Kreis-Wochenblatt für den Kreis Adenau und Umgegend	Rhineland
Germany	Adenau	Wochenblatt für den Kreis Adenau und Umgegend	Rhineland
Germany	Ahrweiler	Ahrweiler Kreisblatt	Rhineland
Germany	Aichach	Amtsblatt für das Bezirksamts und Amtsgericht Aichach	Bavaria
Germany	Altenburg	Gnädigst privilegirtes Altenburgisches Intelligenz-Blatt	Thuringia
Germany	Altenburg	Zeitung für den deutschen Adel	nobility paper
Germany	Altona	Altonaer Nachrichten	Hamburg
Germany	Altona	Amtsblatt der Stadt Altona	Hamburg
Germany	Altona	Der Jude	Jewish
Germany	Altona	Jahres-Bericht der Vereinigung der Mennoniten-Gemeinden im deutschen Reich	Mennonite
Germany	Altona	Schleswig-Holsteinische Provinzialblätter	Schleswig-Holstein
Germany	Amberg	Amberger Tagblatt	Bavaria
Germany	Amberg	Amberger Tagblatt	Bavaria
Germany	Amberg	Amberger Volkszeitung (für Stadt und Land)	Bavaria

Country	Published at	Title	Notes
Germany	Amberg	Jahresbericht über die Gewerbschule Amberg	school report
Germany	Amberg	Wochenblatt der Stadt Amberg	Bavaria
Germany	Ammendorf	Kriegs-Zeitung	wartime paper
Germany	Amorbach	Jahresbericht über die Fürstl.-Leining. Lateinschule zu Amorbach	school report
Germany	Anclam see Anklam		
Germany	Andernach	Andernacher Burger-Blatt	Rhineland
Germany	Anklam	Anclamer Kreis-, Volks- und Wochenblatt	Pomerania
Germany	Anklam	Anclamer Wochenblatt	Pomerania
Germany	Anklam	Gemeinnütziges Anclammer Wochenblatt für alle Stände	Pomerania
Germany	Anklam	Kreis- und Volksblatt für den Kreis Anclam	Pomerania
Germany	Anklam	Pommersches Volks- und Anzeigeblatt	Pomerania
Germany	Ansbach	Ansbacher Intelligenz-Zeitung	Bavaria
Germany	Ansbach	Ansbacher Morgenblatt	Bavaria
Germany	Ansbach	Ansbacher Tagblatt	Bavaria
Germany	Ansbach	Intelligenzblatt des Rezat-Kreises	Bavaria
Germany	Ansbach	Königlich Bayerisches Intelligenzblatt für Mittelfranken	Bavaria
Germany	Arendsee	Arendseer Wochenblatt	Saxony

Country	Published at	Title	Notes
Germany	Arnsberg	Amtsblatt für den Regierungs-Bezirk Arnsberg	Westphalia
Germany	Arnsberg	Amtsblatt für den Regierungs-Bezirk Arnsberg	Westphalia
Germany	Arnsberg	Arnsberger Intelligenz-Blatt	Westphalia
Germany	Arolsen/Bad Arolsen	Waldeckisches Intelligenz-Blatt	Waldeck
Germany	Arolsen/Bad Arolsen	Waldeckisches Intelligenz-Blatt	Waldeck
Germany	Arolsen/Bad Arolsen	Wöchentlich Oekonomisches Intelligenz-Blatt	Waldeck
Germany	Aschaffenburg	Aschaffenburger Wochenblatt	Bavaria
Germany	Aschaffenburg	Aschaffenburger Zeitung	Bavaria
Germany	Aschaffenburg	Herold des Glaubens	Bavaria
Germany	Aschaffenburg	Intelligenzblatt von Unterfranken und Aschaffenburg	Bavaria
Germany	Aschaffenburg	Königlich Bayerisches Kreis-Amtsblatt von Unterfranken und Aschaffenburg	Bavaria
Germany	Aschaffenburg	Neue Aschaffenburger Zeitung und Aschaffenburger Anzeiger	Bavaria
Germany	Augsburg	Ahasverus, der ewige Jude	Jewish
Germany	Augsburg	Allerneuestes Gradaus oder deutsches Volk	Bavaria
Germany	Augsburg	Allgemeine Zeitung	Bavaria
Germany	Augsburg	Allgemeine Zeitung	Bavaria
Germany	Augsburg	Allgemeiner bayerischer National-Korrespondent	Bavaria
Germany	Augsburg	Augsburger Abendzeitung	Bavaria

Country	Published at	Title	Notes
Germany	Augsburg	Augsburger allgemeine Zeitung	Bavaria
Germany	Augsburg	Augsburger Anzeigeblatt	Bavaria
Germany	Augsburg	Augsburger Neuester Nachrichten	Bavaria
Germany	Augsburg	Augsburger Post-Zeitung	Bavaria
Germany	Augsburg	Augsburger Sonntagsblatt	Bavaria
Germany	Augsburg	Augsburger Tagblattt	Bavaria
Germany	Augsburg	Augsburger Unterhaltungs-Blatt	Bavaria
Germany	Augsburg	Augspurgische Extra-Zeitung	Bavaria
Germany	Augsburg	Augspurgische Ordinari Postzeitung	Bavaria
Germany	Augsburg	Bayerische Landtags-Zeitung	Bavaria government paper
Germany	Augsburg	Der Hausfreund	Bavaria
Germany	Augsburg	Der Lechbote	Bavaria
Germany	Augsburg	Deutsches Wochenblatt für constitutionelle Monarchie	monarchy paper
Germany	Augsburg	Gründtliche und warhafftige newe Zeitung	early paper
Germany	Augsburg	Intelligenz-Blatt der königlichen Regierung von Schwaben und Neuburg	Bavaria
Germany	Augsburg	Intelligenz-Blatt und wöchentlicher Anzeiger der königlich bairischen Stadt Augsburg	Bavaria
Germany	Augsburg	Königlich Bayerisches Intelligenz-Blatt für den Ober-Donau Kreis	Bavaria

Country	Published at	Title	Notes
Germany	Augsburg	Königlich-Bayerisches Kreis-Amtsblatt von Schwaben und Neuburg	Bavaria
Germany	Augsburg	Neue Augsburger Zeitung	Bavaria
Germany	Augsburg	Newe Zeitung. Wie der Türck Die Statt Nicosiam...	early paper
Germany	Augsburg	Sion, eine Stimme in der Kirche für unsere Zeit	Catholic
Germany	Augsburg	Tagblatt für die Kreishauptstadt Augsburg	Bavaria
Germany	Augsburg	Verhandlungen des Landraths im Ober-Donau Kreis	Bavaria
Germany	Augsburg	Newe Zeytung. Die Widerteuffer zu Münster belangende ...	early paper
Germany	Aurich	Ostfriesische Anzeigen und Nachrichten von allerhand zum gemeinen Besten überhaupt auch zur Beförderung Handels und Wandels dienenden Sachen	East Frisia
Germany	Aurich	Wöchentliche Anzeigen und Nachrichten	East Frisia
Germany	Backnang	Der Berg	family newsletter
Germany	Bad Berleburg	Landsturm's Krieg's Bote	WW I paper
Germany	Bad Godesberg	Godesberger Volkszeitung	Rhineland
Germany	Bad Reichenhall	Reichenhaller Badeblatt	spa paper
Germany	Bad Sobernheim	Anzeiger für Sobernheim, Kirn und Umgegend	Rhineland
Germany	Bad Sobernheim	Sobernheim-Kirner Intelligenz-Blatt	Rhineland
Germany	Bad Wimpfen	Wimpfener Zeitung	WW I paper
Germany	Baden-Baden	Badewochenblatt für die großherzogliche Stadt Baden	spa paper

Country	Published at	Title	Notes
Germany	Bamberg	Allgemeines Amtsblatt	Bavaria
Germany	Bamberg	Bamberger Journal	Bavaria
Germany	Bamberg	Bamberger Neueste Nachrichten	Bavaria
Germany	Bamberg	Bamberger Tagblatt	Bavaria
Germany	Bamberg	Der Freund der Wahrheit und des Volkes	Bavaria
Germany	Bamberg	Die fränkischen Zuschauer	Franconia
Germany	Bamberg	Fränkischer Merkur	Franconia
Germany	Bamberg	Tag-Blatt der Stadt Bamberg	Bavaria
Germany	Bamberg	Wöchentlicher Anzeiger für die katholische Geistlichkeit	Catholic clergy
Germany	Barmen	Barmer Wochenblatt	Rhineland
Germany	Barmen	Barmer Zeitung	500 years U Heidelberg
Germany	Barmen	Jahresbericht über die Realschule Barmen	school report
Germany	Baruth	Baruther Anzeiger	Brandenburg
Germany	Baruth	Baruther Heimatland	Brandenburg
Germany	Bayreuth	Bayreuther Intelligenz-Zeitung	Bavaria
Germany	Bayreuth	Bayreuther Zeitung	Bavaria
Germany	Bayreuth	Deutsche Reichs- und Gesetz-Zeitung	Bavaria
Germany	Bayreuth	Die braune Sonntagszeitung	National Socialist paper
Germany	Bayreuth	Fränkische Provinzialblätter	Bavaria

Country	Published at	Title	Notes
Germany	Bayreuth	Königlich bayerisches Intelligenz-Blatt für Oberfranken	Bavaria
Germany	Bayreuth	Sinai	Jewish paper
Germany	Bayreuth	Sudetendeutsche Zeitung	Sudetenland
Germany	Bayreuth	Sudetenland	Sudetenland Germans
Germany	Bensberg	Bensberger Volkszeitung	Rhineland
Germany	Bensberg	Bensberg-Gladbacher Anzeiger	Rhineland
Germany	Bensheim	Bergsträßer Anzeigeblatt	Hesse
Germany	Bergisch-Gladbach	Bergische Wacht	Rhineland
Germany	Bergisch-Gladbach	Bergisch-Gladbacher Volkszeitung	Rhineland
Germany	Bergisch-Gladbach	Rheinisch-Bergische Zeitung	Rhineland
Germany	Bergisch-Gladbach	Volksblatt für Bergisch-Gladbach und Umgegend	Rhineland
Germany	Berlin	Allerneueste Mannigfaltigkeiten	Berlin
Germany	Berlin	Allgemeine deutsche Gärtnerzeitung	gardener paper
Germany	Berlin	Allgemeine Militär-Zeitung	Brandenburg
Germany	Berlin	Allgemeine preußische Staats-Zeitung	Brandenburg
Germany	Berlin	Allgemeine Uhrmacher-Zeitung	clockmaker paper
Germany	Berlin	Amtsblatt der deutschen Reichs-Postverwaltung	Brandenburg
Germany	Berlin	Amtsblatt der königlichen Regierung zu Berlin	Brandenburg
Germany	Berlin	Amtsblatt des preußischen Post-Departements	Prussia

Country	Published at	Title	Notes
Germany	Berlin	Arbeiterwohlfahrt	labor paper
Germany	Berlin	Arbeiter-Zeitung für Schlesien und Oberschlesien	Communist paper
Germany	Berlin	Aufwärts	youth trade newspaper
Germany	Berlin	Bar Kochba	Jewish
Germany	Berlin	Beiblatt der Freisinnigen Zeitung	500 years U Heidelberg
Germany	Berlin	Bericht was sich zu anfang dieß itzt angehenden Jahres ... = Frischmanns Berichte	historic 17th century newpaper
Germany	Berlin	Bericht waß sich zugetragen und begeben = Frischmanns Berichte	historic 17th century newpaper
Germany	Berlin	Berichte für die Lehranstalt für die Wissenschaft des Judentums	Jewish
Germany	Berlin	Berichte für die Lehranstalt für die Wissenschaft des Judentums	Jewish
Germany	Berlin	Berliner Börsen-Courier	500 years U Heidelberg
Germany	Berlin	Berliner Börsen-Zeitung	stock market paper
Germany	Berlin	Berliner Courier	500 years U Heidelberg
Germany	Berlin	Berliner Gerichts-Zeitung	judicial newspaper
Germany	Berlin	Berliner Krakehler	humor
Germany	Berlin	Berliner Lokal-Anzeiger	Berlin
Germany	Berlin	Berliner Morgenpost	Brandenburg
Germany	Berlin	Berliner Musikzeitung	music

Country	Published at	Title	Notes
Germany	Berlin	Berliner Politisches Wochenblatt	political
Germany	Berlin	Berliner Tageblatt und Handels-Zeitung	Brandenburg
Germany	Berlin	Berliner Vereinsbote	Jewish
Germany	Berlin	Berliner Volkszeitung	Brandenburg
Germany	Berlin	Berliner Volks-Zeitung	Brandenburg
Germany	Berlin	Berliner Zeitung	DDR paper
Germany	Berlin	Berlinische Nachrichten von Staats- und gelehrten Sachen	Berlin
Germany	Berlin	Berlinische privilegierte Zeitung	Brandenburg
Germany	Berlin	Berlinisches litterarisches Wochenblatt	literary
Germany	Berlin	Bestimmung und Aufbruch	socialist monthly
Germany	Berlin	Betriebsräte-Zeitschrift des DMV	metal worker paper
Germany	Berlin	Blau-Weiß-Blätter	Jewish hiking paper
Germany	Berlin	Blau-Weiß-Blätter (Neue Folge)	Jewish hiking paper
Germany	Berlin	Blau-Weiß-Blätter Führerheft	Jewish hiking paper
Germany	Berlin	Botanische Zeitung	botany
Germany	Berlin	Bulletin des Parteitags der KPD	Communist paper
Germany	Berlin	Cameralistische Zeitung	German government
Germany	Berlin	Centralblatt der Bauverwaltung	building industry paper
Germany	Berlin	Central-Blatt für das deutsche Reich	German government
Germany	Berlin	Central-Verein Zeitung	Jewish

Country	Published at	Title	Notes
Germany	Berlin	Constitutionelle Zeitung	extra
Germany	Berlin	Courier	trade union paper
Germany	Berlin	Das Echo	political
Germany	Berlin	Das Kleine Journal	Brandenburg
Germany	Berlin	Das neue Reich	Brandenburg
Germany	Berlin	Das Recht der Feder	literary
Germany	Berlin	Das rote Berlin	Brandenburg
Germany	Berlin	Der ärztliche Hausfreund	medical paper
Germany	Berlin	Der Bazar	fashion
Germany	Berlin	Der Brummbär	Brandenburg
Germany	Berlin	Der Bureauangestellte	office worker paper
Germany	Berlin	Der Demokrat	supplement
Germany	Berlin	Der freie Angestellte	employees paper
Germany	Berlin	Der freie Arbeiter	socialist paper
Germany	Berlin	Der Funke	socialist daily
Germany	Berlin	Der Gewerkverein	trade union paper
Germany	Berlin	Der jüdische Student	Jewish student publication
Germany	Berlin	Der jüdische Student (Neue Folge)	Jewish student publication

Country	Published at	Title	Notes
Germany	Berlin	Der jüdische Wille (Alte Folge)	Jewish
Germany	Berlin	Der jüdische Wille (Neue Folge)	Jewish
Germany	Berlin	Der junge Jude	Jewish youth publication
Germany	Berlin	Der Kämpfer	Brandenburg
Germany	Berlin	Der Kampfruf	Brandenburg
Germany	Berlin	Der Montag	Brandenburg
Germany	Berlin	Der Morgen	Jewish
Germany	Berlin	Der Papierfabrikant	papermaker weekly
Germany	Berlin	Der preußische Staatsanzeiger	Brandenburg
Germany	Berlin	Der Sozialist	socialist paper
Germany	Berlin	Der Stahlhelm	Brandenburg
Germany	Berlin	Der Sturm	Brandenburg
Germany	Berlin	Der Syndikalist	anarchist paper
Germany	Berlin	Der Tag	Brandenburg
Germany	Berlin	Der Tagesspiegel	Brandenburg
Germany	Berlin	Der Textilarbeiter	trade union paper
Germany	Berlin	Deutsche allgemeine Zeitung	Brandenburg
Germany	Berlin	Deutsche Bau-Zeitung	construction paper
Germany	Berlin	Deutsche Fleischbeschauer-Zeitung	German meat inspector

Country	Published at	Title	Notes
Germany	Berlin	Deutsche Gemeinde-Zeitung	municipalities paper
Germany	Berlin	Deutsche Kolonialzeitung	German colonial paper
Germany	Berlin	Deutsche Kriegszeitung	WW I
Germany	Berlin	Deutsche Schriftsteller-Zeitung	paper for authors
Germany	Berlin	Deutsche Uhrmacher-Zeitung	clockmaker paper
Germany	Berlin	Deutscher Reichs-Anzeiger	Brandenburg
Germany	Berlin	Deutscher Verkehrsbund	union paper
Germany	Berlin	Deutsches Kolonialblatt	German colony administration
Germany	Berlin	Deutsches Nachrichtenbüro	National Socialist press agency
Germany	Berlin	Deutsches Tageblatt	500 years U Heidelberg
Germany	Berlin	Die Ameise	trade union paper
Germany	Berlin	Die Arbeit	trade union paper
Germany	Berlin	Die Archäologische Zeitung	archaeology paper
Germany	Berlin	Die Baugewerkschaft	trade union paper
Germany	Berlin	Die Deutsche Zucker-Industrie: Wochenblatt	sugar industry
Germany	Berlin	Die Eiche	trade union paper
Germany	Berlin	Die Feder	for authors and journalists
Germany	Berlin	Die Freie Generation	anarchist paper

Country	Published at	Title	Notes
Germany	Berlin	Die Gewerkschaft	trade union paper
Germany	Berlin	Die Internationale	Communist paper
Germany	Berlin	Die jüdische Presse	Jewish
Germany	Berlin	Die Kämpferin	Communist party paper
Germany	Berlin	Die KPD	Communist party paper
Germany	Berlin	Die Kreatur	Jewish
Germany	Berlin	Die literarische Praxis	literary
Germany	Berlin	Die Post aus Deutschland	Voss
Germany	Berlin	Die Redaktion	literary
Germany	Berlin	Die Rote Front	Brandenburg
Germany	Berlin	Die Schwarze Fahne	Brandenburg
Germany	Berlin	Die Schwarze Front	Brandenburg
Germany	Berlin	Die Voss	Brandenburg
Germany	Berlin	Dramaturgisches Wochenblatt	teacher paper
Germany	Berlin	Eiserne Front	Brandenburg
Germany	Berlin	Garten-Zeitung	gardener paper
Germany	Berlin	Germania	500 years U Heidelberg
Germany	Berlin	Gewissen	journalism

Country	Published at	Title	Notes
Germany	Berlin	Hausangestellten-Zeitung	domestic worker paper
Germany	Berlin	Heimat und Ferne	Brandenburg
Germany	Berlin	Im Deutschen Reich	Jewish
Germany	Berlin	Israelitische Rundschau	Jewish
Germany	Berlin	Jahrbuch für jüdische Geschichte und Literatur	Jewish literary publication
Germany	Berlin	Jeschurun (Neue Folge)	Jewish
Germany	Berlin	Jüdische Arbeits- und Wanderfürsorge	Jewish
Germany	Berlin	Jüdische Rundschau	Jewish
Germany	Berlin	Kameralistische Zeitung	government paper
Germany	Berlin	Kampfsignal	Brandenburg
Germany	Berlin	Kartell-Convent Blätter	Jewish
Germany	Berlin	Kartell-Mitteilungen	Jewish
Germany	Berlin	Keramischer Bund	trade union paper
Germany	Berlin	Kladderadatsch	satire
Germany	Berlin	Königlich preußische Staats-Anzeiger	Brandenburg
Germany	Berlin	Königlich preußisches Central-Polizei-Blatt	Brandenburg
Germany	Berlin	Königlich privilegirte Berlinische Zeitung von Staats- und gelehrten Sachen	Brandenburg
Germany	Berlin	Kyffhäuser	military veteran paper

63

Country	Published at	Title	Notes
Germany	Berlin	Linnaea	botany
Germany	Berlin	Locomotive	political
Germany	Berlin	Magazin für die Wissenschaft des Judentums	Jewish
Germany	Berlin	Medizinische Zeitung	medical paper
Germany	Berlin	Militär-Wochenblatt	military paper
Germany	Berlin	Militär-Zeitung	military paper
Germany	Berlin	Mitteilungen aus dem Verband der Vereine für jüdische Geschichte und Literatur in Deutschland	Jewish
Germany	Berlin	Mitteilungen der Arbeitsgemeinschaft jüdisch-liberale Jugendvereine Deutschlands	Jewish youth publication
Germany	Berlin	Mitteilungen der Gesellschaft für jüdische Volkskunde [Neue Folge]	Jewish
Germany	Berlin	Mitteilungsblatt der Arbeitsgemeinschaft freier Angestelltenverbände	employees union paper
Germany	Berlin	Mitteilungsblatt der Berliner Mennoniten-Gemeinde	Mennonite
Germany	Berlin	Montagspost	Berlin
Germany	Berlin	Nachrichtendienst	Jewish
Germany	Berlin	National-Zeitung	500 years U Heidelberg
Germany	Berlin	National-Zeitung	Brandenburg
Germany	Berlin	Neue jüdische Monatshefte	Jewish

Country	Published at	Title	Notes
Germany	Berlin	Neue Mannigfaltigkeiten	Berlin
Germany	Berlin	Neue preußische Zeitung	500 years U Heidelberg
Germany	Berlin	Neue preußische Zeitung	Brandenburg
Germany	Berlin	Neue Zeit	CDU paper in DDR
Germany	Berlin	Neues Deutschland	official paper in DDR (SED)
Germany	Berlin	Neueste Mittheilungen	Prussian official press
Germany	Berlin	Norddeutsche Allgemeine Zeitung	500 years U Heidelberg
Germany	Berlin	Norddeutsche allgemeine Zeitung	Brandenburg
Germany	Berlin	Ost und West	Jewish
Germany	Berlin	Palästina	Jewish
Germany	Berlin	Palästina Nachrichten	Jewish
Germany	Berlin	Permanente Revolution	Berlin
Germany	Berlin	Preußisches Zentral-Polizei-Blatt	Prussian police gazette
Germany	Berlin	Protestantische Kirchenzeitung	500 years U Heidelberg
Germany	Berlin	Protokoll der Sitzung des Kuratoriums der Vereinigung der Mennonien-Gemeinden im Deutschen Reich	Mennonite
Germany	Berlin	Provinzial-Correspondenz	Prussian official press
Germany	Berlin	Reichswart	political
Germany	Berlin	Rundschau der Frau	women's labor paper

Country	Published at	Title	Notes
Germany	Berlin	Sattler- und Portefeuiller Zeitung	saddler paper
Germany	Berlin	Sattler- und Tapezierer Zeitung	saddler paper
Germany	Berlin	Sattler-Tapezierer- und Portefeuiller Zeitung	saddler paper
Germany	Berlin	Sattler-Zeitung	saddler paper
Germany	Berlin	Sichel und Hammer	Communist
Germany	Berlin	Solidarität	labor paper
Germany	Berlin	Sonntagsblatt	religious paper
Germany	Berlin	Sonntagsruhe	Brandenburg
Germany	Berlin	Tägliche Rundschau	500 years U Heidelberg
Germany	Berlin	Tribunal	Berlin
Germany	Berlin	Ulk	satire
Germany	Berlin	Unser Teltow	Brandenburg
Germany	Berlin	Urwähler-Zeitung	Prussian political
Germany	Berlin	Verband der Brauerei- und Mühlenarbeiter und Verwandter Berufsgenossen	trade union paper
Germany	Berlin	Verbandszeitung Verband der Lebensmittel- und Getränkearbeiter Deutschlands	trade union paper
Germany	Berlin	Volk und Land	Jewish political
Germany	Berlin	Volkszeitung	Brandenburg

Country	Published at	Title	Notes
Germany	Berlin	Volks-Zeitung	Brandenburg
Germany	Berlin	Vossische Zeitung	Brandenburg
Germany	Berlin	Wirtschaftliche Rundschau	economic paper
Germany	Berlin	Wochenblatt der Johanniter-Ordens-Balley Brandenburg	Teutonic Knights
Germany	Berlin	Zeitbilder	a Voss paper
Germany	Berlin	Zeitschrift für Demographie und Statistik der Juden [Alte Folge]	Jewish statistics
Germany	Berlin	Zeitschrift für Demographie und Statistik der Juden [Neue Folge]	Jewish statistics
Germany	Berlin	Zeitschrift für die Wissenschaft der Juden	Jewish
Germany	Berlin	Zeitung auß Deutschlandt, Welschlandt, Franckreich, Böhmen, Hungarn, Niederlandt und andern Orten = Frischmanns Berichte	historic 17th century newpaper
Germany	Berlin	Zeitung des Vereins deutscher Eisenbahn-Verwaltungen	railroad administration
Germany	Berlin	Zeitung imm ... Jhaar einkommen und wöchentlichzusammen getragen worden = Frischmanns Berichte	historic 17th century newpaper
Germany	Berlin	Zeitung so im ... Jahr von wochen zu wochen colligirt und zusammen getragen worden = Frischmanns Berichte	historic 17th century newpaper
Germany	Berlin	Zentralblatt der Bauverwaltung	building industry paper
Germany	Berlin	Zion	Jewish
Germany	Berlin; Hamburg	Der Maler	trade union paper
Germany	Berlin; Hamburg	Vereinsanzeiger Vereinigung der Maler, Lackierer,	trade union paper

Country	Published at	Title	Notes
Germany	Berlin; Leipzig	Anstreicher und Verwandter Berufsgenossen Deutschlands	labor paper
Germany	Berlin; Stuttgart	Korrespondent für Deutschlands Buchdrucker und Schriftgießer	
Germany	Berlin; Wien/Vienna	Metallarbeiter-Jugend	labor youth paper
Germany	Berlin-Charlottenburg	Der Jude	Jewish
Germany	Berlinchen	Der Judenkenner	anti-Semitic
Germany	Berlin-Neukölln	General-Anzeiger für Berlinchen, Bernstein und Umgegend	Brandenburg
Germany	Bieberach	Neubau und Siedlung	
Germany	Bielefeld	Wochenblatt für Papierfabrikation	papermaker weekly
Germany	Bingen	Jahresbericht über das Schuljahr 1873–1874	school report
Germany	Bingen	Intelligenzblatt für den Kreis Bingen	Hesse
Germany	Birkenfeld	Rhein- und Nahe-Zeitung	Hesse
Germany	Birkenwerder	Amtsblatt für den Landesteil Birkenfeld	Rhineland
Germany	Bitburg	Briesetal-Bote	Brandenburg
Germany	Blieskastel	Bitburger Kreis- und Intelligenzblatt	Rhineland
Germany	Bochum	Jahresbericht über die lateinische Schule Blieskastel	school report
Germany	Bochum	Bergarbeiter-Zeitung	trade union paper
Germany	Bochum	Bergarbeiter-Zeitung und Jungkamerad	trade union paper
Germany	Bochum	Bochumer Kreisblatt	Westphalia
Germany	Bochum	Deutsche Berg- und Hüttenargeiterzeitung	trade union paper

Country	Published at	Title	Notes
Germany	Bochum	Die Bergbau-Industrie	trade union paper
Germany	Bockenheim	Bockenheimer Anzeiger	Frankfurt am Main
Germany	Bockenheim	Frankfurt-Bockenheimer Anzeige-Blatt	Frankfurt am Main
Germany	Bonn	Allgemeiner Bonner Anzeiger für Industrie, Handel und Gewerbe	Rhineland
Germany	Bonn	Annalen	Rhineland
Germany	Bonn	Beiträge zur Ausbreitung nützlicher Kenntnisse	Rhineland
Germany	Bonn	Blätter für religiöse Erziehung	more coming
Germany	Bonn	Bonner Anzeiger	Rhineland
Germany	Bonn	Bonner Chronik	Rhineland
Germany	Bonn	Bonner Dekadenschrift	Rhineland
Germany	Bonn	Bonner Tageblatt	Rhineland
Germany	Bonn	Bonner Volksblatt	Rhineland
Germany	Bonn	Bonner Volkszeitung	Rhineland
Germany	Bonn	Bonner Wochenblatt	Rhineland
Germany	Bonn	Bonner Zeitung	Rhineland
Germany	Bonn	Bönnischer Sitten, Staats- und Geschichtskalender	Rhineland
Germany	Bonn	Bönnisches Wochenblatt	Rhineland
Germany	Bonn	Deutsche demokratische Zeitung	Rhineland

Country	Published at	Title	Notes
Germany	Bonn	Deutsche Reichszeitung	Rhineland
Germany	Bonn	Feuilles d'affiches annonces et avis divers de Bonn	Rhineland; bilingual
Germany	Bonn	General-Anzeiger für Bonn und Umgegend	Bonn area
Germany	Bonn	Gnädigst privilegirtes Bönnisches Intelligenz-Blatt	Rhineland
Germany	Bonn	Mittelrheinische Landeszeitung	Rhineland
Germany	Bonn	Neue Bonner Zeitung	Rhineland
Germany	Bonn	Rheinische Allgemeine Zeitung	Rhineland
Germany	Bonn	Spartacus	Rhineland; political
Germany	Bonn	Volksblatt für die Kreise Bonn und Sieg	Rhineland
Germany	Bonn	Volksmund	Rhineland
Germany	Bonn	Wochenblatt des Bönnischen Bezirks	Rhineland
Germany	Bonndorf	Der Lindenbuck	Baden
Germany	Braunschweig	Braunschweigische landwirtschaftliche Zeitung	agricultural paper
Germany	Braunschweig	Braunschweigisches Journal	literary
Germany	Braunschweig	Naturwissenschaftliche Rundschau	science
Germany	Braunschweig	Zeitschrift für die Geschichte der Juden in Deutschland	Jewish history
Germany	Bremen	Bremer Zeitung	Bremen
Germany	Bremen	Deutsche Auswanderer-Zeitung	emigration paper
Germany	Bremen	Milchwirtschaftliches Zentralblatt	dairy paper
Germany	Bremen	Weser-Zeitung	Bremen

Country	Published at	Title	Notes
Germany	Brilon	Sauerländischer Anzeiger	Rhineland
Germany	Brünsbüttel	Kanal-Zeitung	Schleswig-Holstein canal paper
Germany	Bückeburg	Anzeigen des Fürstenthums Schaumburg-Lippe	Schaumburg-Lippe
Germany	Buckow	Buckower Local-Anzeiger	Brandenburg
Germany	Budissen	Budissener Nachrichten	Saxony
Germany	Burghausen	Jahresbericht über die kgl. Bayerische Studienanstalt in Burghausen	school report
Germany	Bütow	Bütower Anzeiger	Brandenburg
Germany	Celle	Jahresbericht über das Gymnasium Celle	school report
Germany	Charlottenburg	Charlottenburger Zeitung	Berlin
Germany	Charlottenburg	Kornblumen	Sunday supplement
Germany	Chemnitz	Die Spinnmaschine	industry paper
Germany	Chemnitz; Leipzig	Deutsche Industrie-Zeitung	industry paper
Germany	Coburg	Allgemeine deutsche Arbeiter-Zeitung	labor paper
Germany	Coburg	Bayerische Ostmark Coburger National-Zeitung	Bavaria
Germany	Coburg	Coburger Nationalzeitung	Bavaria
Germany	Coburg	Coburger Regierungs-Blatt	Bavaria
Germany	Coburg	Coburger Regierungs-Blatt / Bezirksamt Coburg	Bavaria
Germany	Coburg	Coburger Tagblatt	Bavaria

Country	Published at	Title	Notes
Germany	Coburg	Coburger Zeitung	Bavaria and Saxony
Germany	Coburg	Coburgische wöchentliche Anzeige	Bavaria and Saxony
Germany	Coburg	Herzogl. Sachsen-Coburgisches Regierungs- und Intelligenzblatt	Bavaria and Saxony
Germany	Coburg	Herzogl. Sachsen-Coburg-Saalfeldes Regierungs- und Intelligenzblatt	Bavaria and Saxony
Germany	Coburg	Regierungs-Blatt für das Herzogtum Coburg	Bavaria and Saxony
Germany	Cochem	Cochemer Anzeiger	Rhineland
Germany	Cöthen/Koethen	Chemische Zeitung	chemical paper
Germany	Dachau	Amper-Bote	Bavaria
Germany	Darmstadt	Allgemeine Kirchenzeitung	church paper
Germany	Darmstadt	Amtsblatt der großherzoglichen Oberstudiendirektion	Hesse school council
Germany	Darmstadt	Amtsblatt des großherzoglichen Ministerium der Finanzen	Hesse finance ministry
Germany	Darmstadt	Amtsblatt des großherzoglichen Oberschulraths	Hesse school council
Germany	Darmstadt	Darmstädter Freie Presse	Hesse
Germany	Darmstadt	Darmstädter Tageblatt	500 years U Heidelberg
Germany	Darmstadt	Darmstädter Zeitung	Hesse
Germany	Darmstadt	Großherzoglich Hessisches Regierungsblatt	Hesse
Germany	Darmstadt	Hessische landwirtschaftliche Zeitschrift	agricultural paper
Germany	Darmstadt	Illustriertes Unterhaltungs-Blatt	Hesse entertainment section

Country	Published at	Title	Notes
Germany	Darmstadt	Intelligenzblatt für die Provinz Oberhessen	Friedberg Hesse area
Germany	Darmstadt	Lauterbacher Anzeiger	Lauterbach Hesse area
Germany	Darmstadt	Neue Militär-Zeitung	Hesse
Germany	Darmstadt	Neuer Anzeiger	Hesse
Germany	Darmstadt	Oberhessische Volkszeitung	Alsfeld Hesse area
Germany	Darmstadt	Regierungsblatt des Großherzogtums Hessen	Hesse
Germany	Darmstadt	Wochenbeilage der Darmstädter Zeitung	Hesse
Germany	Deggendorf	Bauern-Zeitung	Bavarian farmer paper
Germany	Deggendorf	Deggendorfer Donaubote	Bavaria
Germany	Demmin	Demminer Tagblatt	Mecklenburg
Germany	Deßau/Dessau	Der preußische Postfreund für Norddeutschland	postal paper
Germany	Deßau/Dessau	Sulamith	Jewish
Germany	Detmold	Die Wage	Lippe
Germany	Detmold	Fürstlich-Lippisches Regierungs- und Anzeigeblatt	Lippe
Germany	Detmold	Lippische Landes-Zeitung	500 years U Heidelberg
Germany	Detmold	Lippische Tages-Zeitung	wartime paper
Germany	Detmold	Lippisches Volksblatt	Lippe
Germany	Detmold	Westfälisch-Schaumburgische Zeitung	500 years U Heidelberg
Germany	Dillingen	Jahresbericht von der Königlichen Studien-Anstalt zu Dillingen	school report

Country	Published at	Title	Notes
Germany	Dillingen	Tagblatt für die Städte Dillingen, Lauingen, Höchstadt, Wertingen und Gundelfingen	Bavaria
Germany	Dillingen	Wochenblatt der Stadt Dillingen	Bavaria
Germany	Dinglingen	Der Schatzgräber	paper for mixed-religion marriages
Germany	Dinkelsbühl	Dinkelsbühlisches Intelligenzblatt	Bavaria
Germany	Dortmund	Amtsblatt für die Provinz Westfalen	Westphalia
Germany	Dortmund	Dortmunder Zeitung	Rhineland
Germany	Dortmund	Glück-Auf!	trade union paper
Germany	Dresden	Abend-Zeitung	Saxony
Germany	Dresden	Amtsblatt der königlichen Direktion der sächsischen Eisenbahnen	Saxony
Germany	Dresden	Arbeiterstimme	labor paper
Germany	Dresden	Betriebsgemeinschaft Renner	factory paper
Germany	Dresden	Der Calculator an der Elbe	Saxony
Germany	Dresden	Der Freiheitskampf	Saxony
Germany	Dresden	Der letzte Appell	Saxony
Germany	Dresden	Der Sonntag	Saxony
Germany	Dresden	Der Zeitgeist	Saxony
Germany	Dresden	Dresdner Anzeiger	500 years U Heidelberg

Country	Published at	Title	Notes
Germany	Dresden	Dresdner fliegende Blätter	Saxony
Germany	Dresden	Dresdner Journal	500 years U Heidelberg
Germany	Dresden	Dresdner Journal	Saxony
Germany	Dresden	Dresdner Morgenzeitung	Saxony
Germany	Dresden	Dresdner Nachrichten	500 years U Heidelberg
Germany	Dresden	Dresdner neueste Nachrichten	Saxony
Germany	Dresden	Dresdner Zeitung	500 years U Heidelberg
Germany	Dresden	Dresdner Zeitung	Saxony
Germany	Dresden	Feierabend	Saxony
Germany	Dresden	Für unsere Frauen	women's paper
Germany	Dresden	Haus und Herd	women's paper
Germany	Dresden	Monatsschrift für Geschichte und Wissenschaft des Judentums	Jewish
Germany	Dresden	Neueste Nachrichten	Saxony
Germany	Dresden	Sachsenstimme	Saxony
Germany	Dresden	Spartakus	socialist paper
Germany	Dresden	St.-Benno-Blatt	Catholic
Germany	Dresden	Wochenblatt	Saxony agricultural paper
Germany	Dresden	Wöchentlicher Anzeiger	Saxony
Germany	Duisburg	Der deutsche Metallarbeiter	trade union paper

Country	Published at	Title	Notes
Germany	Duisburg	Duisburger Intelligenz-Zeitung	Rhineland
Germany	Duisburg	Jahresbericht über das Königliche Gymnasium zu Duisburg	Rhineland
Germany	Düren	Dürener Anzeiger und Unterhaltungsblatt	Rhineland
Germany	Düren	General-Anzeiger für Stadt und Kreis Düren	Rhineland
Germany	Düren	Verkündiger für den Kreis Düren	Rhineland
Germany	Dürkheim/Bad Dürkheim	Jahresbericht über die Lateinische Schule zu Dürkheim	school report
Germany	Dürkheim/Bad Dürkheim	Wöchentliches Unterhaltungs-Blatt für den Kanton Dürkheim	Bavarian Palatinate
Germany	Düsseldorf	Amtsblatt für den Regierungsbezirk Düsseldorf	Rhineland
Germany	Düsseldorf	Bergischer Türmer	Rhineland
Germany	Düsseldorf	Düsseldorfer Erzähler	Rhineland
Germany	Düsseldorf	Düsseldorfer Intelligenz- und Adreß-Blatt	Rhineland
Germany	Düsseldorf	Düsseldorfer Literarisch-Merkantilisches Intelligenz- und Adreß-Blatt	Rhineland
Germany	Düsseldorf	Düsseldorfer Sonntagsblatt	Rhineland
Germany	Düsseldorf	Düsseldorfer Volksblatt	Rhineland
Germany	Düsseldorf	Düsseldorfer Zeitung	Rhineland
Germany	Düsseldorf	Erinnerungsblätter der 211. Infanterie-Division	WW I paper
Germany	Düsseldorf	Gülich und bergische wöchentliche Nachrichten	Rhineland

Country	Published at	Title	Notes
Germany	Düsseldorf	Holzarbeiterzeitung	trade union paper
Germany	Düsseldorf	Jüdische Allgemeine	Jewish
Germany	Düsseldorf	Königliches Düsseldorfer Intelligenzblatt	Rhineland
Germany	Düsseldorf	Rheinisches Land	Rhineland tourism
Germany	Düsseldorf	Rheinisches Volksblatt	Rhineland
Germany	Düsseldorf	Textilarbeiterzeitung	trade union paper
Germany	Düsseldorf	Textilarbeiterzeitung für die Interessen der Textilarbeiter und -Arbeiterinnen aller Branchen	trade union paper
Germany	Edenkoben	Jahresbericht über die kgl. Bayerische Studienanstalt in Edenkoben	school report
Germany	Ehrenbreitstein	Allgemeines Intelligenzblatt für die Fürstlich-Nassau-Weilburgischen und Nassau-Sayn-Hachenburgischen Lande	Rhineland
Germany	Ehrenbreitstein	Ehrenbreitsteiner Intelligenzblatt	Rhineland
Germany	Eichstätt	Eichstätter Intelligenzblatt	Bavaria
Germany	Eichstätt	Eichstätter Tagblatt	Bavaria
Germany	Eisenach	Stimme der Kirche	religious paper
Germany	Eisenberg	Der deutsche Patriot	Saxony
Germany	Eisenberg	Eisenbergisches Nachrichtsblatt	Saxony
Germany	Eisenstadt	Burgenländische Freiheit	Burgenland

Country	Published at	Title	Notes
Germany	Eisleben	Jahresbericht von Ostern 1863 bis dahin 1864 (Gymnasium Eisleben)	Saxony-Anhalt
Germany	Elberfeld	Conservative Provinzial-Zeitung für Rheinland und Westphalen	Rhineland
Germany	Elberfeld	Elberfelder Intelligenzblatt	Rhineland
Germany	Elberfeld	Elberfelder Zeitung	500 years U Heidelberg
Germany	Elberfeld	Rheinisches conservatives Volksblatt	Rhineland
Germany	Ellrich	Journal von und für Deutschland	Thuringia
Germany	Ellwangen	Königlich Württembergisches Allgemeines Amts- und Intelligenz-Blatt für den Jaxt-Kreis	Württemberg
Germany	Emmerich	Bürger-Blatt für die Kreise Rees, Borken und Cleve	Rhineland
Germany	Engelskirchen	Bergische Wacht	Rhineland
Germany	Erfurt	Amtsblatt der Königlichen Regierung zu Erfurt	Thuringia
Germany	Erfurt	Erfurtisches Intelligenz-Blatt	Thuringia
Germany	Erfurt	Möllers deutsche Gärtner-Zeitung	gardener paper
Germany	Erfurt	Neues Journal für die Botanik	botany
Germany	Erfurt	Regierungsblatt für das Land Thüringen	Thuringia
Germany	Erfurt	Regierungsblatt für Thüringen	Thuringia
Germany	Erlangen	Allgemeiner Kameral-, Oekonomie-, Forst- und Technologie-Korrespondent	Bavaria
Germany	Erlangen	Erlanger Mittwochs-Blatt	Bavaria

Country	Published at	Title	Notes
Germany	Erlangen	Erlanger Real-Zeitung	Bavaria
Germany	Erlangen	Erlanger Tagblatt	Bavaria
Germany	Erlangen	Erlanger Zeitung	Bavaria
Germany	Erlangen	Jahresbericht der lateinischen Vorbereitungsschulen zu Erlangen	Bavaria
Germany	Eschweiler; Berlin-Steglitz	Die Freistatt	Jewish cultural paper
Germany	Essen & Dortmund	Rheinisch Westfälische Zeitung	500 years U Heidelberg
Germany	Euskirchen	Erfa, Kreis-Intelligenzblatt für Euskirchen, Rheinbach und Ahweiler	Rhineland
Germany	Eutin	Ostholsteinischer Anzeiger	Schleswig-Holstein
Germany	Fechenheim	Fechenheimer Anzeiger	Frankfurt am Main suburb
Germany	Fehrbellin	Fehrbelliner Zeitung	agricultural
Germany	Flörsheim	Flörsheimer Zeitung	Hesse
Germany	Forchheim	Amtsblatt für die königlichen Bezirksämter Forchheim und Ebermannstadt	Bavaria
Germany	Frankenthal	Frankenthaler Wochen-Blatt	Bavarian Palatinate
Germany	Frankenthal	Jahresbericht über die Königliche Bayerische Lateinische Schule … Frankenthal	annual school report
Germany	Frankfurt am Main	Allgemeine Abeiterzeitung	labor paper
Germany	Frankfurt am Main	Amts-Blatt der freien Stadt Frankfurt	Frankfurt am Main

Country	Published at	Title	Notes
Germany	Frankfurt am Main	Amtsblatt für den Stadtkreis Frankfurt a. M.	Frankfurt am Main
Germany	Frankfurt am Main	Anzeigeblatt der städtischen Behörden zu Frankfurt am Main	Frankfurt am Main
Germany	Frankfurt am Main	Badener Lazarett-Zeitung	war hospital paper
Germany	Frankfurt am Main	Central-Anzeiger für jüdische Literatur	Jewish literary paper
Germany	Frankfurt am Main	Das illustrierte Blatt	Frankfurt am Main
Germany	Frankfurt am Main	Der israelitische Volkslehrer	Jewish
Germany	Frankfurt am Main	Der teutsche Reichs-Herold	Frankfurt am Main
Germany	Frankfurt am Main	Diarium Hebdomadale, oder wöchentliche auiso	Frankfurt am Main
Germany	Frankfurt am Main	Die Fackel	Frankfurt am Main
Germany	Frankfurt am Main	Die Maabrick	satire
Germany	Frankfurt am Main	Franckfurtische gelehrte Zeitungen	Frankfurt am Main
Germany	Frankfurt am Main	Frankfurt-Bockenheimer Anzeige-Blatt	Frankfurt am Main
Germany	Frankfurt am Main	Frankfurter Aerzte-Correspondenz	physicians
Germany	Frankfurt am Main	Frankfurter Bürgerzeitung Sonne	Frankfurt am Main
Germany	Frankfurt am Main	Frankfurter Illustrierte	Hesse
Germany	Frankfurt am Main	Frankfurter Israelitisches Familienblatt	Jewish
Germany	Frankfurt am Main	Frankfurter Journal	500 years U Heidelberg
Germany	Frankfurt am Main	Frankfurter Konversationsblatt	Frankfurt am Main
Germany	Frankfurt am Main	Frankfurter Krebbel-Zeitung	Frankfurt am Main

Country	Published at	Title	Notes
Germany	Frankfurt am Main	Frankfurter Leben	Frankfurt am Main
Germany	Frankfurt am Main	Frankfurter Nachrichten	Frankfurt am Main
Germany	Frankfurt am Main	Frankfurter Nachrichten und Intelligenzblatt	Frankfurt am Main
Germany	Frankfurt am Main	Frankfurter Oberpostamts-Zeitung	postal paper
Germany	Frankfurt am Main	Frankfurter Reform	Frankfurt am Main
Germany	Frankfurt am Main	Frankfurter Universitäts-Zeitung	university paper
Germany	Frankfurt am Main	Frankfurter Volksfreund	Frankfurt am Main
Germany	Frankfurt am Main	Frankfurter Wohlfahrtsblätter	Frankfurt am Main
Germany	Frankfurt am Main	Frankfurter Zeitung	500 years U Heidelberg
Germany	Frankfurt am Main	Frankfurter Zeitung und Handelsblatt	Frankfurt am Main
Germany	Frankfurt am Main	Gemeindeblatt der Israelitischen Gemeinde Frankfurt am Main	Jewish congregational paper
Germany	Frankfurt am Main	Großherzoglich frankfurtisches Regierungsblatt	Frankfurt
Germany	Frankfurt am Main	Hessisch-Nassauischer Volksbote	Hesse-Nassau
Germany	Frankfurt am Main	Intelligenz-Blatt der freien Stadt Frankfurt	Frankfurt
Germany	Frankfurt am Main	Israelitische Annalen	Jewish
Germany	Frankfurt am Main	Israelitische Religionsgesellschaft Frankfurt a.M.	Jewish
Germany	Frankfurt am Main	Jahrbuch der Jüdisch-Literarischen Gesellschaft	Jewish literary publication
Germany	Frankfurt am Main	Jahrbücher für jüdische Geschichte und Literatur	Jewish literary publication
Germany	Frankfurt am Main	Jeschurun (Alte Folge)	Jewish

Country	Published at	Title	Notes
Germany	Frankfurt am Main	Jüdische Zeitschrift für Wissenschaft und Leben	Jewish
Germany	Frankfurt am Main	Kleine Presse	Frankfurt am Main
Germany	Frankfurt am Main	Korrespondenzblatt des Vereins zur Gründung und Erhaltung einer Akademie für die Wissenschaft des Judentums	Jewish
Germany	Frankfurt am Main	Liberales Judentum	Jewish
Germany	Frankfurt am Main	Medizinisches Wochenblatt	medical
Germany	Frankfurt am Main	Mitteldeutsche Rundschau	Frankfurt am Main
Germany	Frankfurt am Main	Nachalath Zewi	Jewish
Germany	Frankfurt am Main	Neues Bürgerblatt: eine Wochenschrift	Frankfurt am Main
Germany	Frankfurt am Main	Neueste preußische Zeitung	Frankfurt am Main
Germany	Frankfurt am Main	Neueste Zeitung	Frankfurt am Main
Germany	Frankfurt am Main	Öffentlicher Anzeiger. Amtsblatt für den Stadtkreis Frankfurt a. M.	Frankfurt am Main
Germany	Frankfurt am Main	Olympiade-Pressedienst	workers' Olympics
Germany	Frankfurt am Main	Ordentliche wöchentliche Franckfurter Frag- und Anzeigungs-Nachrichten	Frankfurt am Main
Germany	Frankfurt am Main	Philanthropin	Jewish school publication
Germany	Frankfurt am Main	Populär-wissenschaftliche Monatsblätter zur Belehrung über das Judentum für Gebilldete aller Confessionen	Jewish
Germany	Frankfurt am Main	Sonntagsgruß: Kirchlicher Anzeiger für Frankfurt a.M. und Umgebung	religious paper
Germany	Frankfurt am Main	Turner-Schnaken	gymnastics paper

Country	Published at	Title	Notes
Germany	Frankfurt am Main	Wissenschaftliche Zeitschrift für jüdische Theologie	Jewish theology
Germany	Frankfurt am Main	Wochenblatt der Frankfurter Zeitung	Frankfurt am Main
Germany	Frankfurt am Main	Zeitung der freien Stadt Frankfurt	Frankfurt am Main
Germany	Frankfurt am Main	Zeitung des Großherzogthums Frankfurt	Frankfurt am Main
Germany	Frankfurt am Main and Leipzig	Didaskalia: Blätter für Geist, Gemüth und Publizität	literary
Germany	Frankfurt an der Oder	Amtsblatt der Regierung zu Frankfurt an der Oder	Brandenburg
Germany	Frankfurt an der Oder	Amtsblatt der Regierung zu Frankfurt an der Oder	Brandenburg
Germany	Frankfurt an der Oder	Dibre Emeth	Christian paper for Jewish readers
Germany	Frauendorf	Allgemeine deutsche Garten-Zeitung	gardener paper
Germany	Frauendorf	Bauern-Zeitung aus Frauendorf	farm paper
Germany	Freiberg	Berg- und Hüttenmännische Zeitung	miner paper; Saxony
Germany	Freiburg	Badisches Volksblatt	Baden
Germany	Freiburg	Breisgauer Zeitung	Baden
Germany	Freiburg	Freiburger Pfennigblatt	Baden
Germany	Freiburg	Freiburger Wochenblatt	Baden
Germany	Freiburg	Freiburger Zeitung	Baden
Germany	Freiburg	Großherzoglich badisches Amts- und Regierungsblatt für den Oberrhein-Kreis	Baden laws and regulations

Country	Published at	Title	Notes
Germany	Freiburg	Notariatsblatt für das Großherzogthum Baden	notary paper for Baden
Germany	Freiburg	Sammlung der Administrativ-Verordnungen und Bekanntmachungen für den Oberrhein-Kreis	Baden laws and regulations
Germany	Freiburg	Volkswacht	socialist paper
Germany	Freysing/Freising	Freisinger Tagblatt	Bavaria
Germany	Freysing/Freising	Freysinger Wochenblatt	Bavaria
Germany	Fulda	Fuldaisches Intelligenz-Blatt	Hesse
Germany	Fulda	Fürstlich-Oranien-Nassau-Fuldaische wöchentliche Polizei-, Kommerz- und Zeitungsanzeigen	Hesse
Germany	Fulda	Kreisblatt	Hesse
Germany	Fulda	Kreisblatt des vorhinnigen Regierungsbezirkes Fulda	Hesse
Germany	Fulda	Provinzial-Blatt für das Großherzogthum Fulda	Hesse
Germany	Fulda	Wochenblatt für die Provinz Fulda	Hesse
Germany	Fürstenfeldbruck	Fürstenfeldbrucker Zeitung	Bavaria
Germany	Fürth/Fuerth	Fürther Abendzeitung	Bavaria
Germany	Fürth/Fuerth	Fürther Tagblatt	Bavaria
Germany	Fürth/Fuerth	Fürther Tagblatt/Erzähler	Bavaria
Germany	Fürth/Fuerth	Jahresbericht der Königlichen Gewerb- und Handelsschule zu Fürth	annual school report

Country	Published at	Title	Notes
Germany	Geilenkirchen	Gemeinnütziges Wochenblatt für Geilenkirchen und Umgegend	Rhineland
Germany	Geilenkirchen	Gemeinnütziges Wochenblatt für Geilenkirchen, Heinsberg und die Umgegend	Rhineland
Germany	Gelsenkirchen	Zeitung deutscher Bergleute	trade union paper
Germany	Gera	Die Frauen-Zeitung	women's paper
Germany	Germersheim	Jahresbericht über die Königliche Bayerische Lateinschule ... Germersheim	annual school report
Germany	Germersheim	Wöchentliches Unterhaltungs-Blatt für den Land-Commissariats-Bezirk Germersheim	Bavaria
Germany	Gießen	ordentliche wöchentliche Franckfurter Frag- und Anzeigungs-Nachrichten	500 years U Heidelberg
Germany	Görlitz/Zgorzelec	Görlitzer Anzeiger	Saxony
Germany	Görlitz/Zgorzelec	Muskauer Wochenblatt	journalism
Germany	Görlitz/Zgorzelec	Neuer Görlitzer Anzeiger	Saxony
Germany	Görlitz/Zgorzelec	Newe Zeytung: Oder Kurtzer Discour von dem jetzigen	early paper
Germany	Görlitz/Zgorzelec	Oberlausitzische Fama	Saxony
Germany	Görlitz/Zgorzelec; Ronneburg	Der Anzeiger	Saxony
Germany	Gößnitz	Wochenblatt für Gößnitz und Umgebung	Thuringia
Germany	Gotha	Allgemeiner Anzeiger der Deutschen	Thuringia

Country	Published at	Title	Notes
Germany	Gotha	Allgemeiner Anzeiger und National-Zeitung der Deutschen	Thuringia
Germany	Gotha	Allgemeiner Polizei-Anzeiger	police gazette
Germany	Gotha	Anzeiger: ein Tagblatt	Thuringia
Germany	Gotha	Der Schuhmacher (Gotha)	trade union paper
Germany	Gotha	Gothaische gelehrte Zeitungen	scholarly
Germany	Gotha	Intelligenzblatt zur deutschen Zeitung	scholarly
Germany	Gotha	Kaiserlich privilegirte Reichs-Anzeiger	official imperial paper
Germany	Gotha	Schuhmacherfachblatt	trade union paper
Germany	Göttingen	Göttingische Anzeigen von gelehrten Sachen	scholarly
Germany	Göttingen	Göttingische gelehrte Anzeigen	scholarly
Germany	Göttingen	Göttingische Zeitung von gelehrten Sachen	scholarly
Germany	Göttingen	Göttingsche Policey-Amts Nachrichten	police gazette
Germany	Göttingen	Mennonitenbrief aus Göttingen	Mennonite
Germany	Göttingen	Mitteilungen des Sippenverbandes der Danziger Mennoniten-Familien	Mennonite families
Germany	Göttingen	Zeitschrift für deutsche Mythologie und Sittenkunde	Mennonite
Germany	Grafing	Grafinger Zeitung	some limited
Germany	Greifswald	Greifswalder gemeinnütziges Wochenblatt	Pomerania
Germany	Greifswald	Greifswaldisches Wochen-Blatt von allerhand gelehrten und nützlichen Sachen	Pomerania

Country	Published at	Title	Notes
Germany	Greifswald	Intelligenzblatt von täglichen Vorkommenheiten in Pommern und Rügen	Pomerania
Germany	Greifswald	Kreis-Anzeiger für den Kresi Greifswald	Pomerania
Germany	Greifswald	Kriegs-Zeitung	Pomerania
Germany	Greifswald	Landwirthschaftliche Beilage der Greifswalder Zeitung	agricultural paper for Pomerania
Germany	Greifswald	Neue critische Nachrichten	Pomerania
Germany	Greifswald	Neueste critische Nachrichten	Pomerania
Germany	Greifswald	Schwedisches ökonomisches Wochenblatt	Pomerania and Sweden
Germany	Greiz	Fürstlich Reuß-plauisches Amts-und Verordnungsblatt	Thuringia
Germany	Greiz	Heimat	Thuringia
Germany	Greiz	Kirchlicher Gemeindeblatt für Reuss	church
Germany	Greiz	Landes-Zeitung für das Fürstenthum Reuß	Thuringia
Germany	Greiz	Sonntagsgruss unserer Heimatkirche	religious paper
Germany	Grevenbroich	Geschäfts- und Unterhaltungsblatt für den Kreis Grevenbroich und dessen Umgebung	Rhineland
Germany	Grevenbroich	Grevenbroicher Kreisblatt	Rhineland
Germany	Grevenbroich	Grevenbroicher Kreisblatt und landwirthschaftlicher Anzeiger für das Jülicher Land	Rhineland
Germany	Grevenbroich	Grevenbroicher Kreisblatt und Organ für die Gilbach	Rhineland
Germany	Grevesmühlen	Grevesmühlener Wochenblatt	Mecklenburg

Country	Published at	Title	Notes
Germany	Gronau	Unser Blatt	Mennonite
Germany	Großenhain	Großenhainer Unterhaltungs- und Anzeigeblatt	Saxony
Germany	Grünstadt	Jahresbericht von dem Königlichen Progymnasium zu Grünstadt im Rheinkreise	annual school report
Germany	Guben	Gubener Kriegs-Zeitung	WW I paper
Germany	Gummersbach	Agger-Blatt	Rhineland
Germany	Gummersbach	Gummersbacher Kreisblatt	Rhineland
Germany	Günzburg	Amtsblatt für das Bezirksamt Günzburg	Bavaria
Germany	Günzburg	Jahresbericht über die Königlich Bayerische Lateinschule in Günzbug	Bavaria
Germany	Haan	Haaner Zeitung	Rhineland
Germany	Halle an der Saale	Allgemeine Literatur-Zeitung	literary
Germany	Halle an der Saale	Allgemeines Journal der Uhrmacherkunst	clockmaker paper
Germany	Halle an der Saale	Der Klassenkampf	Communist party paper
Germany	Halle an der Saale	Hallisches patriotisches Wochenblatt	Saxony
Germany	Halle an der Saale	Hallisches Tageblatt	Saxony
Germany	Halle an der Saale	Hallisches Wochenblatt	Saxony
Germany	Halle an der Saale	Journal für Prediger	preacher journal
Germany	Hamburg	Allgemeine deutsche naturhistorische Zeitung	natural history

Country	Published at	Title	Notes
Germany	Hamburg	Amtsblatt der freien und Hansestadt Hamburg	Hamburg
Germany	Hamburg	Börsen-Halle: Hamburgische Abendzeitung für Handel, Schiffahrt und Politik	business paper
Germany	Hamburg	Correspondenzblatt der Generalkommission der Gewerkdhften Deutschlands	trade union paper
Germany	Hamburg	Der Spiegel	major weekly newsmagazine
Germany	Hamburg	Der treue Zions-Wächter	Jewish
Germany	Hamburg	Deutsche Bäcker- und Konditoren-Zeitung	trade union paper
Germany	Hamburg	Deutsche Bäckerzeitung	trade union paper
Germany	Hamburg	Deutsche Levante-Zeitung	shipping lines
Germany	Hamburg	Deutscher Beobachter oder Hanseatische privilegirte Zeitung	
Germany	Hamburg	Die rote Fahne	Communist
Germany	Hamburg	Die Zeit	news and commentary
Germany	Hamburg	Gemeindebrief der Mennonitengemeinde zu Hamburg und Altona	Mennonite
Germany	Hamburg	Hamburger Abendblatt	Hamburg
Germany	Hamburg	Hamburger Anzeiger	Hamburg
Germany	Hamburg	Hamburger Börsenhalle	business paper
Germany	Hamburg	Hamburger Fremdenblatt	500 years U Heidelberg
Germany	Hamburg	Hamburger Garten- und Blumenzeitung	gardener paper

Country	Published at	Title	Notes
Germany	Hamburg	Hamburger Musikalische Zeitung	music paper
Germany	Hamburg	Hamburger Nachrichten	Hamburg
Germany	Hamburg	Hamburger neueste Nachrichten	Hamburg
Germany	Hamburg	Hamburger Zeitung	Hamburg
Germany	Hamburg	Hamburgischer Correspondent	500 years U Heidelberg
Germany	Hamburg	Hamburgischer Correspondent	largest circulation in Europe
Germany	Hamburg	Hamburgisches Gesetz- und Verordnungsblatt	Hamburg official paper
Germany	Hamburg	Handlungsgehülfen-Blatt	deliveryman paper
Germany	Hamburg	Jahresbericht der Taufgesinnten Missionsgesellschaft	Mennonite
Germany	Hamburg	Jahresberichte der Verwaltungsbehörden der freien Stadt Hamburg	government reports
Germany	Hamburg	Jüdische Schulzeitung	Jewish teacher publication
Germany	Hamburg	Kampf	socialist paper
Germany	Hamburg	Kritische Blätter der Börsen-Halle	stocks paper
Germany	Hamburg	Mitteilungen der Gesellschaft für jüdische Volkskunde [Alte Folge]	Jewish
Germany	Hamburg	Neue Hamburger Zeitung	Hamburg
Germany	Hamburg	Neue Tischlerzeitung	trade union paper
Germany	Hamburg	Norddeutsche Nachrichten (coming)	Hamburg
Germany	Hamburg	Staats- und Gelehrte-Zeitung des hamburgischen	Hamburg; international

Country	Published at	Title	Notes
Germany	Hamburg	unpartheyischen Correspondenten	
Germany	Hamburg	Staats- und Gelehrte-Zeitung des unpartheyischen Correspondenten	Hamburg; international
Germany	Hamburg	Staats- und Regierungsblatt für Hamburg	Hamburg
Germany	Hamburg; Berlin	Der Grundstein	trade union paper
Germany	Hamburg; Berlin	Der Zimmerer	trade union paper
Germany	Hamburg; Breslau	Die neue Welt	trade union paper
Germany	Hameln	Deister- und Weser-Zeitung	500 years U Heidelberg
Germany	Hamm	Hammsches Wochenblatt	Westphalia
Germany	Hamm	Jahresbericht des Königlichen Gymnasiums und des Realgymnasiums zu Hamm	Westphalia
Germany	Hammelburg	Jahresbericht über die königlich Bayerische Lateinschule in Hammelburg	Bavaria
Germany	Hanau	Hanauer neue europäische Zeitung	Hesse
Germany	Hanau	Jahresbericht über das Kurfürstliche Gymnasium zu Hanau	annual school report
Germany	Hannover	Amtsblatt für Hannover	Lower Saxony
Germany	Hannover	Brauereiarbeiterzeitung	trade union paper
Germany	Hannover	Der Proletarier	Communist party paper
Germany	Hannover	Deutsche Brauerzeitung	trade union paper
Germany	Hannover	Hannoverscher Courier	500 years U Heidelberg

Country	Published at	Title	Notes
Germany	Hannover	Hannoversches Polizeiblatt	Hannover police gazette
Germany	Hannover	Hannoversches Tagblatt	500 years U Heidelberg
Germany	Hannover	Jahresbericht des Lyceums 1 zu Hannover	Lower Saxony
Germany	Hannover	Notiz-Blatt des Architekten- und Ingenieur-Verein für das Königreich Hannover	architect and engineer paper
Germany	Hannover	Zeitblatt für die Angelegenheiten der Lutherischen Kirche	Lutheran paper
Germany	Hannover-Linden	Brauerzeitung	trade union paper
Germany	Hannover-Linden	Zentralorgan der deutschen Brauer	trade union paper
Germany	Haßfurt	Jahresbericht über die K. Bayer. Lateinschule zu Hassfurt	annual school report
Germany	Heidelberg	Badische Post	Baden
Germany	Heidelberg	Der Heidelberger Student	university student paper
Germany	Heidelberg	Heidelberger Neueste Nachrichten	Baden
Germany	Heidelberg	Heidelberger Tagblatt	dairy paper
Germany	Heidelberg	Heidelberger Zeitung	Baden
Germany	Heidelberg	Jahresbericht über das grossh. Lyceum zu Heidelberg	annual school report
Germany	Heidelberg	Zeitung für Einsiedler	literary paper
Germany	Heidelberg; Frankfurt am Main	Deutsche Zeitung	general newspaper
Germany	Heiligenhaus; Düsseldorf	Velberter Morgen-Zeitung	Rhineland
Germany	Heiligenstadt	Eichsfelder Generalanzeiger	Lower Saxony

Country	Published at	Title	Notes
Germany	Heiligenstadt	Eichsfelder Tageblatt	Lower Saxony
Germany	Heiligenstadt	Eichsfelder Volksblätter	Lower Saxony
Germany	Heiligenstadt	Eichsfeldia	Lower Saxony
Germany	Heinsberg	Der Heinsberger Bote	Rhineland
Germany	Heinsberg	Heinsberger Kreisblatt	Rhineland
Germany	Helmstedt	Helmstedter Kreisblatt	Lower Saxony; 125 year edition
Germany	Henneberg; Suhl	Henneberger Zeitung	Thuringia
Germany	Heppenheim	Verordnungs-Anzeigeblatt für den Kreis Heppenheim	Thuringia
Germany	Herford	Conivn- und Avgirte Wöchentliche Avisen	Lower Saxony
Germany	Herford	Herforder öffentlicher Anzeiger	Herford area
Germany	Hersbruck	Jahresbericht über die Lateinische Schule zu Hersbruck	annual school report
Germany	Hilden	Hildener Rundschau	Rhineland
Germany	Hilden	Rheinisches Volksblatt	Rhineland
Germany	Hildesheim	Molkerei-Zeitung	dairy paper
Germany	Hochheim am Main	Hochheimer Stadtanzeiger	Hesse
Germany	Hof	Hofer Zeitung	Bavaria
Germany	Holzminden	Holzmindisches Wochenblatt	Lower Saxony
Germany	Homburg	Jahresbericht über die Königlich Bayerische Lateinschule zu Homburg in der Pfalz	annual school report

Country	Published at	Title	Notes
Germany	Honnef	Honnefer Volkszeitung	Rhineland
Germany	Hückeswagen	Volksblatt für Berg und Mark	Rhineland
Germany	Ingolstadt	Ingolstädter Anzeiger	Bavaria
Germany	Ingolstadt	Ingolstädter Tagblatt	Bavaria
Germany	Ingolstadt	Ingolstädter Wochen-Blatt	Bavaria
Germany	Ingolstadt	Ingolstädter Zeitung	Bavaria
Germany	Ingolstadt	Süddeutscher Anzeiger	Bavaria
Germany	Itzehoe	Holsteinische Stände-Zeitung	Holstein nobility
Germany	Jena	Allgemeine academische Zeitung	academic paper
Germany	Jena	Am Wege	tourist paper
Germany	Jena	Blätter von der Saale	Thuringia
Germany	Jena	Das Volk: Thüringer Zeitung	Thuringia
Germany	Jena	Deutsche Blätter aus Thüringen	Thuringia
Germany	Jena	Gemeinnütziges Justiz- und Polizeiblatt der Teutschen	Thuringia
Germany	Jena	Glaube und Heimat	Thuringia religious paper
Germany	Jena	Intelligenzblatt der Jenaischen allgemeinen Literatur-Zeitung	literary
Germany	Jena	ISIS, oder, Enzyclopaedische Zeitung von Oken	scholarly
Germany	Jena	Jenaer Literaturzeitung	literary
Germany	Jena	Jenaer Volksblatt	Thuringia

Country	Published at	Title	Notes
Germany	Jena	Jenaische Beyträge zur neuesten gelehrten Gechichte	Thuringia
Germany	Jena	Jenaische gelehrte Anzeigen	Thuringia
Germany	Jena	Jenaische gelehrte Zeitungen	scholarly
Germany	Jena	Jenaische Nachrichten von Gelehrten und andere Sachen	scholarly
Germany	Jena	Jenaische Zeitung	Thuringia
Germany	Jena	Neue jenaische allgemeine Literatur-Zeitung	Thuringia
Germany	Jena	Neuer Rheinischer Merkur	
Germany	Jena	Privilegirte jenaische Wochenblätter	Thuringia
Germany	Jena	Privilegirte jenaische wöchentliche Anzeiger	Thuringia
Germany	Jena	Thüringer Kirchenblatt	religious paper
Germany	Jena	Thüringer Volksfreund	Thuringia
Germany	Jena	Volk	Thuringia
Germany	Jena	Volkszeitung für Sachsen-Weimar-Eisenach	Thuringia
Germany	Jena	Volkszeitung Großherzogtum Sachsen-Weimar-Eisenach	Thuringia
Germany	Jena	Weimarische Volkszeitung	Thuringia
Germany	Jena & Halle	Allgemeine Literatur-Zeitung	literary
Germany	Jülich	Jülicher Kreis-, Correspondenz und Wochenblatt	Rhineland
Germany	Kaiserslautern	Amts- und Intelligenzblatt der Provisorischen Regierung der Rheinpfalz	Bavarian Palatinate
Germany	Kaiserslautern	Christlicher Gemeinde-Kalender	Mennonite

Country	Published at	Title	Notes
Germany	Kaiserslautern	Jahresbericht der K. Studienanstalt zu Kaiserslautern	annual school report
Germany	Kaiserslautern	Pfälzer Demokrat und Sonntags-Blatt	political paper
Germany	Kaiserslautern	Pfälzer Sonntagsblatt	Bavarian Palatinate
Germany	Kaiserslautern	Pfälzer Unterhaltungsblatt	cultural supplement
Germany	Kaiserslautern	Pfälzische Post	Bavarian Palatinate
Germany	Kaiserslautern	Pfälzische Volkszeitung	Bavarian Palatinate
Germany	Kaiserslautern	Pfälzisches Sonntags-Blatt	cultural supplement
Germany	Kaiserslautern	Plauderstübchen	Rhine Bavaria
Germany	Karlsruhe	Allgemeines Intelligenz-Blatt für sämtlich-hochfürstlich-badische Lande	Baden
Germany	Karlsruhe	Badische Chronik	Baden
Germany	Karlsruhe	Badische Landeszeitung	Baden
Germany	Karlsruhe	Badische Presse	Baden
Germany	Karlsruhe	Badischer Beobachter	Baden
Germany	Karlsruhe	Badischer Landsmann	Baden
Germany	Karlsruhe	Badisches Gesetz- und Verordnungsblatt	Baden laws and regulations
Germany	Karlsruhe	Badisches Intelligenzblatt	Baden
Germany	Karlsruhe	Der Führer	Baden National Socialist
Germany	Karlsruhe	Der Volksfreund	Baden
Germany	Karlsruhe	Die Biene	Baden

Country	Published at	Title	Notes
Germany	Karlsruhe	Die Pyramide	Baden
Germany	Karlsruhe	Gesetzes- und Verordnungsblatt für das Großherzogthum Baden	Baden laws and regulations
Germany	Karlsruhe	Großherzoglich-Badische Staats-Zeitung	Baden
Germany	Karlsruhe	Großherzoglich-Badisches Regierungs-Blatt	Baden
Germany	Karlsruhe	Großherzoglich-Badisches Staats- und Regierungs-Blatt	Baden
Germany	Karlsruhe	Junge Gemeinde	Mennonite
Germany	Karlsruhe	Karlsruher Tagblatt	Baden
Germany	Karlsruhe	Karlsruher Unterhaltungsblatt	Baden
Germany	Karlsruhe	Karlsruher Zeitung	Baden
Germany	Karlsruhe	Landwirthschaftliches Centralblatt	Baden agricultural paper
Germany	Karlsruhe	Landwirthschaftliches Wochenblatt für das Großherzogthum Baden	Baden agricultural paper
Germany	Karlsruhe	Notariats-Blatt für das Großherzogthum Baden	Baden
Germany	Karlsruhe	Regierungsblatt der Militär-Regierung Württemberg-Baden	Baden laws and regulations
Germany	Karlsruhe	Sammelband der badischen Presse	special editions for Grand Duke's 70th
Germany	Karlsruhe	Staats-Anzeiger für das Grossherzogtum Baden	Baden
Germany	Karlsruhe	Sterne und Blumen	Baden
Germany	Karlsruhe	Verordnungsblatt für die Beamten und Angestellten der Steuerverwalgung	Baden official tax paper

Country	Published at	Title	Notes
Germany	Karlsruhe	Volksfreund	Baden socialist
Germany	Kassel	Amtsblatt der königlichen Regierung zu Cassel	Hesse
Germany	Kassel	Amtsblatt der königlichen Regierung zu Cassel	Hesse
Germany	Kassel	Casselische Polizey- und Commerzien-Zeitung	Hesse
Germany	Kassel	Hessische Morgenzeitung	500 years U Heidelberg
Germany	Kassel	Kasselsches Journal	extra edition
Germany	Kassel; Leipzig	Journal für Ornithologie	ornithology
Germany	Kastellaun	Castellauner Zeitung	Rhineland
Germany	Kaufbeuren	Jahresbericht über die Lateinische Schule zu Kaufbeuren	annual school report
Germany	Kempten	Allgäuer Volksblatt	Bavaria
Germany	Kempten	Allgäuer Zeitung	Bavaria
Germany	Kempten	Intelligenzblatt der königlich baierischen Stadt Kempten	Bavaria
Germany	Kempten	Intelligenzblatt des königlich baierischen Iller-Kreises	Bavaria
Germany	Kempten	Kemptner Zeitung	Bavaria
Germany	Kempten	Neueste Weltbegebenheiten	Bavaria
Germany	Kiel	Amtsblatt für das Herzogtum Holstein	Holstein
Germany	Kiel	Amtsblatt für die Herzogthümer Schleswig und Holstein	Schleswig-Holstein
Germany	Kiel	Landwirthschaftliches Wochenblatt für Schleswig-Holstein	Schleswig-Holstein agricultural
Germany	Kiel	Neue kielische gelehrte Zeitung	Schleswig-Holstein

Country	Published at	Title	Notes
Germany	Kirchheimbolanden	Jahresbericht über die Königl. Bayer. Lateinische Schule zu Kirchheimbolanden	annual school report
Germany	Kissingen/Bad Kissingen	Jahresbericht der königlichen Gewerbschule zu Kissingen	annual school report
Germany	Kissingen/Bad Kissingen	Kissinger Tagblatt	daily
Germany	Kitzingen	Jahresbericht über die Kgl. Bayerische Katholische Lateinschule zu Kitzingen	annual school report
Germany	Kleve/Cleves	Amtsblatt der königlichen Regierung zu Cleve	Rhineland
Germany	Kleve/Cleves	Clevisches Volksblatt	Rhineland
Germany	Kleve/Cleves	öffentlicher Anzeiger der königlich preussischen Regierung zu Cleve	Rhineland
Germany	Koblenz/Coblenz	Amtsblatt der königlichen Regierung zu Coblenz	Rhineland
Germany	Koblenz/Coblenz	Coblenzer Tageblatt	Rhineland
Germany	Koblenz/Coblenz	Fest-Zeitung	gymnastics paper
Germany	Koblenz/Coblenz	Jocusstädtische Carnevals-Zeitung	humor
Germany	Koblenz/Coblenz	Rhein- und Mosel-Bote	Rhineland
Germany	Koblenz/Coblenz	Rheinischer Merkur	Rhineland
Germany	Köln/Cologne	Allgemeines Organ für Handel und Gewerbe	business paper
Germany	Köln/Cologne	Amtsblatt für den Regierungsbezirk Köln	Rhineland
Germany	Köln/Cologne	Bekleidungsgewerkschaft	clothier and hatter paper
Germany	Köln/Cologne	Der Berggeist	miner paper

Country	Published at	Title	Notes
Germany	Köln/Cologne	Der deutsche Holzarbeiter	trade union paper
Germany	Köln/Cologne	Der Gemeindearbeiter	community employees paper
Germany	Köln/Cologne	Der Holzarbeiter	trade union paper
Germany	Köln/Cologne	Der Wächter am Rhein	Rhineland
Germany	Köln/Cologne	Deutsche Zinngießer-Zeitung	tinsmith/pewterer paper
Germany	Köln/Cologne	Die Gegenwart	Rhineland
Germany	Köln/Cologne	Die Rheinische Volks-Halle	supplement
Germany	Köln/Cologne	Gewerkschaftliche Rundschau	trade union paper
Germany	Köln/Cologne	Graphische Stimmen	printing worker paper
Germany	Köln/Cologne	Jahresbericht des königlichen katholischen Gymnasiums an Marzellen zu Cöln	annual school report
Germany	Köln/Cologne	Kaiserliche Reichs-Ober-Post-Amts-Zeitung zu Köln	postal paper
Germany	Köln/Cologne	Köln-Bergheimer Zeitung	Rhineland
Germany	Köln/Cologne	Kölner Arbeiterzeitung	labor paper
Germany	Köln/Cologne	Kölner Local-Anzeiger	Rhineland
Germany	Köln/Cologne	Kölner Nachrichten	Rhineland
Germany	Köln/Cologne	Kölner Sonntags-Anzeiger	Rhineland
Germany	Köln/Cologne	Kölnische Zeitung	500 years U Heidelberg
Germany	Köln/Cologne	Kölnischer Anzeiger	Rhineland

Country	Published at	Title	Notes
Germany	Köln/Cologne	Kreisblatt für Mülheim, Sieg und Landkreis Köln	Rhineland
Germany	Köln/Cologne	Niederrheinische Musik-Zeitung für Kunstfreunde und Künstler	music paper
Germany	Köln/Cologne	Rheinische Allgemeine Zeitung	Rhineland
Germany	Köln/Cologne	Rheinische Volkszeitung	Rhineland
Germany	Köln/Cologne	Schneider-Zeitung	trade union paper
Germany	Köln/Cologne; Gummersbach	Oberbergischer Bote	Rhineland
Germany	Königswinter	Echo des Siebengebirges	Rhineland
Germany	Königswinter	Königswinterer Zeitung	Rhineland
Germany	Konstanz	Großherzoglich badisches Anzeigeblatt für den Seekreis	Baden
Germany	Konstanz	Konstanzer Zeitung	Baden
Germany	Krefeld	Christlicher Textilarbeiter	trade union paper
Germany	Krefeld	Monatsblätter der Mennonitengemeinde Crefeld	Mennonite
Germany	Kreuznach	Unterhaltungen	Rhineland
Germany	Kronach	Fränkischer Wald	Franconia
Germany	Kusel	Jahresbericht über die Lateinische Schule zu Cusel	annual school report
Germany	Kusel	Königlich-bayerisches Kreisamtsblatt der Pfalz	Bavarian Palatinate
Germany	Kusel	Neue Didaskalia	Bavarian Palatinate
Germany	Kusel	Pfälzer-Bote für das Glantal und Anzeige-Blatt für den Bezirk Kusel	cultural supplement

Country	Published at	Title	Notes
Germany	Kusel	Westricher Tagblatt	daily
Germany	Kusel	Westricher Zeitung	Bavarian Palatinate
Germany	Landau in der Pfalz	Der Eilbote	Bavarian Palatinate
Germany	Landau in der Pfalz	Der Eilbote aus dem Bezirk	Bavarian Palatinate
Germany	Landau in der Pfalz	Kreis-Anzeiger von Landau	Bavarian Palatinate
Germany	Landau in der Pfalz	Landauer Wochenblatt	Bavarian Palatinate
Germany	Landau in der Pfalz	Neues Volksblatt	Bavarian Palatinate
Germany	Landau in der Pfalz	Palatina	Bavarian Palatinate
Germany	Landsberg am Lech	Jahresbericht von der Lateinischen Stadtschule in Landsberg im Isarkreis	annual school report
Germany	Landshut	Amts-Blatt für die Gemeinden des Bezirksamts Landshut	Bavaria
Germany	Landshut	Königlich-Bayerisches Kreis-Amtsblatt für Niederbayern	Bavaria
Germany	Landshut	Kurier fur Niederbayern	Bavaria
Germany	Landshut	Landshuter Wochenblatt	Bavaria
Germany	Landshut	Landshuter Zeitung	Bavaria
Germany	Landshut	Tagblatt für Landshut und Umgegend	daily
Germany	Langenberg	Der Zeitungs-Bote	Rhineland
Germany	Langenberg	Velberter Zeitung	Rhineland
Germany	Langensalza	Langensalzaer Kreis- und Nachrichtenblatt	Thuringia

Country	Published at	Title	Notes
Germany	Langensalza	Langensalzaer Kreisblatt	Thuringia
Germany	Langensalza	Langensalzaer Kreis-Wochenblatt	Thuringia
Germany	Langensalza	Langensalzaer Tageblatt	Thuringia
Germany	Langensalza	Langensalzaer Wochenblatt	Thuringia
Germany	Langensalza	Langensalzaisches Wochenblat	Thuringia
Germany	Langensalza	Wochenblat für den Langensalzaer Kreis	Thuringia
Germany	Lauenburg an der Elbe	Jahresbericht	Schleswig-Holstein
Germany	Leipzig	Allgemeine deutsche Lehrerzeitung	teacher paper
Germany	Leipzig	Allgemeine Literatur-Zeitung	literary
Germany	Leipzig	Allgemeine musikalische Zeitung	music paper
Germany	Leipzig	Allgemeine Preßzeitung	press newspaper
Germany	Leipzig	Allgemeine Zeitung des Judenthums	Jewish
Germany	Leipzig	Allgemeines Repertorium der Literatur	literary
Germany	Leipzig	Allgemeiner Anzeiger für Mechanik, Optik, Elektrotechnik, Glasinstrumenten und Uhrmacherbranche	mechanical and technological
Germany	Leipzig	An Flanderns Küste	wartime field paper
Germany	Leipzig	Ben-Chananja	Jewish
Germany	Leipzig	Blätter für literarische Unterhaltung	literary
Germany	Leipzig	Börsenblatt für den deutschen Buchhandel	bookseller paper

Country	Published at	Title	Notes
Germany	Leipzig	Cholera-Zeitung	cholera paper
Germany	Leipzig	Der Correspondent	printer and typesetter paper
Germany	Leipzig	Der Genealogische Archivarius	genealogy of upper class
Germany	Leipzig	Der Herold	Saxony
Germany	Leipzig	Der Jude	Jewish
Germany	Leipzig	Der Leuchtturm	Saxony
Germany	Leipzig	Der Orient	Jewish
Germany	Leipzig	Deutsche Buchbinderzeitung	bookbinder paper
Germany	Leipzig	Deutsche Reichs-Bremse	satire
Germany	Leipzig	Die Bauhuette: Illustrierte Freimaurerzeitung	Masonic paper
Germany	Leipzig	Die Betriebsgemeinschaft der Leipziger Funkgerätebau	trade union paper
Germany	Leipzig	Die Grenzboten	Saxony
Germany	Leipzig	Die Laterne	Saxony
Germany	Leipzig	Die Leipziger Zeitung	Saxony
Germany	Leipzig	Die neue Zeit	Saxony
Germany	Leipzig	Die Uhrmacher-Woche	clockmaker paper
Germany	Leipzig	Die Wartburg	Saxony
Germany	Leipzig	Extract der eingelauffenen Nouvellen	Saxony
Germany	Leipzig	Freimaurer-Zeitung	Masonic paper

Country	Published at	Title	Notes
Germany	Leipzig	Graphische Presse	lithographer paper
Germany	Leipzig	Handels-Zeitung für die gesamte Uhren-Industrie	clockmaker paper
Germany	Leipzig	Illustrirte Zeitung	Saxony
Germany	Leipzig	Jahrbuch für die Geschichte der Juden und des Judenthums	Jewish historical publication
Germany	Leipzig	Jüdisches Jahrbuch für Sachsen	Jewish Saxony publication
Germany	Leipzig	Korrespondent	trade union paper
Germany	Leipzig	Korrespondenzblatt für Deutschlands Buchdrucker und Schriftgießer	trade union paper
Germany	Leipzig	Kunstchronik	art paper
Germany	Leipzig	Leipziger Illustrirte Zeitung	Saxony
Germany	Leipzig	Leipziger Intelligenz-Blatt	Saxony
Germany	Leipzig	Leipziger Lokomotive	Saxony
Germany	Leipzig	Leipziger Mieter-Zeitung	renter paper
Germany	Leipzig	Leipziger Neueste Nachrichten	Saxony
Germany	Leipzig	Leipziger Tageblatt	daily
Germany	Leipzig	Leipziger Tageblatt und Anzeiger	500 years U Heidelberg
Germany	Leipzig	Leipziger Tageszeitung	daily
Germany	Leipzig	Leipziger Uhrmacher-Zeitung	clockmaker paper

Country	Published at	Title	Notes
Germany	Leipzig	Leipziger Völkisches-Echo	Saxony
Germany	Leipzig	Leipziger Volkszeitung	Saxony
Germany	Leipzig	Leipziger Westend-Zeitung	Saxony
Germany	Leipzig	Leipziger Zeitungen	Saxony
Germany	Leipzig	Leipzig's roter Straßenbahner	socialist streetcar union paper
Germany	Leipzig	Literarisches Centralblatt für Deutschland	literary
Germany	Leipzig	Literarisches Conversationsblatt	literary
Germany	Leipzig	Mitteilungen des Gesamtarchivs der deutschen Juden	Jewish
Germany	Leipzig	Mitteilungsblatt des Ortskommittes der RGO Leipzig	socialist paper
Germany	Leipzig	Monatshefte der Comenius Gesellschaft	Mennonite
Germany	Leipzig	Musikalisches Wochenblatt	music paper
Germany	Leipzig	Neue jenaische allgemeine Literatur-Zeitung	literary
Germany	Leipzig	Neue Leipziger Zeitung	Saxony
Germany	Leipzig	Neue Rheinische Zeitung	general newspaper
Germany	Leipzig	Neue Zeitungen von gelehrten Sachen	scholarly
Germany	Leipzig	Sachsenpost	Saxony
Germany	Leipzig	Sachsenzeitung	Saxony
Germany	Leipzig	Seifenblasen	supplement
Germany	Leipzig	Signale für die musikalische Welt	music paper

Country	Published at	Title	Notes
Germany	Leipzig	Theater-Zeitung	theater paper
Germany	Leipzig	Zeitschrift für die Musikwissenschaft	music paper
Germany	Leipzig	Zeitung für den deutschen Adel	nobility
Germany	Leipzig	Zeitung für die Jugend	youth paper
Germany	Leipzig & Dresden	Illustrirtes Familien-Journal	family paper
Germany	Leipzig; Berlin	Allgemeine Zeitung des Judentums	Jewish
Germany	Leipzig; Bremen; Berlin	Der Tabakarbeiter	trade union paper
Germany	Leipzig; Dresden	General-Gouvernements-Blatt fur Sachsen	Saxony
Germany	Leipzig-Gohlis	Freimaurer-Zeitung	Freemasonry paper
Germany	Leipzig-Wahren	Gefolgschaft Pittler	factory newspaper
Germany	Leisnig	Anzeiger und Amtsblatt für das königl. Gerichtsamt und den Stadtrath zu Leisnig	Saxony
Germany	Lemgo	Lippische Intelligenzblätter	Lippe
Germany	Lemgo	Lippisches Intelligenzblatt	Lippe
Germany	Lengsfeld	Der Israelit des neunzehnten Jahrhunderts	Jewish
Germany	Lindau (Bodensee)	Intelligenzblatt der Reichsstadt Lindau	Bavaria
Germany	Lindau (Bodensee)	Lindauer Tagblatt für Stadt und Land	Bavaria
Germany	Lindlar	Bergischer Agent	Rhineland
Germany	Lindlar; Düsseldorf	Bergischer Türmer	Rhineland

Country	Published at	Title	Notes
Germany	Linz am Rhein	Rheinisches Wochenblatt	Rhineland
Germany	Linz am Rhein	Rheinisches Wochenblatt für Stadt und Land	Rhineland
Germany	Linz am Rhein	Sinziger Volksfreund	Rhineland
Germany	Linz am Rhein; Ahrweiler	Rheinisches Wochenblatt für Stadt und Land	Rhineland
Germany	Lippstadt	Alte Nachrichten von Lippstadt und benachbarten Gegenden	Lippe
Germany	Lippstadt	Der Hahn	Lippe
Germany	Lippstadt	Westfälische Lehrer-Zeitung	teacher paper
Germany	Lübeck	Der Volksbote	Luebeck daily
Germany	Ludwigshafen	Berg Frei	miner paper
Germany	Ludwigshafen	Jahresbericht der Konferenz der süddeutschen Mennoniten	Mennonite
Germany	Ludwigshafen	Mennonitische Jugendwarte	Mennonite
Germany	Ludwigshafen	Pfälzer Zeitung	Bavarian Palatinate
Germany	Ludwigshafen	Pfälzischer Kurier	Bavarian Palatinate
Germany	Lüneburg	Juristische Zeitung für das Königreich Hannover	judicial paper
Germany	Lüneburg	Lüneburger Landeszeitung	Lower Saxony
Germany	Magdeburg	Amtsblatt der Regierung zu Magdeburg	Saxony-Anhalt
Germany	Magdeburg	Der Reichsbanner	Saxony-Anhalt
Germany	Magdeburg	Der Zeitungs-Verlag	newspaper publishers' paper
Germany	Magdeburg	General-Anzeiger	500 years U Heidelberg

Country	Published at	Title	Notes
Germany	Magdeburg	Hochzeits-Zeitung	Saxony-Anhalt
Germany	Magdeburg	Magdeburgische Zeitung	Saxony-Anhalt
Germany	Magdeburg	Volksstimme	labor paper
Germany	Magdeburg	Wochenzeitung für Kinder im Magdeburger Land	children's paper
Germany	Mainz	Der Israelit	Jewish
Germany	Mainz	Der Katholik	Catholic
Germany	Mainz	Deutsche Weinzeitung	Rhineland wine newspaper
Germany	Mainz	Die Brennessel	humor
Germany	Mainz	Die neue Mainzer Zeitung	Rhineland
Germany	Mainz	Mainzer Carneval-Zeitung Narrhalla	humor
Germany	Mainz	Mainzer Eulenspiegel	humor
Germany	Mainz	Mainzer Fastnachts-Zeitung	humor
Germany	Mainz	Mainzer Journal	Rhineland
Germany	Mainz	Mainzer Schwewwel	humor
Germany	Mainz	Mainzer Witz-Raketen	humor
Germany	Mainz	Meenzer Klepper-Buwe-Zeitung	humor
Germany	Mainz	Raketen	humor
Germany	Mainz	Rheinischer Humorist	humor

Country	Published at	Title	Notes
Germany	Mainz	Sanct-Paulinus-Blatt für das deutsche Volk	Rhineland
Germany	Mallersdorf	Mallersdorfer Anzeiger	Bavaria
Germany	Mannheim	Großherzoglich Badisches niederrheinisches Provinzialblatt	Baden
Germany	Mannheim	Mannheimer Intelligenzblatt	Baden
Germany	Mannheim; Heidelberg	Charis	cultural paper
Germany	Marienwerder	Amtsblatt für den Regierungs-Bezirk Marienwerder	Brandenburg
Germany	Marnheim	Jahresbericht der Realanstalt am Donnersberg	Mennonite
Germany	Mayen	Illustrierte Sonntags-Zeitung	Rhineland
Germany	Mayen	Mayener Volkszeitung	Rhineland
Germany	Meiningen	Meininger Tageblatt	Thuringia
Germany	Memmingen	Jahresbericht der königlichen Studienschule zu Memmingen	annual school report
Germany	Memmingen	Memminger Bezirksamtsblatt	Bavaria
Germany	Mengeringhausen	Fürstlich Waldeckisches Regierungsblatt	Waldeck
Germany	Mengeringhausen	Fürstlich Waldeckisches Regierungsblätter	Waldeck
Germany	Merseburg	Amts-Blatt der königlich Preußischen Regierung zu Merseburg	Saxony
Germany	Merseburg	Amtsblatt der königlichen Regierung zu Merseburg	Saxony
Germany	Merseburg	General-Gouvernements-Blatt fur das Königlich Preussische Herzogthum Sachsen	Saxony

Country	Published at	Title	Notes
Germany	Metten	Jahresbericht über die lateinische Schule im Benediktiner-Stifte Metten	Bavaria
Germany	Mettmann	Mettmanner Kreisblatt	Rhineland
Germany	Mettmann	Mettmanner Zeitung	Rhineland
Germany	Michelstadt	Der Odenwälder	Hesse
Germany	Miltenberg	Jahresbericht über die Königl. Bayer. Lateinschule zu Miltenberg a. M.	annual school report
Germany	Miltenberg	Miltenberger Tagblatt	Bavaria
Germany	Minden	Amtsblatt der königlich preußischen Regierung zu Minden	Westphalia
Germany	Minden	Wochenschrift für das Fürstenthum Minden und die Grafschaft Ravensburg	Minden area
Germany	Montjoie/Monschau	Montjoiér Volksblatt	Catholic
Germany	Montjoie/Monschau	Stadt- und Landbote	Rhineland
Germany	Mülheim	Mülheimer Volkszeitung	Rhineland
Germany	Mülheim, Waldbröl	Waldbröler Kreisblatt	Rhineland
Germany	München/Munich	Der Nationalsozialist	national socialist
Germany	München/Munich	Münchener Amtsblatt	Bavaria
Germany	München/Munich	Abendblatt von München	Bavaria
Germany	München/Munich	Aerztliches Intelligenzblatt	physicians

Country	Published at	Title	Notes
Germany	München/Munich	Allerneueste Nachrichten oder Münchener Neuigkeits-Kourier	Bavaria
Germany	München/Munich	Allgemeine bayrische Hopfen-Zeitung	beer paper
Germany	München/Munich	Allgemeine deutsche Fischerei-Zeitung	fishery paper
Germany	München/Munich	Allgemeine Rundschau	Bavaria
Germany	München/Munich	Allgemeine Zeitung (München)	Bavaria
Germany	München/Munich	Allgemeiner Anzeiger für Bayern	Bavaria
Germany	München/Munich	Allgemeiner Anzeiger für das Königreich Bayern	Bavaria
Germany	München/Munich	Allgemeines Intelligenzblatt für das Königreich Baiern	Bavaria
Germany	München/Munich	Amtsblatt der königlich Bayerischen General-Zoll-Administration	customs officials
Germany	München/Munich	Baierische Landtags-Zeitung	Bavaria
Germany	München/Munich	Baierische Nationalzeitung	Bavaria
Germany	München/Munich	Baierische Wochenschrift	Bavaria
Germany	München/Munich	Baierischer Eilbote	Bavaria
Germany	München/Munich	Baierisches Wochenblatt	Bavaria
Germany	München/Munich	Bayerische Hochschulzeitung	Bavaria high education
Germany	München/Munich	Bayerische Israelitische Gemeindezeitung	Jewish
Germany	München/Munich	Bayerische Landbötin	Bavaria
Germany	München/Munich	Bayerische Landeszeitung	Bavaria
Germany	München/Munich	Bayerische Schulzeitung	Bavaria

Country	Published at	Title	Notes
Germany	München/Munich	Bayerische Wochenzeitung	Bavaria
Germany	München/Munich	Bayerische Zeitung	Bavaria
Germany	München/Munich	Bayerischer Kurier	Bavaria
Germany	München/Munich	Bayerisches Gesetz- und Verordnungsblatt	Bavaria laws and regulations
Germany	München/Munich	Bayerisches Zentral-Polizei-Blatt	Bavarian police gazette
Germany	München/Munich	Bayern-Warte und Münchener Stadtanzeiger	Bavaria
Germany	München/Munich	Bayerscher Beobachter	Bavaria
Germany	München/Munich	Beiblatt der Fliegenden Blätter	humor
Germany	München/Munich	Beylage zum Münchner Policey-Anzeiger	Bavarian police gazette
Germany	München/Munich	Beylage zur Münchner Politische Zeitung	Bavaria
Germany	München/Munich	Bürger-Zeitung	Bavaria
Germany	München/Munich	Centralblatt des Landwirthschaftlichen Vereins	Bavaria agricultural paper
Germany	München/Munich	Churbaierisches Intelligenzblatt	Bavaria
Germany	München/Munich	Churpfalzbaierisches Regierungsblatt	Bavaria
Germany	München/Munich	Conversernationsblatt für München und Bayern	Bavaria
Germany	München/Munich	Das freie Wort	Bavaria
Germany	München/Munich	Das jüdische Echo	Jewish paper
Germany	München/Munich	Der bayerische Beobachter	Bavaria

113

Country	Published at	Title	Notes
Germany	München/Munich	Der Bayerische Volksfreund	Bavaria
Germany	München/Munich	Der Deutsche Jäger	hunting
Germany	München/Munich	Der gerade Weg	Bavaria
Germany	München/Munich	Der Münchner Gevattersmann	political
Germany	München/Munich	Der neue Anfang	Jewish
Germany	München/Munich	Der Reichsbote	Bavaria
Germany	München/Munich	Deutsche constitutionelle Zeitung	political
Germany	München/Munich	Deutsches Nachrichtenbüro	press bureau
Germany	München/Munich	Die Bewegung	student paper
Germany	München/Munich	Die Nutz- und Lust-erweckende Gesellschafft Der Vertrauten Nachbarn am Isarstrom	Bavaria
Germany	München/Munich	Es muss Tag werden	Bavaria
Germany	München/Munich	Fliegende Blätter	humor
Germany	München/Munich	Gesetzblatt für das Königreich Bayern	Bavaria
Germany	München/Munich	Gradaus mein deutsches Volk!	Bavaria
Germany	München/Munich	Illustrierter Sonntag	Bavaria
Germany	München/Munich	Intelligenzblatt der Königlichen Regierung von Oberbayern	Upper Bavaria
Germany	München/Munich	Intelligenzblatt des pharmaceutischen Vereins in Baiern	pharmacy paper
Germany	München/Munich	Intelligenzblatt für das Königreich Bayern	official paper Bavaria

Country	Published at	Title	Notes
Germany	München/Munich	Jugend	youth paper
Germany	München/Munich	KAIN	socialist paper
Germany	München/Munich	Kaiserlich und kurpfalzbairische privilegirte allgemeine Zeitung	official paper Bavaria
Germany	München/Munich	Königlich Baierische Staats-Zeitung von München	official paper Bavaria
Germany	München/Munich	Königlich Bayerischer Polizey-Anzeiger für München	Bavarian police gazette
Germany	München/Munich	Königlich Bayerisches Intelligenzblatt für den Isar-Kreis	official paper Bavaria
Germany	München/Munich	Königlich Bayerisches Kreis-Amtsblatt für Oberbayern	official paper Upper Bavaria
Germany	München/Munich	Kurfürstlich gnädigst privilegirte Münchner Zeitung	official paper Bavaria
Germany	München/Munich	Münchener Conversations-Blatt	Bavaria
Germany	München/Munich	Münchener Guckkasten	Bavaria
Germany	München/Munich	Münchener Herold	Bavaria
Germany	München/Munich	Münchener Omnibus	Bavaria
Germany	München/Munich	Münchener Post	Bavaria
Germany	München/Munich	Münchener Ratsch-Kathl	humor
Germany	München/Munich	Münchener Stadtanzeiger	Bavaria
Germany	München/Munich	Münchener Stadtanzeiger und Münchener Ratsch-Kathl	Bavaria
Germany	München/Munich	Münchener Wochenblatt für das katholische Volk	Catholic
Germany	München/Munich	Münchener Zeitung	supplement
Germany	München/Munich	Münchner Intelligenzblatt	Bavaria

Country	Published at	Title	Notes
Germany	München/Munich	Münchner Staats-, gelehrte und vermischte Nachrichten	Bavaria
Germany	München/Munich	Münchner Zeitung	Bavaria
Germany	München/Munich	Neue Münchener Zeitung	Bavaria
Germany	München/Munich	Neuer Bayerischer Kurier für Stadt und Land	Bavaria
Germany	München/Munich	Neues Münchener Tagblatt	Bavaria
Germany	München/Munich	Neues Tagblatt für München und Bayern	Bavaria
Germany	München/Munich	Newe Zeitung. Ware vnnd gründtliche anzaygung vnd bericht	early paper
Germany	München/Munich	Octoberfest-Zeitung	Octoberfest paper
Germany	München/Munich	Ordinari-Münchner-Zeitungen	Bavaria
Germany	München/Munich	Politischer Gevattersmann	political
Germany	München/Munich	Regierungs- und Gesetzblatt für das Königreich Bayern	Bavaria
Germany	München/Munich	Regierungs- und Gesetzblatt für das Königreich Bayern	Bavaria parliament paper
Germany	München/Munich	Regierungs- und Intelligenzblatt für das Herzogtum Coburg	official paper Coburg
Germany	München/Munich	Regierungsblatt für das Königreich Bayern	Bavaria
Germany	München/Munich	Schneider-Zeitung	tailor paper
Germany	München/Munich	Schützengraben in den Vogesen	WW I paper
Germany	München/Munich	Simplicissimus	satire
Germany	München/Munich	Staats- und Regierungsblatt für Baiern	Bavaria
Germany	München/Munich	Süddeutscher Anzeiger	Bavaria
Germany	München/Munich	Tags-Blatt für München	Bavaria

Country	Published at	Title	Notes
Germany	München/Munich	Verordnungs- und Anzeigeblatt der königl. Bayerischern Verkehrs-Anstalten	transportation paper
Germany	München/Munich	Verordnungs- und Anzeigeblatt für die königlich postal paper Bayerischen Posten	
Germany	München/Munich	Vorwärts	
Germany	München/Munich	Wochenblatt des Landwirtschaftlichen Vereins in Bayern	Bavaria agricultural paper
Germany	München/Munich	Zeitung für Feuerlöschwesen	fireman paper
Germany	Münnerstadt	Jahresbericht über die Königliche Studien-Anstalt in Münnerstadt	Bavaria
Germany	Münster/Muenster	Allgemeine Chronik der Königlich Preussischen Provinz Rheinland-Westfalen	Westphalia
Germany	Münster/Muenster	Allgemeines Anzeigeblatt	Westphalia
Germany	Münster/Muenster	Amtsblatt der königlich preußischen Regierung zu Münster	Westphalia
Germany	Münster/Muenster	Amtsblatt der westfälischen Wilhelms-Universität Münster	university
Germany	Münster/Muenster	Die Angelegenheiten und Ereignisse Westfalens und der Rheinlande	Westphalia
Germany	Münster/Muenster	Münsterische Universitäts-Zeitung	university
Germany	Münster/Muenster	Münsterisches gemeinnütziges Wochenblatt	Westphalia
Germany	Münster/Muenster	Münsterisches Intelligenzblatt	Westphalia
Germany	Münster/Muenster	Westfälische Nachrichten	Westphalia

Country	Published at	Title	Notes
Germany	Nassau	Herzoglich nassauisches allgemeines Intelligenzblatt	Nassau
Germany	Nauen	Osthavelländisches Kreisblatt	Brandenburg
Germany	Naumburg	Naumburger Briefe	Saxony-Anhalt
Germany	Naumburg	Naumburger Kreisblatt	Saxony-Anhalt
Germany	Naumburg	Naumburger Tageblatt	Saxony-Anhalt; to 1933 planned
Germany	Neuburg	Neuburger Wochenblatt	Bavaria
Germany	Neuburg	Pfalz-Neuburgische Provinzialblätter	Bavaria
Germany	Neustadt an der Haardt/Weinstraße	Jahresbericht von der lateinischen Vorbereitungsschule in Neustadt a. d. Haardt	annual school report
Germany	Neustadt an der Haardt/Weinstraße	Neustädter Kreisblatt	Bavarian Palatinate
Germany	Neustadt an der Haardt/Weinstraße	Neustadter Wochenblatt	Bavarian Palatinate
Germany	Neustadt an der Haardt/Weinstraße	Unterhaltungsblatt der Neustadter Zeitung	cultural supplement
Germany	Neustadt an der Orla	Neustädter Kreisbote	Thuringia
Germany	Neustadt bei Coburg	Provinzialblatt	Bavaria
Germany	Neustrelitz	Neustrelitzer Zeitung	500 years U Heidelberg
Germany	Neuwied	Der Erzähler	Rhineland
Germany	Neuwied	Der unpartheyische Correspondent am Rhein	Rhineland

118

Country	Published at	Title	Notes
Germany	Neuwied	Flugblatt	Rhineland
Germany	Neuwied	Freymaurer-Zeitung	Freemasonry paper
Germany	Neuwied	Neuwieder Intelligenz- und Kreis-Blatt	Rhineland
Germany	Neuwied	Neuwiedische Nachrichten	Rhineland
Germany	Neuwied	Regierungs-Blatt der Fürstlich-Wiedischen Regierung in Wied	Rhineland
Germany	Nördlingen	Amtsblatt für das Bezirksamt Nördlingen	official paper Nördlingen area
Germany	Nördlingen	Bienen-Zeitung	beekeeper paper
Germany	Nördlingen	Der Hausfreund	Bavaria
Germany	Nördlingen	Freimunds Kirchlich-Politisches Wochenblatt für Stadt und Land	religious paper
Germany	Nördlingen	Intelligenzblatt der Königlich bayerischen Stadt Nördlingen	Bavaria
Germany	Nördlingen	Jahresbericht über die Königliche lateinschule zu Nördlingen	annual school report
Germany	Nördlingen	Nördlinger Wochenblatt	weekly
Germany	Nördlingen	Nördlingisches Intelligenz- und Wochenblatt	weekly
Germany	Nördlingen	Nördlingsche wöchentliche Nachrichten	weekly
Germany	Nördlingen	Sonntagsblatt	Bavaria
Germany	Nördlingen	Wochenblatt der Stadt Nördlingen	weekly
Germany	Nürnberg/Nuremberg	Allgemeine bayrische Hopfen-Zeitung	brewers
Germany	Nürnberg/Nuremberg	Allgemeine Handlungszeitung	business paper

Country	Published at	Title	Notes
Germany	Nürnberg/Nuremberg	Allgemeine Handlungs-Zeitung	business paper
Germany	Nürnberg/Nuremberg	Allgemeine Hopfen-Zeitung	brewers
Germany	Nürnberg/Nuremberg	Allgemeine polytechnische Zeitung	technical journal
Germany	Nürnberg/Nuremberg	Allgemeine Zeitung von und für Bayern	Bavaria
Germany	Nürnberg/Nuremberg	Allgemeines Intelligenzblatt der Stadt Nürnberg	Bavaria
Germany	Nürnberg/Nuremberg	Allgemeines merkantilisches Anzeige-, Anfrage- und Zusage-Blatt	Bavaria
Germany	Nürnberg/Nuremberg	Aviso oder Zeitung das ist Kurtze jedoch außfürliche Relation	Bavaria
Germany	Nürnberg/Nuremberg	Bayerische Lehrerzeitung	Bavaria teacher paper
Germany	Nürnberg/Nuremberg	Bayerischer Generalanzeiger	Bavaria
Germany	Nürnberg/Nuremberg	Bayerisches Brauer-Journal	brewers
Germany	Nürnberg/Nuremberg	Blätter für das Volk zunächst in Bayern	Bavaria
Germany	Nürnberg/Nuremberg	Der deutsche Volksbote	Bavaria
Germany	Nürnberg/Nuremberg	Der freie Staatsbürger	Bavaria
Germany	Nürnberg/Nuremberg	Der Friedens- und Kriegs-Kurier	Bavaria
Germany	Nürnberg/Nuremberg	Der Korrespondent von und für Deutschland	Bavaria
Germany	Nürnberg/Nuremberg	Der Schuhmacher (Nürnberg)	trade union paper
Germany	Nürnberg/Nuremberg	Der Stürmer	National Socialist
Germany	Nürnberg/Nuremberg	Die Nürnberger Estaffette	Bavaria
Germany	Nürnberg/Nuremberg	Fränkischer Kurier	Bavaria

Country	Published at	Title	Notes
Germany	Nürnberg/Nuremberg	Fürther Tagblatt	Bavaria
Germany	Nürnberg/Nuremberg	General-Anzeiger für Deutschland	general newspaper
Germany	Nürnberg/Nuremberg	Neue Nürnbergische gelehrte Zeitung	Bavaria
Germany	Nürnberg/Nuremberg	Newe Zeitung von den Widertauffern zu Münster	early paper
Germany	Nürnberg/Nuremberg	Nürnberger Abendblatt	daily
Germany	Nürnberg/Nuremberg	Nürnberger Stadtzeitung	Bavaria
Germany	Nürnberg/Nuremberg	Nürnberger Tagblatt	daily
Germany	Nürnberg/Nuremberg	Süddeutsche Blätter für Leben, Wissenschaft und Kunst	cultural paper
Germany	Nürnberg/Nuremberg	Theatralisches Wochenblatt	teacher paper
Germany	Ober-Ingelheim	Rheinhessischer Beobachter	Hesse
Germany	Oberkassel	Oberkasseler Zeitung	Rhineland
Germany	Oberkirch	Oberkircher Bote	Baden
Germany	Oderberg	Oderberger Zeitung und Wochenblatt	Brandenburg
Germany	Oettingen	Oettingisches Wochenblatt	Bavaria
Germany	Oettingen	Wochenblatt für das Fürstenthum Oettingen-Spielberg	Bavaria
Germany	Oettingen	Wochenblatt für das Fürstenthum Oettingen-Spielberg und die Umgebung	Bavaria
Germany	Oettingen	Wochen-Blatt für die Stadt und den Landgerichts-Bezirk Oettingen	Bavaria
Germany	Offenbach am Main	Der Frieden	wartime paper

Country	Published at	Title	Notes
Germany	Offenbach am Main	Hessische Gemeindebeamten-Zeitung	Hesse
Germany	Offenbach am Main	Kommunist: Organ der Vereinigten Kommunistischen Partei für Südwestdeutschland	Communist party paper
Germany	Offenbach am Main	Neuer Rheinischer Merkur	Hesse
Germany	Offenbach am Main	Offenbacher Abendblatt	Hesse political paper
Germany	Offenbach am Main	Offenbacher Zeitung	Hesse
Germany	Offenburg	Offenburger Nachrichten	Baden
Germany	Oldenburg	Der Oldenburgische Volksfreund	Oldenburg
Germany	Oldenburg	Mittheilungen aus Oldenburg	Oldenburg
Germany	Oldenburg	Nordwestzeitung Oldenburg	Oldenburg
Germany	Osnabrück	Osnabrücker Zeitung	Lower Saxony
Germany	Ottobeuren	Grönenbacher Wochenblatt	Bavaria
Germany	Paderborn	Paderborner Anzeiger	Westphalia
Germany	Paderborn	Paderbornsches Intelligenzblatt für den Appellationsgerichts-Bezirk	Westphalia
Germany	Parchim	Mecklenburgische gemeinnützige Blätter	Mecklenburg
Germany	Passau	Der Obstbaum-Freund	orchardists
Germany	Passau	Donau-Zeitung	Bavaria
Germany	Passau	Königlich bayerisches Intelligenzblatt für Niederbayern	Bavaria
Germany	Passau	Kourier an der Donau: Zeitung für Niederbayern	Bavaria

Country	Published at	Title	Notes
Germany	Passau	Neue Passauer Zeitung	Bavaria
Germany	Passau	Passauer Neue Presse	Bavaria
Germany	Passau	Passauer Tagblatt	daily
Germany	Passau	Passavia	Bavaria
Germany	Pfarrkirchen	Der Rotthaler Bote	Bavaria
Germany	Pirmasens	Sickinger Bote	Bavarian Palatinate
Germany	Plauen	Vogtländischer Anzeiger und Tageblatt	500 years U Heidelberg
Germany	Potsdam	Amtsblatt der churmärkischen Regierung	Brandenburg
Germany	Potsdam	Amtsblatt der Königlichen Regierung zu Potsdam und der Stadt Berlin	Brandenburg
Germany	Potsdam	Gemeinnütziges Volksblatt	Brandenburg
Germany	Potsdam	Jahresbericht über die höhere Knaben-Schule	annual school report
Germany	Prenzlau	Jahresbericht über das Gymnasium zu Prenzlau	annual school report
Germany	Prüm	Intelligenz-Blatt für die Kreise Prüm, Bitburg, Daun und den ehemaligen Kreis St. Vith	Prüm area
Germany	Ratzeburg	Wöchentliche Anzeigen für das Fürstenthum Ratzeburg	Mecklenburg
Germany	Regensburg	Abensberger Wochenblatt	Abensberg region
Germany	Regensburg	Flora	botanical paper
Germany	Regensburg	Königlich bairisches Intelligenzblatt für den Regen-Kreis	Bavaria

123

Country	Published at	Title	Notes
Germany	Regensburg	Königlich Bayerisches Kreis-Amts-Blatt der Oberpfalz und von Regensburg	Bavaria
Germany	Regensburg	Kreisblatt-Repertorium der Oberpfalz und von Regensburg	Bavaria
Germany	Regensburg	Mittelbayerische Zeitung	post-WW II
Germany	Regensburg	Regensburger Anzeiger	Bavaria
Germany	Regensburg	Regensburger Conversations-Blatt	Bavaria
Germany	Regensburg	Regensburger Intelligenzblatt	Bavaria
Germany	Regensburg	Regensburger Morgenblatt	daily
Germany	Regensburg	Regensburger Neueste Nachrichten	Bavaria
Germany	Regensburg	Regensburger Wochenblatt	weekly
Germany	Regensburg	Regensburger Zeitung	Bavaria
Germany	Regensburg	Regensburgisches Diarium	Bavaria
Germany	Regensburg	Gründliche Warhafftige Newe Zeitung	calendar change 10 days
Germany	Regensburg, Hamburg	Deutsche Israelitische Zeitung	Jewish
Germany	Reihen	Gemeindeblatt der Mennoniten	Mennonite
Germany	Rendsburg	Rendsburger Tagespost	Schleswig-Holstein
Germany	Rendsburg	Schleswig-Holsteinische Tageszeitung	Schleswig-Holstein
Germany	Rheda	Gemeinnütziges Hausarchiv	Westphalia
Germany	Rheinbach	Intelligenzblatt für Euskirchen und Rheinbach	Rhineland

Country	Published at	Title	Notes
Germany	Rheinbach	Rheinbacher Anzeiger	Rhineland
Germany	Rheinbach	Rheinbacher Kreisblatt	Rhineland
Germany	Rheinberg	Rheinberger Wochenblatt	Rhineland
Germany	Rheine	Jahresbericht über das Gymnasium Dionysianum zu Rheine	annual school report
Germany	Rheinsberg	HJ im Vormarsch	Hitler youth paper
Germany	Rheinsberg	Rheinsberger Zeitung	Brandenburg
Germany	Rheinsberg	Rheinsberger Zeitung: Illustrirte Unterhaltungsbeilage	supplement
Germany	Rheinsberg	Unterhaltung, Wissen und Heimat	Brandenburg
Germany	Rheydt	Kreis- und Intelligenblatt zunächst für Rheydt, Gladbach, Odenkirchen, Giesenkirchen, Wickrath und Dahlen	Rhineland
Germany	Ried	Rieder Intelligenzblatt	Bavaria
Germany	Rinteln	Jahresbericht über das Königliche Gymnasium zu Rinteln	annual school report
Germany	Rixdorf; Berlin; Leipzig	Der Steinarbeiter	trade union paper
Germany	Rosenheim	Rosenheimer Anzeiger	Bavaria
Germany	Rosenheim	Rosenheimer Tagblatt Wendelstein	Bavaria
Germany	Rosenheim	Rosenheimer Wochenblatt	Bavaria
Germany	Rostock	Etwas von gelehrten Rostockschen Sachen	Pomerania
Germany	Rostock	Neue wöchentliche Rostock'sche Nachrichten und Anzeigen	Pomerania

Country	Published at	Title	Notes
Germany	Rostock	Officielle Beilage für amtliche Bekanntmachungen	Pomerania
Germany	Rostock	Rostocker Zeitung	500 years U Heidelberg
Germany	Rothenburg ob der Tauber	Amts- und Anzeigenblatt für die Stadt und das königl. Bezirksamt Rothenburg	Bavaria
Germany	Rothenburg ob der Tauber	Fränkischer Anzeiger	Bavaria
Germany	Rothenburg ob der Tauber	Jahresbericht über das Königliche Progymnasium zu Rothenburg	Bavaria
Germany	Rudolstadt	Allgemeine Auswanderungs-Zeitung	emigration paper
Germany	Rudolstadt	Schwarzburger Bote	Thuringia
Germany	Saarbrücken	Amtsblatt des Saarlandes	Saarland
Germany	Saarbrücken	Der Stoßtrupp	WW I paper
Germany	Saarbrücken	Jahresbericht über das Königliche Gymnasium und die Vorschule zu Saarbrücken	annual school report
Germany	Sangerhausen	Sangerhäuser Kreisblatt	Saxony-Anhalt
Germany	Sankt Wendel	Nahe-Blies-Zeitung	Saarland
Germany	Sankt Wendel	Wochenblatt für die Kreise St. Wendel und Ottweiler	Saarland
Germany	Schewinfurt	Schweinfurter Tagblatt	Bavaria
Germany	Schleiden	Unterhaltungsblatt und Anzeiger für den Kreis Schleiden und Umgegend	Rhineland
Germany	Schleiden	Wochenblatt und Anzeiger für den Kreis Schleiden und Umgegend	Rhineland

Country	Published at	Title	Notes
Germany	Schleiz	Jahresbericht über das Schuljahr von Ostern 1878 - Ostern 1879	Thuringia
Germany	Schleswig	Amtsblatt der preussischen Regierung zu Schleswig	Schleswig-Holstein
Germany	Schleswig	Amtsblatt für die Verhandlungen der Provinzialstände des Herzogthums Schleswig	Schleswig-Holstein
Germany	Schleswig	Schleswig-Holsteinische Blätter	Schleswig-Holstein
Germany	Schnepfenthal	Der Bote aus Thüringen	Thuringia
Germany	Schrobenhausen	Amts-Blatt für den Verwaltungs- und Gerichts-Bezirk Schrobenhausen	Bavaria
Germany	Schrobenhausen	Wochenblatt für die königlich bayerischen Landgerichtsbezirke Pfaffenhofen und Schrobenhausen	Bavaria
Germany	Schwabach	Jahresbericht für die Landwirthschafts- und Gewerbsschule zu Schwabach	annual school report
Germany	Schwandorf	Der Naabthal-Bote	Bavaria
Germany	Schwedt an der Oder	Schwedter Tageblatt	Brandenburg
Germany	Schweinfurt	Jahresbericht der Königlichen Landwirthschafts- und Gewerbsschule zu Schweinfurt	annual school report
Germany	Schweinfurt	Schweinfurter Anzeiger	Bavaria
Germany	Schweinfurt	Schweinfurter Tagblatt	Bavaria
Germany	Schwerin	Der Wächter: Polizeiblatt für Mecklenburg	Mecklenburg
Germany	Schwerin	Herzoglich Mecklenburg-Schwerinisches officieles Wochenblatt	Mecklenburg

Country	Published at	Title	Notes
Germany	Schwerin	Mecklenburgische Anzeigen	500 years U Heidelberg
Germany	Schwerin	Mode und Heim	fashion
Germany	Schwerin	Regierungsblatt für Mecklenburg	Mecklenburg
Germany	Schwerin	Regierungsblatt für Mecklenburg–Schwerin Amtliche Beilage	Mecklenburg
Germany	Schwerte	Schwerter Zeitung	Rhineland
Germany	Seelow	Seelower Tageblatt	Brandenburg wartime paper
Germany	Seesen am Harz, Goslar	Jahresberichte der Jacobson-Schule	Jewish/Christian school report
Germany	Siegburg	Anzeiger des Siegkreises	Rhineland
Germany	Siegburg	Sieg-Bote	Rhineland
Germany	Siegburg	Siegburger Kreisblatt	Rhineland
Germany	Siegen	Jahresbericht der Realschule erster Ordnung zu Siegen	annual school report
Germany	Sigmaringen	Amtsblatt der preußischen Regierung zu Sigmaringen	Hohenzollern Prussia
Germany	Sigmaringen	Wochenblatt für das Fürstenthum Sigmaringen	Hohenzollern Prussia
Germany	Simmern	Der Hunsrücken	Rhineland
Germany	Simmern	Hunsrücker Erzähler	Rhineland
Germany	Simmern	Intelligenz-Blatt für den Kreis Simmen	Rhineland
Germany	Simmern	Intelligenz-Blatt für den Kreis Simmen und dessen Umgegend	Rhineland
Germany	Solingen	Bergisches Volks-Blatt	Rhineland
Germany	Solingen	Solinger Kreis-Intelligenzblatt	Rhineland
Germany	Sondershausen	Der Deutsche: Sondershäuser Zeitung	Thuringia

Country	Published at	Title	Notes
Germany	Sondershausen	Jahresbericht über das Schwarzburgische Gymnasium zu Sondershausen	annual school report
Germany	Spandau	Anzeiger für das Havelland	Brandenburg
Germany	Spandau	Spandauer Zeitung	Brandenburg
Germany	Speyer	Allgemeiner Anzeiger für die Pfalz	Bavarian Palatinate
Germany	Speyer	Amts- und Intelligenzblatt der Königlich-bayerischen Regierung des Rheinkreises	Bavarian Palatinate
Germany	Speyer	Amtsblatt der Königlich-Baierischen Regierung des Rheinkreises	Bavarian Palatinate
Germany	Speyer	Amtsblatt für das Königlich-Baierische Gebiet auf dem linken Rheinufer	Bavarian Palatinate
Germany	Speyer	Anzeige der Beamten und Angestellte im Staats- und Communal-Dienste des Rheinkreises	list of officials
Germany	Speyer	Beilage zum Amts- und Intelligenz-Blatte des Rheinkreises	Bavarian Palatinate
Germany	Speyer	Der Rheinbayer	Bavarian Palatinate
Germany	Speyer	Die Rheinpfalz	Bavarian Palatinate
Germany	Speyer	Feuilleton zum Pfälzischer Kurier	cultural supplement
Germany	Speyer	Intelligenz-Blatt des Rheinkreises	Bavarian Palatinate
Germany	Speyer	Jahresbericht über das Gymnasium und die Lateinische Schule zu Speyer	musical paper
Germany	Speyer	Königlich bayerisches Amts- und Intelligenzblatt für die Pfalz	Bavarian Palatinate

Country	Published at	Title	Notes
Germany	Speyer	Königlich-Bayerisches Kreis-Amtsblatt der Pfalz	Bavarian Palatinate
Germany	Speyer	Musikalische Real-Zeitung	musical paper
Germany	Speyer	Neue Speyerer Zeitung	Bavarian Palatinate
Germany	Speyer	Pfälzischer Kurier	Bavarian Palatinate
Germany	Speyer	Pfälzischer Zeitung	Bavarian Palatinate
Germany	Speyer	Speyerer Tagblatt	Bavarian Palatinate
Germany	Speyer	Speyerer wöchentliches Anzeige-Blatt	Bavarian Palatinate
Germany	St. Goar	St. Goarer Kreisblatt	Rhineland
Germany	St. Wendel	Wochenblatt für die Kreise St. Wendel und Ottweiler	Rhineland
Germany	Stadtamhof	Wochen- und Amts-Blatt der königlichen Bezirks-Aemter Stadtamhof und Regensburg	Bavaria
Germany	Stargard	Amtsblatt der Königlichen Regierung von Pommern	Pomerania
Germany	Staufen	Staufener Volksblatt	Baden
Germany	Staufen	Staufener Wochenblatt	Baden
Germany	Stettin	Allgemeiner Wohnungsanzeiger für Stettin	Pomerania
Germany	Stettin	Neue Pommersche Provinzialblätter	Pomerania
Germany	Stralsund	Amtsblatt der preußischen Regierung zu Stralsund	Pomerania
Germany	Stralsund	Stralsundische Zeitung	Pomerania
Germany	Stralsund	Stralsundischer RelationsCourier	Pomerania
Germany	Stralsund	Sundine	Pomerania

Country	Published at	Title	Notes
Germany	Straubing	Jahresbericht über die königliche Gewerbschule zu Straubing	annual school report
Germany	Straubing	Straubinger Tagblatt	Bavaria
Germany	Strelitz	Großherzoglich Mecklenburgisch-Strelitzer officieler Anzeiter für Gesetzgebung und Staatsverwaltung	Mecklenburg
Germany	Stuttgart	Allgemeine Familien-Zeitung	family paper
Germany	Stuttgart	Allgemeiner Anzeiger für Buchbindereien	bookbinding paper
Germany	Stuttgart	Der Horchposten	WW I paper
Germany	Stuttgart	Deutsche Metall-Arbeiter-Zeitung	trade union paper
Germany	Stuttgart	Deutsches Kunstblatt	art
Germany	Stuttgart	Die Kommunistin	communist women
Germany	Stuttgart	Die Sonntags-Zeitung	Württemberg
Germany	Stuttgart	Eisenbahn-Zeitung	railroad paper
Germany	Stuttgart	Illustrierte Garten-Zeitung	gardener paper
Germany	Stuttgart	Illustriertes Sonntags-Blatt	supplement for East Africa
Germany	Stuttgart	Literaturblatt des Deutschen Kunstblattes	art literature
Germany	Stuttgart	Metallarbeiter Jugend	metal worker paper
Germany	Stuttgart	Neckar-Zeitung	Württemberg
Germany	Stuttgart	Polytechnisches Journal	technical journal
Germany	Stuttgart	Regierungsblatt für das Königreich Württemberg	Württemberg
Germany	Stuttgart	Regierungsblatt für Württemberg	Württemberg

131

Country	Published at	Title	Notes
Germany	Stuttgart	Schwäbischer Merkur	Württemberg
Germany	Stuttgart	über Land und Meer	Stuttgart
Germany	Stuttgart	Wochenblatt für Land- und Hauswirthschaft, Gewerbe und Handel	agricultural and trade paper
Germany	Stuttgart; Augsburg	Allgemeine Zeitung	Württemberg
Germany	Stuttgart; Berlin	Buchbinder-Zeitung	bookbinding paper
Germany	Stuttgart; Tübingen	Morgenblatt für gebildete Stände	art
Germany	Suhl	Suhler Zeitung	Thuringia
Germany	Sulzbach	Sulzbacher Wochenblatt	Bavaria
Germany	Sulzbach	Wochenblatt der Stadt Sulzbach	Bavaria
Germany	Teltow	Teltower Kreisblatt	Prussian official press
Germany	Thurnau	Jahresbericht der Lateinschule zu Thurnau	annual school report
Germany	Traunstein	Jahresbericht über die königliche Gewerbschule in Traunstein	annual school report
Germany	Traunstein	Traun-Alz Bote	Bavaria
Germany	Trier	Allgemeiner Anzeiger	Rhineland
Germany	Trier	Allgemeiner Anzeiger und Kunst-, Handels- und Gewerbezeitung für den Regierungsbezirk Trier	Trier district
Germany	Trier	Amtsblatt der preußischen Regierung in Trier	Rhineland
Germany	Trier	Der Beobachter an der Saar	Rhineland
Germany	Trier	Kurier von der Mosel und den belgischen und französischen Gränzen	Rhineland

Country	Published at	Title	Notes
Germany	Trier	Politische Zeitung im Saar-Departement	Saarland
Germany	Trier	Saar- und Mosel-Zeitung	500 years U Heidelberg
Germany	Trier	Treviris	Rhineland
Germany	Trier	Trierische Staats- und gelehrte Zeitungen	Rhineland
Germany	Trier	Trierisches Wochen-Blättgen	Rhineland
Germany	Triesdorf	Jahresbericht der Königlichen Kreisackerbauschule	Bavaria
Germany	Trostberg	Der Traunbote	Bavaria
Germany	Trostberg	Traun-Alz-Salzach Bote	Bavaria
Germany	Tübingen	Blätter für Polizei und Kultur	police paper
Germany	Tübingen	Der Kinderfreund	child welfare
Germany	Tübingen	Tübinger Blätter	Württemberg
Germany	Tübingen	Tübingische gelehrte Anzeigen	Württemberg
Germany	Tübingen	Kriegs-Zeitung des Nationalenstudendienstes Tübingen	wartime paper
Germany	Vacha	Rhön-Zeitung	Thuringia, Hesse, Bavaria
Germany	various articles	Zeitungszeugen	historical commentary
Germany	Velbert	Langenberger Zeitung	Rhineland
Germany	Verden an der Aller	Die Kauwenhoven	family newsletter
Germany	Vetschau	Neue Vetchauer Zeitung	Brandenburg
Germany	Waldbröl	Waldbröler Kreisblatt	Rhineland

133

Country	Published at	Title	Notes
Germany	Waldeck	Fürstlich Waldeckisches Regierungsblatt, -blätter	Waldeck
Germany	Wasserburg	Anzeiger für den Bezirk Wasserburg	Bavaria
Germany	Wasserburg	Wasserburger Anzeiger	Bavaria
Germany	Wasserburg	Wasserburger Wochenblatt	Bavaria
Germany	Weierhof	Bericht über unsere mennonitische Hilfskasse	Mennonite
Germany	Weierhof	Mennonitische Geschichtsblätter	Mennonite
Germany	Weilheim	Weilheimer Tagblatt für Stadt und Land	Bavaria
Germany	Weilheim	Weilheim-Werdenfelser Wochenblatt	Bavaria
Germany	Weimar	Amts- und Nachrichtenblatt für Thüringen	Thuringia
Germany	Weimar	Der Neue Teutsche Merkur	Thuringia
Germany	Weimar	Großherzoglich Sachsen-Weimar-Eisenachisches Regierungs-Blatt	Thuringia
Germany	Weimar	Kirchenblatt für Sachsen-Weimar-Eisenach	Thuringia
Germany	Weimar	Kirchlicher Anzeiger für Thüringen	Thuringia
Germany	Weimar	Kirchliches Verordnungsblatt für Sachsen-Weimar-Eisenach	Thuringia
Germany	Weimar	Oppositions-Blatt oder Weimarische Zeitung	Thuringia
Germany	Weimar	Regierungs- und Nachrichtenblatt für Sachsen-Weimar-Eisenach	Thuringia
Germany	Weimar	Regierungsblatt für das Großherzogthum Sachsen-Weimar-Eisenach	Saxony
Germany	Weimar	Regierungsblatt für Sachsen-Weimar-Eisenach	Saxony

Country	Published at	Title	Notes
Germany	Weimar	Thüringer Kirchenblatt und Kirchlicher Anzeiger	religious paper
Germany	Weimar	Thüringer Kirchenblatt: Gesetz- und Verordnungsblatt	religious paper
Germany	Weimar	Thüringer Lehrerzeitung	teacher paper
Germany	Weimar	Thüringer Volk	Thuringia
Germany	Weimar	Wartburg Herold	Thuringia
Germany	Weimar	Weimarer Zeitung	Thuringia
Germany	Weimar	Weimarische wöchentliche Anzeigen	Thuringia
Germany	Weimar	Weimarische Zeitung	Thuringia
Germany	Weimar	Weimarisches Allerlei	Thuringia
Germany	Weimar	Weimarisches Wochenblatt	Thuringia
Germany	Weinheim	Weinheimer Anzeiger	Baden
Germany	Weißenburg Bayern	Jahresbericht über die Königliche Realschule zu Weißenburg a. Sd.	annual school report
Germany	Weissensee	Blumen-Zeitung	flower paper
Germany	Weissensee	Numismatische Zeitung	coin collecctors
Germany	Wernigerode	Dein Reich Komme	Mennonite
Germany	Wernigerode	Russische Blätter	Mennonite
Germany	Wesel	Der Volksfreund	Rhineland
Germany	Wesel	Kreisblatt für den Kreis Rees	Rhineland

Country	Published at	Title	Notes
Germany	Wetzlar	Wetzlarer Kreis- und Amtsblatt	Hesse
Germany	Wetzlar	Wetzlarer Kreis- und Anzeigeblatt	Hesse
Germany	Wiedenbrück	Der Bote an der Ems	Westogakua
Germany	Wiesbaden	Amtsblatt der Königlichen Regierung zu Wiesbaden	Nassau
Germany	Wiesbaden	Die Gemeinde	church paper
Germany	Wiesbaden	Intelligenzblatt für Nassau	Nassau
Germany	Wiesbaden	Rheinische Blätter	Nassau
Germany	Wiesbaden	Wiesbadener Badeblatt	Rhineland
Germany	Wiesbaden	Wiesbadener Tagblatt	daily
Germany	Wilhelmshaven	Wilhelmshavener Tageblatt	500 years U Heidelberg
Germany	Wipperfürth	Wipperfürther Kreis-Intelligenz-Blatt	Rhineland
Germany	Wittenberg	Das Wittenbergsche Wochenblatt	Saxony-Anhalt
Germany	Wittenberg	Wittenbergisches Wochenblatt	Saxony-Anhalt
Germany	Worbis	Treffurter Wochenblatt	Thuringia
Germany	Worms	Blumen-Zeitung	Rhineland
Germany	Worms	Mittelrheinische Sportzeitung	sports paper
Germany	Worms	Wormser Sport=Zeitung	Hesse sports paper
Germany	Worms	Wormser Tageblatt	Worms area
Germany	Worms	Wormser Zeitung	Rhineland

Country	Published at	Title	Notes
Germany	Wunsiedel	Jahresbericht der königlichen Bewerbschule in Wunsiedel	annual school report
Germany	Wuppertal	Täglicher Anzeiger für Berg und Mark	Rhineland
Germany	Würzburg	Der Postbote aus Franken: eine Würzburger politische Zeitung	Bavaria
Germany	Würzburg	Frankenzeitung	Bavaria
Germany	Würzburg	Fränkische Zeitung	Bavaria
Germany	Würzburg	Fränkisches Bürgerblatt	Bavaria
Germany	Würzburg	Herold des Glaubens	religious
Germany	Würzburg	Intelligenz-Blatt für den Unter-Mainkreis des Königreichs Bayern	Bavaria
Germany	Würzburg	Intelligenzblatt für Kunst und Literatur	literary
Germany	Würzburg	Intelligenzblatt für Unterfranken und Aschaffenburg	Bavaria
Germany	Würzburg	Neue Fränkische Zeitung	Bavaria
Germany	Würzburg	Neue Würzburger Zeitung	Bavaria
Germany	Würzburg	Teutsches Volksblatt	Bavaria
Germany	Würzburg	Würzburger Abendblatt	Bavaria
Germany	Würzburg	Würzburger Anzeiger	Bavaria
Germany	Würzburg	Würzburger Diözesanblatt	Catholic diocesan paper
Germany	Würzburg	Würzburger Intelligenzblatt	Bavaria
Germany	Würzburg	Würzburger Regierungsblatt	Bavaria
Germany	Würzburg	Würzburger Stadt- und Landbote	Bavaria

Country	Published at	Title	Notes
Germany	Würzburg	Würzburger Tagblatt	Bavaria
Germany	Xanten	Kreis-Blatt für den Kreis Geldern	Rhineland
Germany	Zeulenroda	Sonntagsgruß: Reußisches Kirchenblatt für Stadt und Land	religious paper
Germany	Zittau	Der arme Teufel aus der Oberlausitz	Saxony
Germany	Zittau	Lausizisches Wochenblatt	Saxony
Germany	Zittau	Zeitung des Landsturm-Infanterie-Bataillon Zittau	wartime field paper
Germany	Zülpich	Anzeiger und Unterhaltungsblatt für Zülpich, Lechenich und Umgegend	Rhineland
Germany	Zülpich	Zülpicher Anzeiger	Rhineland
Germany	Zweibrücken	Pfälzische Blätter	cultural paper
Germany	Zweibrücken	Polyhymnia	cultural supplement
Germany	Zweibrücken	Rheinbayerisches Volksblatt	Bavarian Palatinate
Germany	Zweibrücken	Zweibrücker Tagblatt	daily
Germany	Zweibrücken	Zweibrücker Zeitung	Bavarian Palatinate
Germany	Zweibrücken	Zweybrückische Zeitung	Bavarian Palatinate
Germany	Zweibrücken	Zweybrückisches Wochenblatt (and variants)	weekly
Germany	Zwickau	Jahresbericht des Gymnasiums zu Zwickau	annual school report
Greece	Athens	Regierungsblatt des Königreichs Griechenland	translation of Greek government paper
Hungary	Altenburg	Der Heideboden	Christian weekly

Country	Published at	Title	Notes
Hungary	Budapest	Abendblatt des Pester Lloyd	500 years U Heidelberg
Hungary	Budapest	Allgemeine illustrierte Judenzeitung	Jewish
Hungary	Budapest	Der katholische Christ	Catholic paper
Hungary	Budapest	Der ungarische Israelit	Jewish
Hungary	Budapest	Deutsches Bauernblatt	farm paper one issue
Hungary	Budapest	Deutsches Tageblatt	daily
Hungary	Budapest	Hamechaker	Jewish theology and history
Hungary	Budapest	Jahresberichte der Landes-Rabbinnerschule in Budapest	Jewish rabbinical school report
Hungary	Budapest	Jüdische Gemeinde- und Schulzeitung	Jewish school publication
Hungary	Budapest	Jüdische Pester Zeitung	Jewish
Hungary	Budapest	Jüdischer Pester Lloyd	Jewish
Hungary	Budapest	Neue jüdische Pester Zeitung	Jewish
Hungary	Budapest	Neue jüdische Zeitung	Jewish
Hungary	Budapest	Neue Post	four issues
Hungary	Budapest	Neues Budapester Abendblatt	one issue
Hungary	Budapest	Pester Lloyd	Hungary
Hungary	Budapest	Pesther Tageblatt	Hungary
Hungary	Budapest	Pesth-Ofener Localblatt und Landbote	Hungary
Hungary	Budapest	Ungarisch-jüdische Wochenschrift	Jewish

Country	Published at	Title	Notes
Hungary	Budapest	Ungarländische jüdische Zeitung	Jewish
Hungary	Budapest	Vereinigte Ofner-Pester Zeitung	Hungary
Hungary	Budapest	Volksstimme	Hungary
Hungary	Mohács	Mohácser Wochenblatt	Hungary
Hungary	Ödenburg/Sopron	Der Proletarier	socialist paper
Hungary	Ödenburg/Sopron	Oedenburger Arbeiterrat	Hungary
Hungary	Ödenburg/Sopron	Oedenburger Proletariat	Hungary
Hungary	Ödenburg/Sopron	Oedenburger Zeitung	Hungary
Hungary	Ödenburg/Sopron	Weckruf	one issue
Hungary	Szeged	Ben Chananja: Blätter für israelitisch-ungarische Angelegenheiten	Jewish
Israel; France	Jerusalem; Paris	Jüdische Welt-Rundschau	Jewish
Italy	Bozen/Bolzano	Alpenzeitung	Fascist paper
Italy	Bozen/Bolzano	Bozner Nachrichten	South Tirol
Italy	Bozen/Bolzano	Bozner Tagblatt	South Tirol
Italy	Bozen/Bolzano	Bozner Zeitung	South Tirol
Italy	Bozen/Bolzano	Das Bozner Kriegsblättchen	South Tirol
Italy	Bozen/Bolzano	Der Bote für Tirol	South Tirol
Italy	Bozen/Bolzano	Der Fortschritt	South Tirol
Italy	Bozen/Bolzano	Der Tiroler	South Tirol

Country	Published at	Title	Notes
Italy	Bozen/Bolzano	Dolomiten	South Tirol
Italy	Bozen/Bolzano	Dolomiten Landausgabe	South Tirol
Italy	Bozen/Bolzano	Rundschreiben des Präfekten von Bozen	wartime government
Italy	Bozen/Bolzano	Südtiroler Nachrichten	political paper
Italy	Bozen/Bolzano	Südtiroler Volksblatt	South Tirol
Italy	Bozen/Bolzano	Tiroler Volksblatt	South Tirol
Italy	Bozen/Bolzano	Volksblatt	South Tirol
Italy	Bozen/Bolzano	Volksbote	South Tirol
Italy	Bozen/Bolzano	Volksrecht	political paper
Italy	Brixen/Bressenone	Brixener Chronik	South Tirol
Italy	Brixen/Bressenone	Das Brixener Diözesanblatt	Catholic diocesan paper
Italy	Brixen/Bressenone	Der Ladiner	one issue
Italy	Brixen/Bressenone	Tiroler Volksbote	South Tirol
Italy	Bruneck/Brunico	Anzeiger zum Pustertaler Boten	South Tirol
Italy	Bruneck/Brunico	Beilage zum Pustertaler Boten	South Tirol
Italy	Bruneck/Brunico	Der Hausfreund	South Tirol
Italy	Bruneck/Brunico	Handels, Geschäfts-, Verkehrs- und Intelligenzblatt	South Tirol
Italy	Bruneck/Brunico	Jedem Etwas	South Tirol
Italy	Bruneck/Brunico	Kleiner Gasthof- und Geschäftsanzeiger	South Tirol

Country	Published at	Title	Notes
Italy	Bruneck/Brunico	Praktische Mitteilungen	South Tirol
Italy	Bruneck/Brunico	Pustertaler Bote	South Tirol
Italy	Bruneck/Brunico	Sonntagsblatt	South Tirol
Italy	Bruneck/Brunico	Volkswirtschaftliche Blätter	South Tirol
Italy	Görz	Jahresbericht des K. K. Ober-Gymnasiums in Görz	annual school report
Italy	Kaltern/Caldaro	Überetscher Gemeindeblatt für Eppan und Kaltern	South Tirol
Italy	Mais	Maiser Wochenblatt	South Tirol
Italy	Meran/Merano	Alpenländische Fachschrift	South Tirol
Italy	Meran/Merano	Alpenländische Gewerbe-Zeitung	South Tirol
Italy	Meran/Merano	Der Burggräfler	South Tirol
Italy	Meran/Merano	Der Standpunkt	South Tirol
Italy	Meran/Merano	Meraner Zeitung	South Tirol
Italy	Meran/Merano	Südtiroler Landeszeitung	South Tirol
Italy	Sterzing/Vipiteno	Sterzinger Bezirks-Anzeiger	South Tirol
Italy	Triest	Journal des österreichischen Lloyd	South Tirol
Latvia	Goldingen/Kuldiga	Anzeiger für Goldingen und Windau	Latvia
Latvia	Goldingen/Kuldiga	Goldingenscher Anzeiger	Latvia
Latvia	Mitau/Jelgava	Mitausche Zeitung	Latvia
Latvia	Pernau/Pärnu	Rigasche Zeitung	Latvia

Country	Published at	Title	Notes
Latvia	Riga/Riia	Livländische Gouvernements-Zeitung	Latvia
Latvia	Riga/Riia	Rigaische Rundschau	Latvia
Latvia	Riga/Riia	Rigasche Hausfrauen-Zeitung	housewives
Latvia	Riga/Riia	Rigasche Industrie-Zeitung	industry
Latvia	Riga/Riia	Rigasche Stadtblätter	Latvia
Latvia	Riga/Riia	Rigische Novellen	Latvia
Latvia	Windau/Ventspils	Windausche Zeitung	Latvia
Liechtenstein	Vaduz	Der Umbruch	Liechtenstein
Liechtenstein	Vaduz	Liechtensteiner Heimatdienst	Liechtenstein
Liechtenstein	Vaduz	Liechtensteiner Landeszeitung	Liechtenstein
Liechtenstein	Vaduz	Liechtensteiner Nachrichten	Liechtenstein
Liechtenstein	Vaduz	Liechtensteiner Vaterland	Liechtenstein
Liechtenstein	Vaduz	Liechtensteiner Volkblatt	Liechtenstein
Liechtenstein	Vaduz	Liechtensteiniche Wochenzeitung	Liechtenstein
Liechtenstein	Vaduz	Oberrheinische Nachrichten	Liechtenstein
Lithuania	Memel	Memeler Dampfboot	Lithuania
Lithuania	Vilnius	Armeezeitung-Scholze	WW I paper
Lithuania	Vilnius	Zeitung der 10. Armee	WW I paper
Luxembourg	Hollerich	Bürger- und Beamten-Zeitung	Luxembourg

Country	Published at	Title	Notes
Luxembourg	Luxemburg	A-Z: Luxemburger Illutrierte Wochenschrift	Luxembourg
Luxembourg	Luxemburg	Das Luxemburger Land	multilingual
Luxembourg	Luxemburg	Das Vaterland	Luxembourg
Luxembourg	Luxemburg	Luxemburger Illustrierte	Luxembourg
Luxembourg	Luxemburg	Luxemburger Wochenblatt	Luxembourg
Luxembourg	Luxemburg	Luxemburger Wort	Luxembourg
Mexico	Mexiko/Mexico City	Deutsche Zeitung von Mexiko	Mexico
Montenegro	Cetinje	Cetinjer Zeitung	WW I paper
Morocco	Tanger/Tangier	Deutsche Marokko-Zeitung	Morocco
Namibia	Lüderitz	Lüderitzbuchter Zeitung	was German Southwest Africa
Namibia	Swakopmund	Swakopmunder Echo	was German Southwest Africa
Namibia	Swakopmund	Swakopmunder Zeitung	was German Southwest Africa
Netherlands	Amsterdam	ITF	transport workers paper
Norway	Oslo	Lappland-Kurier	Posen/Poznań
Paraguay	Fernheim	Mennoblatt	Mennonite
Poland	Adelnau/Odolandów	Kreis-Blatt für den Kreis Adelnau	Posen/Poznań
Poland	Beuthen/Bytom	Oberschlesische Zeitung	Upper Silesia
Poland	Beuthen/Bytom	Oberschlesisches Wochenblatt	Upper Silesia
Poland	Beuthen/Bytom	Ostdeutsche Morgenpost	Upper Silesia

Country	Published at	Title	Notes
Poland	Bialystok/Bialystok	Bialystoker Zeitung	Podlachia/Podlasie
Poland	Bialystok/Bialystok	Neu-Ostpreußisches Intelligenzblatt	East Prussia
Poland	Bielitz/Bilsko	Die evangelische Kirchen-Zeitung für Oesterreich	Lutheran church paper for Austria
Poland	Braunsberg/Braniewo	Ermländische Zeitung	Ermland/Warmia
Poland	Braunsberg/Braniewo	Jahresbericht über das Königlich Katholische Gymnasium zu Braunsberg	school report
Poland	Breslau/Wrocław	Amtsblatt der Königlichen Regierung zu Breslau	Lower Silesia
Poland	Breslau/Wrocław	Breslauer jüdisches Gemeindeblatt	Lower Silesia
Poland	Breslau/Wrocław	Breslauer Zeitung	500 years U Heidelberg
Poland	Breslau/Wrocław	Breslauer Zeitung	Lower Silesia
Poland	Breslau/Wrocław	Der Breslauer Erzähler	Lower Silesia
Poland	Breslau/Wrocław	Die freie Meinung	political weekly
Poland	Breslau/Wrocław	Illustrierte Wochenbeilage der Schlesischen Zeitung	Lower Silesia
Poland	Breslau/Wrocław	Jahresberichte des jüdisch-theologischen Seminars Fraenkelische Stiftung	Jewish rabbinical school report
Poland	Breslau/Wrocław	Jüdische Zeitung	Jewish
Poland	Breslau/Wrocław	Jüdische Zeitung für Ostdeutschland	Jewish
Poland	Breslau/Wrocław	Jüdisches Volksblatt	Jewish
Poland	Breslau/Wrocław	Jüdisch-liberale Zeitung	Jewish

Country	Published at	Title	Notes
Poland	Breslau/Wrocław	Kunst und Volk	community theater paper
Poland	Breslau/Wrocław	Neue Breslauer Zeitung	Lower Silesia
Poland	Breslau/Wrocław	Schlesische Landarbeiter	Silesian farm worker
Poland	Breslau/Wrocław	Schlesische Privilegirte Staats-, Kriegs- und Friedens-Zeitung	Lower Silesia
Poland	Breslau/Wrocław	Schlesische Zeitung	500 years U Heidelberg
Poland	Breslau/Wrocław	Schlesische Zeitung	Lower Silesia
Poland	Breslau/Wrocław	Schlesisches Pastoralblatt	pastor publication
Poland	Breslau/Wrocław	Schlesisische Arbeiterzeitung	Silesia labor paper
Poland	Breslau/Wrocław	Sozialistische Arbeiter-Zeitung	labor paper
Poland	Breslau/Wrocław	Volkswacht für Schlesien	labor paper
Poland	Brieg/Brzeg	Brieger Zeitung	Silesia
Poland	Brieg/Brzeg	el	Silesia
Poland	Bromberg/Bydgoszcz	Amtsblatt der königlich preußischen Regierung zu Bromberg	Posen/Poznań
Poland	Bromberg/Bydgoszcz	Amtsblatt der königlichen Regierung zu Bromberg	Posen/Poznań
Poland	Bromberg/Bydgoszcz	Bromberger Tageblatt	500 years U Heidelberg
Poland	Bromberg/Bydgoszcz	Bromberger Wochenblatt	Posen/Poznań
Poland	Bromberg/Bydgoszcz	Oeffentlicher Anzeiger	Posen/Poznań
Poland	Bublitz/Bobolice	Kreisblatt für den Kreis Bublitz	Pomerania

Country	Published at	Title	Notes
Poland	Danzig/Gdańsk	Amtsblatt der königlichen Regierung zu Danzig	Danzig
Poland	Danzig/Gdańsk	Danziger Allgemeine Zeitung	Danzig
Poland	Danzig/Gdańsk	Danziger Dampfboot	literature, humor
Poland	Danzig/Gdańsk	Danziger Volksstimme	Danzig labor paper
Poland	Danzig/Gdańsk	Danziger Volks-Zeitung	Danzig
Poland	Danzig/Gdańsk	Danziger Zeitung	Danzig
Poland	Danzig/Gdańsk	Danziger Zeitung: Organ für Handel	Danzig
Poland	Danzig/Gdańsk	Feldzeitung der Armee-Abteilung Scheffer	army paper WW I
Poland	Danzig/Gdańsk	Mennonitische Blätter	Mennonite
Poland	Danzig/Gdańsk	Neue Wogen der Zeit	Danzig
Poland	Danzig/Gdańsk	Volkswacht	West Prussia labor paper
Poland	Deutsch Krone/Wałcz	Deutsch-Kroner Zeitung	500 years U Heidelberg
Poland	Elbing/Elbląg	Blätter für Religion und Erziehung	Mennonite
Poland	Elbing/Elbląg	Die Kahlberger Woche	Poland
Poland	Elbing/Elbląg	Elbinger Anzeiger	West Prussia
Poland	Elbing/Elbląg	Elbinger Volksblatt	West Prussia
Poland	Elbing/Elbląg	Neuer Elbinger Anzeiger	West Prussia
Poland	Frankenstein/Lonsky	Frankensteiner Kreisblatt	Silesia
Poland	Frankenstein/Lonsky	Frankensteiner Wochenblatt	Silesia

Country	Published at	Title	Notes
Poland	Fraustadt/Wschowa	Fraustädter Kreisblatt	Posen/Poznań
Poland	Glatz/Kłodzko	Jahresbericht des Königl. Katholischen Gymnasiums zu Glatz	annual school report
Poland	Gleiwitz/Gliwice, Rybnik	Der Oberschlesische Wanderer	Upper Silesia
Poland	Gleiwitz/Gliwice, Rybnik	Jahrbuch der k. kath. Gymnasiums zu Gleiwitz	annual school report
Poland	Gleiwitz/Gliwice, Rybnik	Rybniker Kreisblatt	Silesia
Poland	Glogau/Glogow	Der niederschlesische Anzeiger	Lower Silesia
Poland	Glogau/Glogow	Schlesische Provinzialblätter	Silesia
Poland	Gnesen/Gniezno	Kirchliches Amtsblatt für die Erzdiözesen Gnesen und Posen	Catholic bilingual
Poland	Goldap/Goldap	Goldaper Kreisblatt	Masuria
Poland	Görlitz/Zgorzelec	Görlitzer Anzeiger	Lusatia
Poland	Görlitz/Zgorzelec	Görlitzer Fama	Lusatia
Poland	Greifenhagen/Gryfino	Greifenhagener Kreisblatt	Pomerania
Poland	Greifenhagen/Gryfino	Greifenhagener Kreiszeitung	Pomerania
Poland	Greifenhagen/Gryfino	Kreisblatt für die Kreisstadt Greifenhagen und Umgegend	Pomerania
Poland	Groß-Glogau/Głogów	Jahresbericht des Königlichen Katholischen Gymnasium zu Groß-Glogau	annual school report
Poland	Groß–Strehlitz/Strzelce Opolskie	Gross-Strehlitzer Kreisblatt	Silesia
Poland	Groß-Wartenberg/Sycow	Gross-Wartenberger Kreisblatt	Posen/Poznań
Poland	Grottkau/Grodków	Grottkauer Stadt- und Kreisblatt	Silesia

148

Country	Published at	Title	Notes
Poland	Grottkau/Grodków	Grottkauer Zeitung	Silesia
Poland	Grünberg/Zielona Góra	Grünberger Wochenblatt	Silesia
Poland	Guhrau/Góra	Guhrauer Anzeiger	Silesia
Poland	Guttenberg/Dobrodzień	Guttentager Stadtblatt	Upper Silesia
Poland	Habelschwerdt/Kladská Bystřice	Habelschwerdter Kreisblatt	Lower Silesia
Poland	Hindenburg/Zabrze	Zabrzer Kreisblatt	Upper Silesia; bilingual
Poland	Hindenburg/Zabrze	Zabrzer Kreis-Blatt	Upper Silesia
Poland	Hirschberg/Jelenia Góra	Der Bote aus dem Riesen-Gebirge	Lower Silesia
Poland	Hrubesiev/Hrubieszów	Amtsblatt des k. und k. Kreiskommandos in Hrubieszów	Poland
Poland	Inowroclaw	Kujawisches Wochenblatt	Pomerania
Poland	Janów	Amtsblatt des k. und k. Kreiskommandos in Janów	Poland
Poland	Kalisz/Kalisch	Zeitung der Landsturm-Infanterie-Batterie Zittau	WW I paper
Poland	Kattowitz/Katowice	Anzeiger für den Kreis Pleß	Upper Silesia
Poland	Kattowitz/Katowice	Kattowitzer Zeitung	Upper Silesia
Poland	Kattowitz/Katowice	Oberschlesische Morgen-Zeitung	Upper Silesia
Poland	Kattowitz/Katowice	Wochen-Post	Upper Silesia
Poland	Kielce	Amtsblatt des k. und k. Kreiskommandos in Kielce	Poland
Poland	Kolmar/Chodzież	Kolmarer Kreisblatt	Posen/Poznań

Country	Published at	Title	Notes
Poland	Kolmar/Chodzież	Kolmarer Kreiszeitung	Posen/Poznań
Poland	Koschmin/Koźmiń	Amtliches Kreisblatt für den Kreis Koschmin	Posen/Poznań
Poland	Koschmin/Koźmiń	Amtliches Kreisblatt und Anzeiger für den Kreis und die Stadt Koschmin	Posen/Poznań
Poland	Koschmin/Koźmiń	Koschminer Zeitung und Anzeiger für die Städte Borek und Pogorzela	Posen/Poznań
Poland	Köslin/Koszalin	Amtsblatt der preußischen Regierung zu Köslin	Pomerania
Poland	Köslin/Koszalin	Gendarmerie-Zeitung	Pomerania
Poland	Köslin/Koszalin	Kösliner Volksblatt	Pomerania
Poland	Köslin/Koszalin	Kösliner Zeitung	Pomerania
Poland	Krakau/Kraków	Krakauer Jüdische Zeitung	Jewish paper
Poland	Krakau/Kraków	Pressedienst des Generalgouvernements	wartime paper for Poland
Poland	Lähn/Wlen	Lähner Anzeiger	Silesia
Poland	Lauban/Lubań	Jahresbericht. Evangelisches Städtisches Gymnasium zu Lauban	annual school report
Poland	Laurahütte	Haus und Welt	supplement
Poland	Leobschütz/Głubczyce	Jahresbericht über das Königliche katholische Gymnasium zu Leobschütz	annual school report
Poland	Liegnitz/Lignica	Amts-Blatt der Preußischen Regierung zu Liegnitz	Silesia
Poland	Łódź/Lodz	Deutsche Post	Poland
Poland	Łódź/Lodz	Illustriertes Familienblatt	Poland

Country	Published at	Title	Notes
Poland	Łódź/Lodz	Landwirtschaftliche Beilage zur Deutschen Post	agricultural paper
Poland	Łódź/Lodz	Lodzer Rundschau	Poland
Poland	Łódź/Lodz	Neue Lodzer Zeitung	Poland
Poland	Łódź/Lodz	Unterhaltungs-Beilage der Lodzer Rundschau	Poland
Poland	Łódź/Lodz	Wissen und Kunst	Poland
Poland	Lyck/Ełk	Das Lycker gemeinnützige Unterhaltungsblatt	Masuria
Poland	Lyck/Ełk	Jahresbericht des Königlichen Gymnasiums zu Lyck	annual school report
Poland	Miechów	Amtsblatt des KreisesMiech¢w	Lesser Poland
Poland	Münsterberg/Ziębice	M (just M, not a misprint)	Silesia
Poland	Münsterberg/Ziębice	Münsterberger Kreisblatt	Silesia
Poland	Münsterberg/Ziębice	Münsterberger Wochenblatt	Silesia
Poland	Münsterberg/Ziębice	Stadt- und Wochenblatt	Silesia
Poland	Neisse/Nysa	Jahresbericht des Königl. kath. Gymnasiums zu Neisse	annual school report
Poland	Neustadt/Prudnik	Neustädter Kreisblatt	Upper Silesia
Poland	Neustadt/Wejherowo	Jahresbericht des städtischen Gymnasiums zu Neustadt Ob.-Schl.	annual school report
Poland	Neustadt/Wejherowo	Kreisblatt für den Neustädter Kreis	West Prussia
Poland	Neustettin/Szczecinek	Neustettiner Kreisblatt	Pomerania
Poland	Nowo-Aleksandrya	Amtsblatt des k. und k. Kreiskommandos in Nowo-Alexsandrya	Poland

Country	Published at	Title	Notes
Poland	Noworadomsk	Amtsblatt des k. und k. Kreiskommandos in Noworadomsk	Poland
Poland	Oels/Oleśnica	Lokomotive an der Oder	Silesia
Poland	Oels/Oleśnica	Intelligenzblatt fEr die Städte Oels, Bernstadt, Juliusburg, Hundsfeld und Festenberg	Silesia
Poland	Olkusch/Olkuß	Amtsblatt des Kreises Olkusz	Poland
Poland	Oppeln/Opole	Amtsblatt der königlichen Regierung zu Oppeln	Upper Silesia
Poland	Oppeln/Opole	Jahresbericht des königlichen katholischen Gymnasiums zu Oppeln	Upper Silesia
Poland	Oppeln/Opole	Oppelner Nachrichten	Upper Silesia
Poland	Ostrowo/Ostrów	Amtsblatt des Landrats in Ostrowo	Posen/Poznań
Poland	Ostrowo/Ostrów	Kreisblatt des Kreises Ostrowo	Posen/Poznań
Poland	Pilawy	Amtsblatt des k. und k. Kreiskommandos in Pilawy	Masovia
Poland	Pleschen/Plesczew	Jeschurun	Jewish
Poland	Pleschen/Plesczew	Pleschener Kreisblatt	Posen/Poznań
Poland	Pless/Pszczyna	Der Beobachter an der Weichsel	Silesia
Poland	Posen/Poznań	Amtliches Schul-Blatt für die Provinz Posen	Posen/Poznań
Poland	Posen/Poznań	Amtsblatt der königlichen Regierung zu Posen	Posen/Poznań
Poland	Posen/Poznań	Heimat und Welt	Posen/Poznań
Poland	Posen/Poznań	Kreis-Blatt des Kreises Posen-Ost	Posen/Poznań
Poland	Posen/Poznań	Öffentlicher Anzeiger der königlichen Regierung zu Posen	Posen/Poznań

Country	Published at	Title	Notes
Poland	Posen/Poznań	Posener Tageblatt	Posen/Poznań
Poland	Posen/Poznań	Posener-Zeitung	500 years U Heidelberg
Poland	Ratibor/Racibórz	Oberschlesischer Anzeiger	Upper Silesia
Poland	Reichenbach/Dzierżoniów	Amtsblatt der königlichen preußischen Regierung zu Reichenbach	Silesia
Poland	Rummelsburg/Miastko	Rummelsburger Zeitung	Pomerania
Poland	Sandomierz	Amtsblatt des K. und K. Kreiskommandos in Sandomierz	
Poland	Schneidemühl/Piła	Amtsblatt der preußischen Regierung in Schneidemühl	Pomerania
Poland	Sorau/Żary	Jahresbericht über das Gymnasium zu Sorau	annual school report
Poland	Sorau/Żary	Niederlausitzischer Anzeiger	Lower Lusatia
Poland	Sorau/Żary	Sorauer Kreisblatt	Lower Lusatia
Poland	Sorau/Żary	Sorauer Tageblatt	Lower Lusatia
Poland	Sorau/Żary	Sorauer Wochenblatt für Unterhaltung, Belehrung und Ereignisse der Gegenwart	Lower Lusatia
Poland	Sprottau/Szprotawa	Sprottauer Wochenzeitung	Lower Silesia
Poland	Stettin/Szczecin	Amtsblatt der preußischen Regierung zu Stettin	Pomerania
Poland	Stettin/Szczecin	Börsen-Nachrichten der Ost-See	Pomerania
Poland	Stettin/Szczecin	Die Handels-Marine der Provinzen Pommern, Ost- und Westpreussen	merchant marine of Pomerania, East Prussia, and West Prussia
Poland	Stettin/Szczecin	Entomologische Zeitung	entomology paper

153

Country	Published at	Title	Notes
Poland	Stettin/Szczecin	Greifenhagener Kreisblatt	Pomerania
Poland	Stettin/Szczecin	Jahresbericht des Entomologischen Vereins von Stettin	entomology society
Poland	Stettin/Szczecin	Königlich preußisches Intelligenz-Blatt	Pomerania
Poland	Stettin/Szczecin	Ostsee-Zeitung	Pomerania
Poland	Stettin/Szczecin	Pommersche Zeitung	Pomerania
Poland	Stettin/Szczecin	Pommersche-Zeitung	500 years U Heidelberg
Poland	Stettin/Szczecin	Stettiner Entomologische Zeitung	entomology society
Poland	Stettin/Szczecin	Stettiner General-Anzeiger	Pomerania
Poland	Stettin/Szczecin	Stettiner illustrierte Zeitung	Pomerania
Poland	Stettin/Szczecin	Stettiner Intelligenz-Blatt	Pomerania
Poland	Stettin/Szczecin	Stettiner Zeitung	500 years U Heidelberg
Poland	Stolp/Słupsk	Stolper Neueste Nachrichten	Pomerania
Poland	Stolp/Słupsk	Stolper Wochenblatt	Pomerania
Poland	Strehlen/Strzelin	Strehlener Stadtblatt	Lower Silesia
Poland	Tarnowitz/Tarnowskie Góry	Der Bergfreund	Silesia
Poland	Teschen/Cieszyn	Amts-Blatt der k. k. Bezirkshauptmannschaft zu Teschen	Silesia
Poland	Teschen/Cieszyn	Schlesischer Merkur	Silesia
Poland	Teschen/Cieszyn	Teschner Zeitung	Silesia
Poland	Thorn/Toruń	Thorner Freiheit	Poland

Country	Published at	Title	Notes
Poland	Thorn/Toruń	Thorner Intelligenzblatt	Poland
Poland	Thorn/Toruń	Thorner Wochenblatt	Poland
Poland	Thorn/Toruń	Thorner Zeitung	Poland
Poland	Waldenburg/Wałbrzych	Waldenburger Wochenblatt	Lower Silesia
Poland	Warschau/Warsaw	Warschauer Zeitung	Poland
Poland	Włoszczowa	Amtsblatt des Kreises Włoszczowa	Poland
Poland	Wongrowitz/Wągrowiec	Jahresbericht des Königlichen Gymnasiums zu Wongrowitz	Posen; annual school report
Poland	Znin/Żnin	Zniner Zeitung	Poland
Romania	Focşani	Putna-Zeitung	WWI paper
Romania	Hermannstadt/Sibiu	Der Siebenbürger Bote	Romania
Romania	Hermannstadt/Sibiu	Die Karpathen	Romania
Romania	Hermannstadt/Sibiu	Siebenbürger Bote	Romania
Romania	Hermannstadt/Sibiu	Siebenbürgisch-Deutsches Tageblatt	Romania
Romania	Hermannstadt/Sibiu	Siebenbürgische Provinzialblätter	Romania
Romania	Hermannstadt/Sibiu	Siebenbürgisches Bürgerblatt	Romania
Romania	Hermannstadt/Sibiu	Transsilvania, Beiblatt zum Siebenbürger Boten	Romania
Romania	Kronstadt/Braşov	Kronstädter Zeitung	Romania
Romania	Kronstadt/Braşov	Siebenbürger Wochenblatt	Romania
Romania	Kronstadt/Braşov	Siebenbürgische Zeitung	for society members only

Country	Published at	Title	Notes
Romania	Kronstadt/Braşov	Siebenbürgisches Wochenblatt	Romania
Romania	Szatmár/Satu Mare	Szatmarer allgemeine jüdische Zeitung	Romania
Romania	Temeschburg/Timosoara	Banater Deutsche Zeitung	Banat region
Romania	Temeschburg/Timosoara	Jüdisches Wochenblatt	Jewish
Romania	Temeschburg/Timosoara	Neue jüdische Rundschau	Jewish
Russia	Gerdauen/Zhelezhnodorzhny	Gerdauener Zeitung	East Prussia
Russia	Gumbinnen/Gusev	Amtsblatt der königlichen Litthauischen Regierung	former Lithuania
Russia	Gumbinnen/Gusev	Amtsblatt der Königlichen Regierung in Gumbinnen	East Prussia
Russia	Gumbinnen/Gusev	Gumbinner Allgemeine Zeitung	East Prussia
Russia	Gumbinnen/Gusev	Gumbinner Kreisblatt	East Prussia
Russia	Königsberg/Kaliningrad	Amtsblatt der königlichen preußischen Regierung zu Königsberg	East Prussia
Russia	Königsberg/Kaliningrad	Königsberger allgemeine Zeitung	East Prussia
Russia	Königsberg/Kaliningrad	Königsberger Gelehrte und Politische Zeitungen	East Prussia
Russia	Königsberg/Kaliningrad	Königsberger Hartungsche Zeitung	East Prussia
Russia	Königsberg/Kaliningrad	Mittheilungen aus dem Religiösen Leben	Mennonite
Russia	Königsberg/Kaliningrad	Monatsschrift für die evangelischen Mennoniten	Mennonite
Russia	Königsberg/Kaliningrad	Ostpreußische Zeitung	500 years U Heidelberg
Russia	Königsberg/Kaliningrad	Preußische Provinzial-Blätter	East Prussia

Country	Published at	Title	Notes
Russia	Königsberg/Kaliningrad	Preußische Zeitung	wartime paper
Russia	Moskau/Moscow	Moskauer Deutsche Zeitung	Moscow
Russia	Moskau/Moscow	Moskauer Rundschau	Moscow
Russia	Nordenburg/Krylowo	Nordenburger Anzeiger	East Prussia
Russia	Pillau/Baltiysk	Pillauer Merkur	East Prussia
Russia	Ragnit/Neman	Ragniter Kreis-Anzeiger	East Prussia
Russia	Ragnit/Neman	Ragniter Kreisblatt	East Prussia
Russia	Russia	Freies Deutschland	Communist paper for German POWs
Russia	St. Petersburg	Jahresbericht des deutschen Wohltätigkeits-Vereins St. Petersburg	German benefit society report
Russia	St. Petersburg	Neues St. Petersburgisches Journal	St. Petersburg
Russia	Tilsit/Sovetsk	Tilsiter allgemeine Zeitung	Tilsit
Russia	Tilsit/Sovetsk	Tilsiter Zeitung	Tilsit
Samoa	Apia	Samoanische Zeitung	South Pacific
Scotland	Knockaloe	Lager-Echo	WW I German POW paper
Scotland	Stobs	Stobsiade: Stobser Zeitung	WW I German POW paper
Serbia	Apatin	Die Donau	Catholic
Serbia	Novisad	Deutsche Zeitung / Heimat	Serbia
Slovakia	Kaschau/Košice	Kaschau-Eperieser Kundschaftsblatt	Slovakia

Country	Published at	Title	Notes
Slovakia	Kaschau/Košice	Kaschauer Zeitung	Slovakia
Slovakia	Kesmark/Kežmarok	Die Karpathen-Post	Slovakia
Slovenia	Celje	Deutsche Wacht	Slovakia
Slovenia	Celje	Deutsche Zeitung	Slovakia
Slovenia	Gottschee/Kočevje	Gottscheer Bote	Slovenia
Slovenia	Laibach/ Ljubljana	Laibacher Tagblatt	Slovenia
Slovenia	Laibach/ Ljubljana	Laibacher Wochenblatt	Slovenia
Slovenia	Laibach/ Ljubljana	Laibacher Zeitung	Slovenia
Slovenia	Laibach/ Ljubljana	Landesgesetzblatt für das Herzogtum Krain	Carniola
Slovenia	Laibach/ Ljubljana	Vereinigte Laibacher Zeitung	Slovenia
Slovenia	Laibach/ Ljubljana	Wöchentliches Kundschaftsblatt des Herzogthums Krain	Carniola
Slovenia	Marburg an der Drau/Maribor	Marburger Zeitung	Slovenia
Slovenia	Marburg an der Drau/Maribor	Südsteirische Post	Slovenia
Slovenia	Pettau/Ptuj	Pettauer Zeitung	Slovenia
Spain	Barcelona	Die Soziale Revolution	socialist paper
Switzerland	Aarau	Aarauer Anzeiger	Aargau
Switzerland	Aarau	Aarauer Kurier	Aargau
Switzerland	Aarau	Aarauer Nachrichten	Aargau

Country	Published at	Title	Notes
Switzerland	Aarau	Aarauer Zeitung	Aargau
Switzerland	Aarau	Aargauer Anzeiger	Aargau
Switzerland	Aarau	Aargauer Nachrichten	Aargau
Switzerland	Aarau	Aargauischer Anzeiger	Aargau
Switzerland	Aarau	Das Posthörnchen	Aargau
Switzerland	Aarau	Der Schweizer-Bote	Aargau
Switzerland	Aarau	Hochobrigkeitliches privilegirtes Aargauischen Intelligenz-Blatt	Aargau
Switzerland	Aarau	Schweizerische Bienen-Zeitung	Aargau
Switzerland	Aarau	Täglicher Anzeiger der Stadt Aarau und Umgebung	Aargau
Switzerland	Baden	Schweizerische Volks-Zeitung	Swiss
Switzerland	Basel	Allgemeine Schweizerische Militär-Zeitung	Swiss military paper
Switzerland	Basel	Allgemeines Noth- und Hülfs-Blatt	Swiss
Switzerland	Basel	Baseler Zeitung	Swiss
Switzerland	Basel	Basler Nachrichten	500 years U Heidelberg
Switzerland	Basel	Der Mennonit	Mennonite paper
Switzerland	Bern/Berne	Berner Schulfreund	teacher paper
Switzerland	Bern/Berne	Bernisches Freytags-Blätlein	Swiss
Switzerland	Bern/Berne	Bundesblatt	government register
Switzerland	Bern/Berne	Der Schweizerische Auswanderer	Swiss emigration

Country	Published at	Title	Notes
Switzerland	Bern/Berne	Die Freie Zeitung	Swiss
Switzerland	Bern/Berne	Intelligenzblatt für die Stadt Bern	Swiss
Switzerland	Bern/Berne	Neue Allgemeine Schweizerische Auswanderungszeitung	Swiss emigration
Switzerland	Bern/Berne	Neues Schweizerisches Auswanderungsblatt	Swiss emigration
Switzerland	Bern/Berne	Neu-Helvetia-Amerika-Zeitung	Swiss colony
Switzerland	Chur	Bündner Nachrichten	Canton Grisons
Switzerland	Chur	Der freie Rhätier	Canton Grisons
Switzerland	Chur	Der Liberale Alpenbote	Canton Grisons
Switzerland	Chur	Der Morgenstern	Canton Grisons
Switzerland	Chur	Der Volksfreund	Canton Grisons
Switzerland	Chur	Graubündner General-Anzeiger	Canton Grisons
Switzerland	Döttingen	Die Botschaft	Zurzach region of Aargau
Switzerland	Einsiedeln	Der Pilger	Catholic Sunday paper
Switzerland	Freiburg	Freiburger Nachrichten	Canton Fribourg
Switzerland	Freiburg	Freiburger Zeitung und Anzeiger für die westliche Schweiz	western Switzerland
Switzerland	Freiburg/Fribourg	Freiburger Nachrichten	Swiss
Switzerland	Haldenstein	Bündner Landbote	Canton Grisons
Switzerland	Hottingen	Grütlianer	Swiss
Switzerland	Lichtensteig	Der Kolonist	Swiss emigration

Country	Published at	Title	Notes
Switzerland	Luzern/Lucerne	Jüdisches Jahrbuch für die Schweiz	Jewish Swiss publication
Switzerland	Murten/Morat	Der Landbote des freiburgischen Seebezirks	Canton Fribourg
Switzerland	Olten	Schweizer Schule	Swiss Catholic school weekly
Switzerland	Schaffhausen	Schaffhauser Nachrichen	paid access
Switzerland	Solothurn	Solothurnisches Wochenblatt	Canton Solothurn
Switzerland	Spreitenbach	Die Tat	Swiss
Switzerland	St. Gallen	Der Erzähler	Canton St. Gallen
Switzerland	St. Gallen	Der helvetische Volksfreund	Canton St. Gallen
Switzerland	St. Gallen	Der Wahrheitsfreund	Canton St. Gallen
Switzerland	St. Gallen	Die Ostschweiz	Canton St. Gallen
Switzerland	St. Gallen	Neues Tagblatt aus der östlichen Schweiz	Canton St. Gallen
Switzerland	St. Gallen	Schweizerische Tagblätter	Canton St. Gallen
Switzerland	St. Gallen	St. Galler Volksblatt	Canton St. Gallen
Switzerland	St. Gallen	St. Galler Zeitung	Canton St. Gallen
Switzerland	Steckborn	Bote vom Untersee und Rhein	Canton Thurgau
Switzerland	Wallis	Walliser Bote	Canton Valais
Switzerland	Wallis	Walliser Wochenblatt	Canton Valais
Switzerland	Zug	Der freie Schweizer	Canton Zug
Switzerland	Zug	Der Zugerbieter	Canton Zug

Country	Published at	Title	Notes
Switzerland	Zug	Neue Zuger Zeitung	Canton Zug
Switzerland	Zug	Wochenblatt für die vier löblichen Kantone	Swiss
Switzerland	Zug	Zuger Nachrichten	Canton Zug
Switzerland	Zug	Zuger Volksblatt	Canton Zug
Switzerland	Zug	Zugerisches Kantonsblatt	Canton Zug
Switzerland	Zürich	Amtsblatt des Kantons Zürich	Canton Zürich
Switzerland	Zürich	Der schweizerische Republikaner	Swiss
Switzerland	Zürich	Die Grüne	agricultural paper
Switzerland	Zürich	Eidgenössische Zeitung	Swiss
Switzerland	Zürich	Neue Zürcher Zeitung	500 years U Heidelberg
Switzerland	Zürich	Neue Zürcher Zeitung	Swiss
Switzerland	Zürich	Sechseläuten Tagblatt	Canton Zürich
Switzerland	Zürich	Sonnstagsblatt	Canton Zürich
Switzerland	Zürich	Zürcherisches Wochenblatt	Canton Zürich
Switzerland	Zurzach	Der Aargauer Volks-Bote	Swiss
Syria	Damascus	Armee-Zeitung Jildirim	field paper WWI
Tanzania	Dar-es-Salaam	Der Ostafrikanische Pflanzer	German East Africa
Tanzania	Dar-es-Salaam, Morogoro	Amtlicher Anzeiger für Deutsch-Ostafrika	German East Africa
Tanzania	Dar-es-Salaam, Morogoro	Deutsch-Ostafrikanische Zeitung	German East Africa

Country	Published at	Title	Notes
Turkey	Istanbul	Türkische Post	Turkey
Turkey	Istanbul	Türkische Post Halbmonatliche Wirtschaftsausgabe	business edition
Ukraine	Czernovitz/Czernivtsi	Bukowinaer Fortuna	economic paper
Ukraine	Czernovitz/Czernivtsi	Bukowinaer Landwirtschaftliche Blätter	agricultural paper
Ukraine	Czernovitz/Czernivtsi	Bukowinaer Nachrichten	Ukraine
Ukraine	Czernovitz/Czernivtsi	Bukowinaer Post	Ukraine
Ukraine	Czernovitz/Czernivtsi	Bukowinaer Rundschau	Ukraine
Ukraine	Czernovitz/Czernivtsi	Bukowinaer-Volks-Zeitung	Ukraine
Ukraine	Czernovitz/Czernivtsi	Bukowiner Pädagogische Blätter	Ukraine teacher paper
Ukraine	Czernovitz/Czernivtsi	Bukowiner Schule	Ukraine teacher paper
Ukraine	Czernovitz/Czernivtsi	Bukowiner Volksblatt	Ukraine
Ukraine	Czernovitz/Czernivtsi	Bukowiner Zeitung	Ukraine
Ukraine	Czernovitz/Czernivtsi	Czernowitzer Allgemeine Zeitung	Ukraine
Ukraine	Czernovitz/Czernivtsi	Czernowitzer Gemeinde-Bote	Ukraine
Ukraine	Czernovitz/Czernivtsi	Czernowitzer Presse	Ukraine
Ukraine	Czernovitz/Czernivtsi	Czernowitzer Tagblatt	Ukraine
Ukraine	Czernovitz/Czernivtsi	Der Volksfreund	Ukraine
Ukraine	Czernovitz/Czernivtsi	Die Wahrheit	Ukraine
Ukraine	Czernovitz/Czernivtsi	Freie Lehrer-Zeitung	Ukraine teacher paper

Country	Published at	Title	Notes
Ukraine	Czernovitz/Czernivtsi	Genossenschafts- und Vereins-Zeitung	Ukraine
Ukraine	Czernovitz/Czernivtsi	Ostjüdische Zeitung	Jewish political
Ukraine	Lemberg/Lviv	Amtsblatt zur Lemberger Zeitung	Ukraine
Ukraine	Lemberg/Lviv	Lemberger Allgemeiner Anzeiger	Ukraine
Ukraine	Lemberg/Lviv	Lemberger Zeitung	Ukraine
Ukraine	Melitopol	Deutsche Zeitung für Ost-Taurien	wartime paper
Ukraine	Sewastopol/Sevastopol	Deutsche Zeitung	wartime paper
Ukraine	Stanislau/Ivano-Frankivsk	Evangelisches Gemeindeblatt für Galizien und die Bukowina	Lutheran church paper for Galicia and Bukovina
USA	Allentown, PA	Der Lecha Patriot	Pennsylvania
USA	Allentown, PA	Der Lecha Patriot und Northampton Demokrat	Pennsylvania
USA	Allentown, PA	Der Liberale Beobachter und Northampton Caunty Wöchentlicher Anzeiger	Pennsylvania
USA	Baltimore, MD	Der deutsche Correspondent	Maryland
USA	Breda, IA	Ostfriesische Nachrichten	East Frisian news
USA	Buffalo, NY	Buffalo Volksfreund	New York
USA	Buffalo, NY	Die Aurora	New York; Catholic paper; one issue digital
USA	Buffalo, NY	Täglicher Buffalo Volksfreund	New York
USA	Buffalo, NY	Wöchentlicher Buffalo Volksfreund	New York

Country	Published at	Title	Notes
USA	Canton, OH	Der Vaterlandsfreund und Westliche Beobachter	Ohio
USA	Canton, OH	Ohio Staats-Bote	Ohio
USA	Canton, OH	Vaterlandsfreund	Ohio
USA	Canton, OH	Vaterlandsfreund und Geist der Zeit	Ohio
USA	Carlisle, PA	Freyheits-Fahne	Pennsylvania
USA	Chestnut Hill, PA	Chestnuthiller Wochenschrift	Pennsylvania
USA	Chicago, IL	Abendpost	Illinois
USA	Chicago, IL	Der deutsche Pionier	German-American biography
USA	Chicago, IL	Der Wahrheitsfreund	Mennonite paper
USA	Chicago, IL	Sonntagspost	Illinois
USA	Chicago, IL	Vorbote	Illinois
USA	Cincinnati, OH	Cincinnati Volksblatt	Ohio
USA	Cincinnati, OH	Cincinnati Volksfreund	Catholic
USA	Cincinnati, OH	Die Deborah	Jewish
USA	Cincinnati, OH	Tägliches Cincinnatier Volksblatt	Ohio
USA	Cincinnati, OH	Westliche Blätter	Ohio
USA	Cleveland, OH	Echo: Wochenblatt der Vereingten Deutschen Sozialisten Clevelands	Ohio Socialist
USA	Cleveland, OH	Siebenbürgisch-Amerikanisches Volksblatt	Hungarian/Romanian Germans
USA	Columbus, OH	Columbus Westbote	Ohio

Country	Published at	Title	Notes
USA	Columbus, OH	Ohio Waisenfreund	Catholic
USA	Columbus, OH	Wochenblatt des Westboten	Ohio
USA	Davenport, IA	Der Demokrat	Iowa
USA	Davenport, IA	Der Tägliche Demokrat	Iowa
USA	Denver, CO	Colorado Post	Colorado
USA	Detroit, MI	Detroiter Abend-Post	Michigan
USA	Egg Harbor City, NJ	Beobachter am Egg Harbor River	New Jersey
USA	Egg Harbor City, NJ	Der Wöchentliche Anzeiger	New Jersey
USA	Egg Harbor City, NJ	Der Zeitgeist	New Jersey
USA	Egg Harbor City, NJ	Egg Harbor Aurora	New Jersey
USA	Egg Harbor City, NJ	Egg Harbor Beobachter	New Jersey
USA	Egg Harbor City, NJ	Egg Harbor Pilot	New Jersey
USA	Egg Harbor City, NJ	Pilot	New Jersey
USA	El Reno, OK	Der Oklahoma Courier	Oklahoma
USA	Erie, PA	Erie Tageblatt	Pennsylvania
USA	Eureka, SD	Eureka Post	South Dakota
USA	Fort Scott, KS	Der deutsche Krieger	9th Wisconsin Regt. Civil War
USA	Frankfort, MD	Bartgis's Marylandische Zeitung	Maryland
USA	Frankfort, MD	Freiheitsbothe	Maryland

Country	Published at	Title	Notes
USA	Frederick, MD	Bartgis's Maryland Gazette	Maryland
USA	Frederick, MD	General Staatsbothe	Maryland
USA	Galveston, TX	Die Union	Texas
USA	Galveston, TX	Wochenblatt der Union	Texas
USA	Great Falls, MT	Montana Herold	Montana
USA	Harrisburg, PA	Unparteyische Harrisburg Morgenroethe Zeitung	Pennsylvania
USA	Helena, MT	Montana Herold	Montana
USA	Hermann, MO	Hermanner Zeitung	Missouri
USA	Highland, IL	Highland Union	Illinois
USA	Indianapolis, IN	Deutsch-amerikanische Buchdrucker-Zeitung	German-American printer paper
USA	Indianapolis, IN	Indiana Tribüne	Indiana
USA	Lancaster, PA	Der Wahre Amerikaner	Pennsylvania
USA	Lancaster, PA	Deutsche Porcupein	Pennsylvania
USA	Lancaster, PA	Neue Unpartheyische Lancaster Zeitung	Pennsylvania
USA	Lebanon, PA	Lebanon Weltbothe	Pennsylvania
USA	Louisville, KY	Louisville Anzeiger	one issue; Kentucky
USA	Milwaukee, WI	Jugend-Post	youth paper
USA	Milwaukee, WI	Milwaukeer Socialist	socialist paper
USA	Milwaukee, WI	Milwaukie Flugblätter	Milwaukee

Country	Published at	Title	Notes
USA	Milwaukee, WI	Wahrheit	Wisconsin
USA	Milwaukee, WI	Wiskonsin Banner	Wisconsin
USA	Nauvoo, IL	Der Communist	Icarian society paper
USA	New Berlin, PA	Der christliche Botschafter	Evangelical Association religious
USA	New Braunfels, TX	Neu Braunfelser Zeitung	Texas
USA	New Orleans, LA	New Orleanser Deutsche Zeitung	Louisiana
USA	New Philadelphia, OH	Der deutsche Beobachter	Ohio
USA	New Ulm, MN	Der Fortschritt	Minnesota
USA	New York, NY	Aufbau	Jewish exile journal
USA	New York, NY	Israels Herold	Jewish paper
USA	New York, NY	New Yorker Presse	New York
USA	New York, NY	New Yorker Volkszeitung	labor paper
USA	New York, NY	Sociale Republik	labor paper
USA	Newark, NJ	New Jersey Deutsche Zeitung	New Jersey
USA	Perry, OK	Neuigkeiten	Oklahoma
USA	Perry, OK	Oklahoma Neuigkeiten	Oklahoma
USA	Philadelphia, PA	Amerikanischer Beobachter	Pennsylvania
USA	Philadelphia, PA	Pelican	Pennsylvania
USA	Philadelphia, PA	Pennsylvanische Fama	Pennsylvania

Country	Published at	Title	Notes
USA	Philadelphia, PA	Pennsylvanischer Staatsbote	Pennsylvania; important news
USA	Philadelphia, PA	Philadelphischer Wochenblat	Pennsylvania
USA	Philadelphia, PA	Wöchentliche Philadelphische Staatsbote	Pennsylvania
USA	Pittsburgh, PA	Berlinisches litterarisches Wochenblatt	Pennsylvania
USA	Pittsburgh, PA	Pittsburger Volksblatt	Pennsylvania
USA	Pittsburgh, PA	Volksblatt und Freiheits-Freund	Pennsylvania
USA	Pomeroy, OH	Ohio Waisenfreund	Catholic
USA	Reading, PA	Der Liberale Beobachter und Berks, Montgomery und Schuylkill Counties Anzeiger	Pennsylvania
USA	Reading, PA	Der Weltbothe und wahre Republikaner von Berks, Montgomery und Schuylkill Counties	Pennsylvania
USA	Reading, PA	Reading Adler	Pennsylvania
USA	Reading, PA	Welt-Bothe	Pennsylvania
USA	San Antonio, TX	San Antonio Zeitung	Texas
USA	San Antonio, TX	Verbands-Bote	Texas
USA	Sandusky, OH	Der Bay City Demokrat	Ohio; one issue
USA	Sandusky, OH	Der Baystadt Demokrat	Ohio; one issue
USA	Sandusky, OH	Intelligenz–Blatt	Ohio; one issue
USA	Scranton, PA	Scranton Wochenblatt	Pennsylvania
USA	Seguin, TX	Seguiner Zeitung	Texas

Country	Published at	Title	Notes
USA	Sioux Falls, SD	Deutscher Herold	South Dakota
USA	Sioux Falls, SD	Süd Dakota Nachrichten Herold	South Dakota
USA	Sioux Falls, SD	Süd Dakota Nachrichten und Herold	South Dakota
USA	St. Cloud, MN	Der Nordstern	Minnesota
USA	St. Louis, MO	Deutsch-Amerikanischer Jugendfreund	youth paper
USA	St. Louis, MO	Pastoralblatt	Catholic priest paper
USA	St. Paul, MN	Minnesota Staats-Zeitung	Minnesota
USA	Sunbury, PA	Nordwestliche Post	Pennsylvania
USA	Sunbury, PA	Northumberland Republikaner	Pennsylvania
USA	Wellsburg, IA	Ostfriesen Zeitung	East Frisian news
	place unknown	Appendix Relationis Historicae	early paper
	place unknown	Aus Sundgau und Wasgenwald	wartime field paper
	place unknown	Der Horchposten des Kgl. Württembergischen Gebirgsbattaillions	wartime field paper
	place unknown	Der Kamerad	wartime field paper
	place unknown	Deutsche Kriegszeitung von Brunewitschi	wartime field paper
	place unknown	Die Armierer	wartime field paper
	place unknown	Die Armierer	wartime field paper
	place unknown	Frontpost	wartime field paper

Country	Published at	Title	Notes
	place unknown	Funken-Zeitung der Leichten Funken-Station 1	wartime field paper
	place unknown	Kriegszeitung der 4ten Armee	wartime field paper
	place unknown	Kriegs-Zeitung des Korps-Marschall	wartime field paper
	place unknown	Kriegs-Zeitung Heeresgruppe Scholtz	wartime field paper
	place unknown	Newe Zeitung	early paper
	place unknown	Newe Zeitung des erschrocklichen grossen Wassers	early paper
	place unknown	Newe Zeitung und eigentlicher Bericht ...	early paper
	place unknown	Newe Zeitung von Kaiserlicher Maiestat Kriegsrüstung	early paper
	place unknown	Newe Zeitung, des Türkischen Keisers Absagbrieff	early paper
	place unknown	Newe Zeitunge. Von einem Manne Hans Vader genannt.	early paper
	place unknown	Ordinari Sontags-Zeitung, aus Deutschland, Polen Schweden ...	early paper
	place unknown	PostZeitung	early paper
	place unknown	Resolution, Welche etliche Obristen, mit dem Fürsten von Friedland ...	early paper
	place unknown	Warhafftige Newe Zeitung. Welcher massen die Römische...	early paper
	place unknown	Warhafftige und gründliche Zeitung	early paper
	place unknown	Zeitung auß Wormbs	early paper
	war theatre	Donau-Armee-Zeitung	wartime field paper
	war theatre	Patrouillen-Zeitung	wartime field paper

171

Title	Dates	Key
12 Uhr Blatt	1933–1934	ANNO
84er Zeitung	1931–1941	ANNO
Aachener allgemeine Zeitung	1900–1915	UBONN
Aachener Rundschau	1916	NRW
Aachener Wahrheits-Freund	1814	UDUS
Aarauer Anzeiger	1859	Aargau Dig
Aarauer Kurier	1845–1847	Aargau Dig
Aarauer Nachrichten	1861–1878	Aargau Dig
Aarauer Zeitung	1819	GooBook
Aarauer Zeitung	1817–1821	DigiPress
Aargauer Anzeiger	1840–1900 23 y; gaps	Aargau
Aargauer Nachrichten	1860–1915 25 y; gaps	Aargau Dig
Aargauischer Anzeiger	1840–1900 23 y; gaps	Aargau Dig
Abendblatt des Pester Lloyd	1886 Aug	UHEID
Abendblatt von München	1830	DigiPress
Abendblatt von München	1830	GooBook
Abendpost	1914–1932 5 y; gaps	CRL
Abend-Zeitung	1817–1836 14 y; gaps	ANNO

Title	Dates	Key
Abend-Zeitung (Dresden)	1805–1806; 1822–1826	DigiPress
Abend-Zeitung (Leipzig)	1817–1856	SLUB
Abensberger Wochenblatt	1849–1850	DigiPress
Adelaider Deutsche Zeitung	1851–1862	Trove
Adenauer Kreis- und Wochenblatt	1863–1866	UBONN
Aegyptische Nachrichten	1912	ZEFYS
Aerztliche Correspondenz-Blatt für Böhmen	1873	GooBook
Aerztliches Intelligenzblatt	1858–1907 12 y; gaps	GooBook
Agger-Blatt	1845–1846	UBONN
Agramer Zeitung	1841–1912 33 y; many gaps	ANNO
Agrarische Post	1938–1940; 1942	ANNO
Ahasverus, der ewige Jude	1830–1832	DigiPress
Ahrweiler Kreisblatt	1861–1866	UBONN
Akademische Frauenblätter	1926–1927	ANNO
Allergnädigst-privilegirtes Leipziger Tagblatt	1817–1832	SLUB
Allerneueste Mannigfaltigkeiten	1777–1784	DigiPress
Allerneueste Nachrichten oder Münchener Neuigkeits-Kourier	1848	DigiPress
Allerneuestes Gradaus oder deutsches Volk	1850 Feb 15; 21	DigiPress
Allgäuer Volksblatt	1869–1870	DigiPress

Title	Dates	Key
Allgäuer Zeitung	1852; 1863–1866	DigiPress
Allgäuer Zeitung	1852; 1864; 1866	GooBook
Allgemeine academische Zeitung	1863–1866	DigiPress
Allgemeine Arbeiterzeitung	1848	UFFM
Allgemeine Auswanderungs-Zeitung	1846–1856	UJENA
Allgemeine Auswanderungs-Zeitung	1858–1865	DigiPress
Allgemeine Automobil-Zeitung	1900–1938	ANNO
Allgemeine Bau-Zeitung	1836–1938	ANNO
Allgemeine bayrische Hopfen-Zeitung	1861–1864	GooBook
Allgemeine Chronik der Königlich Preussischen Provinz Rheinland-Westfalen	1832	NRW
Allgemeine deutsche Arbeiter-Zeitung	1863–1866	DigiPress
Allgemeine deutsche Fischerei-Zeitung	1877–1908 31 y; gaps	Bio
Allgemeine deutsche Garten-Zeitung	1826–1831	Bio
Allgemeine deutsche Gärtnerzeitung	1891–1929	FES
Allgemeine deutsche Lehrerzeitung	1862–1870 7 y; gaps	DigiPress
Allgemeine deutsche naturhistorische Zeitung	1846–1857	Bio
Allgemeine deutsche Zeitung	1886–1889	Brazil
Allgemeine Eisenbahn-Zeitung	1928–1932	ANNO
Allgemeine Familien-Zeitung	1869–1874	Ablit

Title	Dates	Key
Allgemeine Feuerwehr-Zeitung	1879–1879	ANNO
Allgemeine Handlungszeitung	1797–1800	DigiPress
Allgemeine Handlungs-Zeitung	1812	GooBook
Allgemeine Handlungs-Zeitung	1803–1804; 1813–1817	DigiPress
Allgemeine Hopfen-Zeitung	1861–1873	DigiPress
Allgemeine illustrierte Judenzeitung	1860–1862	DiFMOE
Allgemeine jüdische Rundschau	1907–1910	DiFMOE
Allgemeine Kirchenzeitung	1822–1872	BavLib
Allgemeine Land- und forstwirthschaftliche Zeitung	1851–1867	ANNO
Allgemeine Literaturzeitung	1785–1786	DigiPress
Allgemeine Literatur-Zeitung	1785–1849	GooBook
Allgemeine Literatur-Zeitung	1785–1849	UJENA
Allgemeine Literatur-Zeitung	1787–1848 39y; gaps	DigiPress
Allgemeine Literatur-Zeitung zunächst für das katholische Deutschland	1785–1816; 1865	ANNO
Allgemeine Militär-Zeitung	1826–1861	ArchOrg
Allgemeine Militär-Zeitung	1826–1873 39 y; gaps	DigiPress
Allgemeine musikalische Zeitung (Leipzig)	1798–1848; 1860–1873	DigiPress
Allgemeine musikalische Zeitung (Wien/Vienna)	1817–1824	ANNO

Title	Dates	Key
Allgemeine Österreichische Gerichts-Zeitung	1851–1918 62 y; gaps	ANNO
Allgemeine Österreichische Gerichts-Zeitung	1856; 1862–1874	DigiPress
Allgemeine Österreichische Zeitschrift für den Landwirth, Forstmann und Gaertner	1829–1845; 1848; 1929	ANNO
Allgemeine polytechnische Zeitung	1834–1837	DigiPress
Allgemeine Preßzeitung	1840–1842; 1844–1845	GooBook
Allgemeine Preßzeitung	1841–1845	DigiPress
Allgemeine preußische Staats-Zeitung	1842	GooBook
Allgemeine preußische Staats-Zeitung	1819–1871 21 y; gaps	DigiPress
Allgemeine Radio-Zeitung	1924–1925	ANNO
Allgemeine Rundschau	1865–1866	DigiPress
Allgemeine Schutzhütten-Zeitung für die Ostalpen	1937–1943	ANNO
Allgemeine Schweizerische Militär-Zeitung	1855–1906; gaps	GooBook
Allgemeine Sport-Zeitung	1880–1919; 1920–1927	ANNO
Allgemeine Theaterzeitung	1822; 1835; 1843–1847	DigiPress
Allgemeine Theaterzeitung und Unterhaltungsblatt	1822; 1835; 1843–1847	DigiPress
Allgemeine Uhrmacher-Zeitung	1891–1893; 1895; 1906–1907	UDRES
Allgemeine Wiener medizinische Zeitung	1856–1875	ANNO
Allgemeine Zeitung	1789–1929	DigiPress
Allgemeine Zeitung	1810–1838; 1907	Hathi

Title	Dates	Key
Allgemeine Zeitung	1841; 1843; 1846–1847	GooBook
Allgemeine Zeitung	1856–1857	CRL
Allgemeine Zeitung des Judenthums	1851	GooBook
Allgemeine Zeitung des Judenthums	1837–1862 15 y; gaps	ANNO
Allgemeine Zeitung des Judenthums	1837–1922	CompMem
Allgemeine Zeitung München	1828–1870 9 y; gaps	GooBook
Allgemeine Zeitung von und für Bayern	1834–1841	DigiPress
Allgemeiner Anzeiger	1860–1861	UBONN
Allgemeiner Anzeiger der Deutschen	1809–1828 7 y; gaps	GooBook
Allgemeiner Anzeiger für Bayern	1822	GooBook
Allgemeiner Anzeiger für Buchbindereien	1897–1907	Hathi
Allgemeiner Anzeiger für das Königreich Bayern	1844	GooBook
Allgemeiner Anzeiger für die Pfalz	1853 Apr	GooBook
Allgemeiner Anzeiger und Kunst-, Handels- und Gewerbezeitung für den Regierungsbezirk Trier	1860–1861	NRW
Allgemeiner Anzeiger und National-Zeitung der Deutschen	1791–1804; 1897; 1809–1850	DigiPress
Allgemeiner Anzeiger und National-Zeitung der Deutschen	1791–1849; gaps	Hathi
Allgemeiner bayerischer National-Korrespondent	1830–1831	DigiPress
Allgemeiner Bonner Anzeiger für Industrie, Handel und Gewerbe	1859–1860	UBONN

Title	Dates	Key
Allgemeiner Kameral-, Oekonomie-, Forst- und Technologie-Korrespondent	1806–1807	GooBook
Allgemeiner Polizei-Anzeiger	1841–1867	DigiPress
Allgemeiner Tiroler Anzeiger	1907–1913; 1915–1938	ANNO
Allgemeiner Wohnungsanzeiger für Stettin	1844–1856 9 y; gaps	Meck
Allgemeines Amts- und Intelligenz-Blatt für den Jaxt-Kreis	1831–1836; 1838–1843; 1849–1850	DigiPress
Allgemeines Amtsblatt	1802	GooBook
Allgemeines Anzeigeblatt	1828–1831	UMST
Allgemeines Intelligenzblatt der Stadt Nürnberg	1818–1828	DigiPress
Allgemeines Intelligenzblatt der Stadt Nürnberg	1826–1827	GooBook
Allgemeines Intelligenzblatt für das Königreich Baiern	1819–1820	Hathi
Allgemeines Intelligenzblatt für die Fürstlich-Nassau-Weilburgischen und Nassau-Sayn-Hachenburgischen Lande	1804–1806	DiLibri
Allgemeines Intelligenz-Blatt für sämtlich-hochfürstlich-badische Lande	1783	DigiPress
Allgemeines Journal der Uhrmacherkunst	1876–1891; 1898–1901; 1907	UDRES
Allgemeines jüdisches Familienblatt	1926–1933	SLUB
Allgemeines merkantilisches Anzeige-, Anfrage- und Zusage-Blatt	1832	DigiPress
Allgemeines Noth- und Hülfs-Blatt	1846–1847	DigiPress
Allgemeines Organ für Handel und Gewerbe (und damit verwandte Gegenstände)	1842	UKLN
Allgemeines Organ für Handel und Gewerbe (und damit verwandte Gegenstände)	1834–1848	DigiPress

179

Title	Dates	Key
Allgemeines Reichs-Gesetz- und Regierungsblatt für das Kaiserthum Oesterreich	1849–1850; 1852	Hathi
Allgemeines Repertorium der Literatur	1819–1832	GooBook
Allgemeiner Anzeiger für Mechanik, Optik, Elektrotechnik, Glasinstrumenten und Uhrmacherbranche	1888–1889; 1895–1896	UDRES
Alpenländische Fachschrift	1908–1909	Tessmann
Alpenländische Gewerbe-Zeitung	1910–1913	Tessmann
Alpenländische Morgen-Zeitung	1933–1934	ANNO
Alpenländische Rundschau	1925–1944	ANNO
Alpenzeitung	1926–1943	Tessmann
Alphabetisches Verzeichnis der in den Verlustlisten ...	1914–1919	Kram
Alte Nachrichten von Lippstadt und benachbarten Gegenden	1787–1788	GooBook
Altonaer Nachrichten	1850–1938	Euro
Am Wege	1924–1932	FES
Amberger Tagblatt	1833 Mar	Amberg
Amberger Tagblatt	1841–1843; 1847–1850; 1863–1873	DigiPress
Amberger Tagblatt	1864; 1869; 1872–1873	GooBook
Amberger Volkszeitung (für Stadt und Land)	1833 Mar	Amberg
Amberger Volkszeitung (für Stadt und Land)	1868–1873	Amberg
Amtliche Linzer Zeitung	1928–1938; 1945–1947	ANNO

Title	Dates	Key
Amtlicher Anzeiger für Deutsch-Ostafrika	1900–1914	Berlin
Amtliches Kreisblatt für den Kreis Koschmin	1909–1911; 1914; 1916–1918	ZEFYS
Amtliches Kreisblatt und Anzeiger für den Kreis und die Stadt Koschmin	1905; 1909	ZEFYS
Amts- und Anzeigeblatt für den Bezirk des Amtsgerichts Eibenstock und dessen Umgebung	1879–1887	SLUB
Amts- und Anzeigeblatt für den Gerichtsbezirk Eibenstock und dessen Umgebung	1872–1879	SLUB
Amts- und Anzeigenblatt für die Stadt und das königl. Bezirksamt Rothenburg	1865–1873	DigiPress
Amts- und Anzeigenblatt für die Stadt und das königl. Bezirksamt Rothenburg	1866–1869	GooBook
Amts- und Intelligenzblatt der Königlich-bayerischen Regierung des Rheinkreises	1831–1837	Bavarica
Amts- und Intelligenzblatt der Provisorischen Regierung des Rheinkreises	1849	DigiPress
Amts- und Intelligenz-Blatt von Salzburg	1818–1822; 1825; 1848	GooBook
Amts- und Nachrichtenblatt für Thüringen	1921–1930	UJENA
Amtsblatt der Bezirkshauptmannschafft Hollabrunn	1935–1941	ANNO
Amtsblatt der churmärkischen Regierung	1812–1813	GooBook
Amtsblatt der deutschen Reichs-Postverwaltung	1872	GooBook
Amts-Blatt der freien Stadt Frankfurt	1857–1864	Hathi
Amtsblatt der freien und Hansestadt Hamburg	1890–1920 19 y; gaps	Hathi
Amtsblatt der großherzoglichen Oberstudiendirektion	1849–1850	UGIE
Amtsblatt der K.K. Österreichischen und K. Baierischen Gemeinschaftlichen Landes-Administrations-Kommission	1816	GooBook

Title	Dates	Key
Amtsblatt der königlich Bayerischen General-Zoll-Administration	1864–1880	UMUN
Amtsblatt der königlich preußischen Regierung zu Bromberg	1815–1851 31 y; gaps	Poznan
Amtsblatt der königlich preußischen Regierung zu Bromberg	1827–1872 46 y; gaps	GooBook
Amtsblatt der königlich preußischen Regierung zu Bromberg	1883–1888	LibPol
Amts-Blatt der königlich Preußischen Regierung zu Merseburg	1816–1822; 1842; 1826–72	UMUN
Amtsblatt der königlich preußischen Regierung zu Minden	1828–1871	GooBook
Amtsblatt der königlich preußischen Regierung zu Münster	1816–1900	UMST
Amtsblatt der Königlich-Baierischen Regierung des Rheinkreises	1818–1819; 1821–1830	Bavarica
Amtsblatt der königlichen Litthauischen Regierung	1811–1816	Gumb
Amtsblatt der königlichen preußischen Regierung zu Königsberg	1814–1830 7 y; gaps	LibPol
Amtsblatt der königlichen preußischen Regierung zu Königsberg	1821–1872	UMUN
Amtsblatt der königlichen preußischen Regierung zu Reichenbach	1819	GooBook
Amtsblatt der Königlichen Regierung in Gumbinnen	1820–1873	UMUN
Amtsblatt der Königlichen Regierung von Pommern	1811	GooBook
Amtsblatt der königlichen Regierung zu Berlin	1821	GooBook
Amtsblatt der Königlichen Regierung zu Breslau	1816–1825; 1827–1872	GooBook
Amtsblatt der Königlichen Regierung zu Breslau	1821–1872 47 y; gaps	UMUN
Amtsblatt der Königlichen Regierung zu Breslau	1859; 1861; 1873; 1877; 1890	Poland
Amtsblatt der königlichen Regierung zu Bromberg	1830	GooBook

Title	Dates	Key
Amtsblatt der königlichen Regierung zu Cassel	1869–1872	UMUN
Amtsblatt der königlichen Regierung zu Cassel	1871–1908 34 y; gaps	Hathi
Amtsblatt der königlichen Regierung zu Cleve	1816–1817; 1820–1821	UMUN
Amtsblatt der königlichen Regierung zu Cleve	1816–1821	DigiPress
Amtsblatt der königlichen Regierung zu Cleve	1816–1821	UDUS
Amtsblatt der königlichen Regierung zu Coblenz	1816–1873 54 y; gaps	UMUN
Amtsblatt der königlichen Regierung zu Danzig	1816–1903	LibPol
Amtsblatt der königlichen Regierung zu Danzig	1820–1872	UMUN
Amtsblatt der Königlichen Regierung zu Erfurt	1827–1851; 1853–1866; 1868–1872	GooBook
Amtsblatt der königlichen Regierung zu Merseburg	1834	GooBook
Amtsblatt der königlichen Regierung zu Oppeln	1816–1865 43 y; gaps	Poland
Amtsblatt der königlichen Regierung zu Oppeln	1817; 1857; 1867	GooBook
Amtsblatt der königlichen Regierung zu Oppeln	1817–1872 46 y; gaps	UMUN
Amtsblatt der königlichen Regierung zu Posen	1815–1910	Poznan
Amtsblatt der Königlichen Regierung zu Potsdam und der Stadt Berlin	1811–1872 58 y; gaps	UMUN
Amtsblatt der Königlichen Regierung zu Potsdam und der Stadt Berlin	1811–1908 86 y; gaps	GooBook
Amtsblatt der Königlichen Regierung zu Potsdam und der Stadt Berlin	1818–1908 40 y; gaps	ArchOrg
Amtsblatt der Königlichen Regierung zu Wiesbaden	1867–1873	DigiPress
Amtsblatt der Königlichen Regierung zu Wiesbaden	1869–1871	UMUN

Title	Dates	Key
Amtsblatt der prdußischen Regierung in Trier	1856; 1870–1872	UMUN
Amtsblatt der preußischen Regierung in Schneidemühl	1937–1939	Pila
Amtsblatt der preußischen Regierung zu Köslin	1816–1843 41 y; gaps	GooBook
Amtsblatt der preußischen Regierung zu Köslin	1821–1872	UMUN
Amtsblatt der preußischen Regierung zu Köslin	1824–1867 13 y; gaps	GooBook
Amtsblatt der preußischen Regierung zu Köslin	1853–1865 10 y; gaps	Hathi
Amts-Blatt der preußischen Regierung zu Köslin	1849	GooBook
Amts-Blatt der Preußischen Regierung zu Liegnitz	1811–1873	DigiPress
Amts-Blatt der Preußischen Regierung zu Liegnitz	1821–1872	GooBook
Amtsblatt der preussischen Regierung zu Schleswig	1870	DigiBib
Amtsblatt der preussischen Regierung zu Schleswig	1869–1873	GooBook
Amtsblatt der preußischen Regierung zu Sigmaringen	1869–1872	GooBook
Amtsblatt der preußischen Regierung zu Stettin	1817–1839; 1841–1872	GooBook
Amtsblatt der preußischen Regierung zu Stettin	1817–1872	UMUN
Amtsblatt der preußischen Regierung zu Stralsund	1827–1872 39 y; gaps	GooBook
Amtsblatt der preußischen Regierung zu Stralsund	1827–1872 41 y; gaps	UMUN
Amtsblatt der Regierung zu Aachen	1845	GooBook
Amtsblatt der Regierung zu Aachen	1817–1906 48 y; gaps	Hathi
Amtsblatt der Regierung zu Aachen	1826–1906 44 y; gaps	GooBook

184

Title	Dates	Key
Amtsblatt der Regierung zu Frankfurt an der Oder	1874	Hathi
Amtsblatt der Regierung zu Frankfurt an der Oder	1816; 1818–1872	UMUN
Amtsblatt der Regierung zu Magdeburg	1823	GooBook
Amtsblatt der Regierung zu Magdeburg	1816–1836	Hathi
Amtsblatt der Regierung zu Magdeburg	1817–1873	UMUN
Amtsblatt der Stadt Altona	1920–1933	UHBG
Amtsblatt der westfälischen Wilhelms-Universität Münster	1938–1944	UMST
Amtsblatt des großherzoglichen Ministerium der Finanzen	1885–1914	Hathi
Amtsblatt des großherzoglichen Oberschulraths	1833–1849	UGIE
Amtsblatt des k. und k. Kreiskommandos in Janów	1915	Polona
Amtsblatt des k. und k. Kreiskommandos in Kielce	1916–1917	Polona
Amtsblatt des k. und k. Kreiskommandos in Nowo-Aleksandrya	1916	Polona
Amtsblatt des k. und k. Kreiskommandos in Noworadomsk	1916–1917	Polona
Amtsblatt des k. und k. Kreiskommandos in Piławy	1916–1918	Polona
Amtsblatt des Kantons Aargau	1838–	Aargau Dig
Amtsblatt des Kantons Zürich	1859–1863, 1865–1884	Hathi
Amtsblatt des Kreises Miechów	1915	Polona
Amtsblatt des Kreises Olkusz	1916	Poland
Amtsblatt des Kreises Włoszczowa	1915–1916	Polona

Title	Dates	Key
Amtsblatt des Landrats in Ostrowo	1943	Poland
Amtsblatt des preußischen Post-Departements	1867	GooBook
Amtsblatt des Saarlandes	1945–2009	UREG
Amtsblatt für das Bezirksamt Günzburg	1869–1873	GooBook
Amtsblatt für das Bezirksamt Nördlingen	1873	GooBook
Amtsblatt für das Bezirksamts und Amtsgericht Aichach	1870	Bavarica
Amtsblatt für das Bezirksamts und Amtsgericht Aichach	1865–1873	DigiPress
Amtsblatt für das Herzogtum Holstein	1851–1852	UMUN
Amtsblatt für das Königlich-Baierische Gebiet auf dem linken Rheinufer	1816–1817	Bavarica
Amtsblatt für den Landesteil Birkenfeld	1858–1859; 1864	DiLibri
Amtsblatt für den Regierungs-Bezirk Arnsberg	1821–1872	UMUN
Amtsblatt für den Regierungs-Bezirk Arnsberg	1821–1872 49 y; gaps	GooBook
Amtsblatt für den Regierungs-Bezirk Arnsberg	1821–1873	DigiPress
Amtsblatt für den Regierungsbezirk Düsseldorf	1816	DigiBib
Amtsblatt für den Regierungsbezirk Düsseldorf	1816–1845;1949–2004	UDUS
Amtsblatt für den Regierungsbezirk Düsseldorf	1820–1830; 1832–1855; 1857–1873	DigiPress
Amtsblatt für den Regierungsbezirk Düsseldorf	1820–1866 44 y; gaps	GooBook
Amtsblatt für den Regierungsbezirk Köln	1827–1872	GooBook
Amtsblatt für den Regierungs-Bezirk Marienwerder	1820–1825; 1828–1869; 1871	UMUN

Title	Dates	Key
Amtsblatt für den Stadtkreis Frankfurt a. M.	1914–1915	UFFM
Amts-Blatt für den Verwaltungs- und Gerichts-Bezirk Schrobenhausen	1863	DigiPress
Amts-Blatt für die Gemeinden des Bezirksamts Landshut	1864; 1866–1867	GooBook
Amtsblatt für die Herzogthümer Schleswig und Holstein	1849	ZEFYS
Amtsblatt für die königlichen Bezirksämter Forchheim und Ebermannstadt (sowie für die Königliche Stadt Forchheim)	1868	Bavarica
Amtsblatt für die königlichen Bezirksämter Forchheim und Ebermannstadt (sowie für die Königliche Stadt Forchheim)	1863; 1865–1873	DigiPress
Amtsblatt für die Provinz Westfalen	1815	Hathi
Amtsblatt für die Verhandlungen der Provinzialstände des Herzogthums Schleswig	1836	GooBook
Amtsblatt für Hannover	1867–1872	UMUN
Amtsblatt zur Lemberger Zeitung	1866	Jag
An der schönen blauen Donau	1886–1895	ANNO
An Flanderns Küste	1916–1918	France
Anclamer Kreis-, Volks- und Wochenblatt	1849–1855	Meck,
Anclamer Wochenblatt	1843–1848	Meck
Andernacher Burger-Blatt	1837; 1855–1862	UBONN
Andreas Hofer Wochenblatt	1878–1906	Tessmann
Anhalt-Cöthensche Zeitung	1813	DigiPress
Annalen	1787	UBONN

187

Title	Dates	Key
Ansbacher Intelligenz-Zeitung	1776–1778; 1800	DigiPress
Ansbacher Morgenblatt	1845–1873	DigiPress
Ansbacher Morgenblatt	1846–1863 6 y; gaps	GooBook
Ansbacher Tagblatt	1844–1845	DigiPress
Anzeige der Beamten und Angestellte im Staats- und Communal-Dienste des Rheinkreises	1827	GooBook
Anzeigeblatt der städtischen Behörden zu Frankfurt am Main	1914	UFFM
Anzeigen des Fürstenthums Schaumburg-Lippe	1850–1859	GooBook
Anzeiger des Siegkreises	1855–1865	NRW
Anzeiger für das Havelland	1905–1908	ZEFYS
Anzeiger für den Bezirk Wasserburg	1872	GooBook
Anzeiger für den Kreis Pleß	1932	Polona
Anzeiger für die Bezirke Bludenz und Montafon	1885–1941	ANNO
Anzeiger für Goldingen und Windau	1927–1929	Latvia
Anzeiger für Sobernheim und Umgegend	1860; 1862	NRW
Anzeiger und Amtsblatt für das königl. Gerichtsamt und den Stadtrath zu Leisnig	1859–1864	UDRES
Anzeiger und Unterhaltungsblatt für Zülpich, Lechenich und Umgegend	1857–1868	NRW
Anzeiger zum Pustertaler Boten	1874–1876; 1878–1882; 1894	Tessmann
Anzeiger: ein Tagblatt	1791–1793	UJENA

Title	Dates	Key
Appendix Relationis Historicae	1632	UBREM
Arbeiter Schachzeitung	1921–1922	ANNO
Arbeiterinnen-Zeitung	1892–1902; 1914–1919	ANNO
Arbeiterstimme	1925–1930	SLUB
Arbeiterwille	1890–1928	ANNO
Arbeiterwohlfahrt	1926–1933	FES
Arbeiter-Zeitung	1889–1937	ANNO
Arbeiter-Zeitung	1945–1989	ArbZtg
Arbeiter-Zeitung für Schlesien und Oberschlesien	1926; 1928–1933	FES
Areler Zeitung	1918 Nov 12	Euro
Arendseer Wochenblatt	1920–1921	UHALL
Argentinisches Wochenblatt	1942–1946	ZEFYS
Armeeblatt	1914; 1916–1919	ANNO
Armee-Zeitung der 2. Armee	1914–1918	France
Armee-Zeitung der IX. Armee	1914	France
Armeezeitung Scholz	1916–1918	France
Arnsberger Intelligenz-Blatt	1803 Sep 27?	WikiComm
Artistisches Notizenblatt	1822–1835	SLUB
Aschaffenburger Wochenblatt	1822–1828; 1832–1873	DigiPress

Title	Dates	Key
Aschaffenburger Wochenblatt	1824; 1826–1828	GooBook
Aschaffenburger Zeitung	1866–1873	GooBook
Aufbau	1951–2004	Baeck
Aufwärts	1932	DHM
Augsburger Abendzeitung	1742–1873 39 y; gaps	DigiPress
Augsburger allgemeine Zeitung	1868	DigiPress
Augsburger Anzeigeblatt	1846–1853; 1855–1873	DigiPress
Augsburger Anzeigeblatt	1861–1862; 1866; 1868	GooBook
Augsburger Neueste Nachrichten	1862–1873	GooBook
Augsburger Neueste Nachrichten	1862–1874	DigiPress
Augsburger Post-Zeitung	1723–1873 110 y; gaps	DigiPress
Augsburger Post-Zeitung	1840; 1854–1855; 1858	GooBook
Augsburger Sonntagsblatt	1873	GooBook
Augsburger Tagblatt	1830–1858; 1860–1871; 1873	DigiPress
Augsburger Tagblatt	1863; 1865–1866; 1868	GooBook
Augsburger Unterhaltungs-Blatt	1846; 1848–1849	DigiPress
Augspurgische Extra-Zeitung	1738	DigiPress
Augspurgische Ordinari Postzeitung	1770–1806	Augsburg
Aus Sundgau und Wasgenwald	1917–1918	France

Title	Dates	Key
Austria: Tagblatt für Handel und Gewerbe	1851	GooBook
Auszug aus der Tagespresse	1917–1918	ANNO
Aviso oder Zeitung das ist Kurtze jedoch außfürliche Relation	1614	UBREM
A–Z: Luxemburger Illustrierte Wochenschrift	1933–1940	Lux
Bacillus verus	1916–1918	USTR
Bade- und Reise-Journal	1876–1930 72 y; gaps	ANNO
Badener Bezirks-Blatt	1880–1896	ANNO
Badener Lazarett-Zeitung	1916–1918	UHEID
Badener Zeitungen	1896–1944	ANNO
Badewochenblatt für die großherzogliche Stadt Baden	1814; 1826	DigiPress
Badische Chronik	1868	Baden
Badische Landeszeitung	1870–1918 25 y; gaps	Baden
Badische Post	1919; 1923	UHEID
Badische Presse	1890–1944 49 y; gaps	Baden
Badischer Beobachter	1860–1935 68 y; gaps	Baden
Badischer Landsmann	1814*	Baden
Badisches Gesetz- und Verordnungsblatt	1803–1921 96 y; gaps	Hathi
Badisches Intelligenzblatt	1756–1831 49 y; gaps	Baden
Badisches Landtags-Zeitung	1819	DigiPress

Title	Dates	Key
Badisches Volksblatt	1832	Hathi
Baierische Nationalzeitung	1807–1820	DigiPress
Baierische Nationalzeitung	1808; 1810–1811; 1813–1819	GooBook
Baierische Wochenschrift	1821–1822	DigiPress
Baierische Wochenschrift	1821–1822	GooBook
Baierischer Eilbote	1837–1840; 1843–1848; 1850	GooBook
Baierisches National-Blatt	1819–1821	DigiPress
Baierisches Wochenblatt	1800	DigiPress
Bamberger Journal	1882	Hathi
Bamberger Neueste Nachrichten	1867–1873	DigiPress
Bamberger Neueste Nachrichten	1869; 1871	GooBook
Bamberger Tagblatt	1866	GooBook
Bamberger Tagblatt	1835; 1845–1868	DigiPress
Bamberger Volksblatt	1872	DigiPress
Bamberger Volksblatt für Stadt und Land	1852	DigiPress
Bamberger Zeitung	1815–1870 37 y; gaps	DigiPress
Banater Deutsche Zeitung	1936–1944	DiFMOE
Bapaumer Zeitung am Mittag	1914 Nov 14	France
Bar Kochba	1919–1921	CompMem

Title	Dates	Key
Barmer Wochenblatt	1838–1859	UBONN
Barmer Zeitung	1886 Aug	UHEID
Bartgis's Maryland Gazette	1792 May 22	NewsBank
Bartgis's Marylandische Zeitung	1789 Feb 18	NewsBank
Baruther Anzeiger	1925–1942	ZEFYS
Baruther Heimatland	1932–1936; 1939	ZEFYS
Basler Nachrichten	1886 Aug	UHEID
Basler Zeitung	1831–1836	DigiPress
Basler Zeitung	1831–1836	GooBook
Bauern-Zeitung	1870–1873	DigiPress
Bauern-Zeitung aus Frauendorf	1826	GooBook
Bayerische Hochschulzeitung	1920–1922; 1924–1934	BavLib
Bayerische Israelitische Gemeindezeitung	1925–1937	CompMem
Bayerische Landbötin	1830–1858; 1860–1863	DigiPress
Bayerische Landeszeitung	1869	GooBook
Bayerische Lehrerzeitung	1867–1873	DigiPress
Bayerische Nationalzeitung	1834–1840	DigiPress
Bayerische Ostmark Coburger National-Zeitung	1939–1940	DigiPress
Bayerische Schulzeitung	1856–1864	DigiPress

Title	Dates	Key
Bayerische Wochenschrift	1859	DigiPress
Bayerische Zeitung	1862–1867	GooBook
Bayerischer Beobachter	1829	GooBook
Bayerischer Generalanzeiger	1862	GooBook
Bayerischer Kurier	1859–1869	GooBook
Bayerischer Kurier	1859–1873	DigiPress
Bayerisches Brauer-Journal	1891–1919	DigiPress
Bayerisches Gesetz- und Verordnungsblatt	1875–1923 40 y; gaps	Hathi
Bayerisches Zentral-Polizei-Blatt	1866–1914	Bavarica
Bayerisches Zentral-Polizei-Blatt	1871–1873	GooBook
Bayerisches Zentral-Polizei-Blatt	1874–1903	Internet Archive
Bayern-Warte und Münchener Stadtanzeiger	1921	DigiPress
Bayreuther Intelligenz-Zeitung	1796	GooBook
Bayreuther Zeitung	1785–1842 8 y; gaps	GooBook
Beiblatt der Fliegenden Blätter	1883–1920 (more coming)	UHEID
Beiblatt der Freisinnigen Zeitung	1886 Aug	UHEID
Beilage zum Amts- und Intelligenz-Blatte des Rheinkreises	1836	GooBook
Beilage zum Pustertaler Boten	1854–1907 32 y; gaps	Tessmann
Beilage zur politischen Chronik	1911–1918	ANNO

Title	Dates	Key
Beiträge zur Ausbreitung nützlicher Kenntnisse	1784–1785	UBONN
Bekleidungsgewerkschaft	1920–1921; 1923–1933	FES
Belehrendes und Unterhaltendes	1895–1896; 1904–1905	ANNO
Ben Chananja	1858–1867	CompMem
Bensberger Volkszeitung	1907–1929	UBONN
Bensberg-Gladbacher Anzeiger	1870–1909	NRW
Berg Frei	1921–1923	FES
Berg- und Hüttenmännische Zeitung	1870–1881	GooBook
Bergarbeiter-Zeitung	1900–1924	FES
Bergarbeiter-Zeitung und Jungkamerad	1925–1928	FES
Bergisch Gladbacher Volkszeitung	1906–1929	NRW
Bergische Wacht	1907–1941	NRW
Bergischer Agent	1903–1905	UBONN
Bergischer Türmer	1903–1912	NRW
Bergisches Volksblatt	1849–1868	NRW
Bergisch-Gladbacher Volkszeitung	1906–1929	UBONN
Bergsträßer Anzeigeblatt	1914–1934 11 y; gaps	UDARM
Bericht über unsere mennonitische Hilfskasse	1892–1898; 1903; 1906	Bethel

195

Title	Dates	Key
Bericht was sich zu anfang dieß itzt angehenden ... Jahres in Deutschlandt, Franckreich, Welschlandt, Böhmen, Ungern, Nederlandt und in andern örten hin unnd wieder zugetragen = Frischmanns Berichte	1617–1618	ZEFYS
Bericht was sich zugetragen und begeben = Frischmanns Berichte	1621	ZEFYS
Berichte für die Lehranstalt für die Wissenschaft des Judentums	1874–1938	CompMem
Berichte und Informationen des österreichischen Forschungsinstituts für Wirtschaft und Politik	1946–1947	ANNO
Berliner Börsen-Courier	1886 Aug	UHEID
Berliner Börsen-Zeitung	1857; 1872–1930	ZEFYS
Berliner Courier	1886 Aug	UHEID
Berliner Gerichts-Zeitung	1853–1898 43 y; gaps	ZEFYS
Berliner Journal	1880–1916	SFU
Berliner Krakehler	1848 May 14	MICHAEL
Berliner Lokal-Anzeiger	1910	ZEFYS
Berliner Morgenpost	1933	ZEFYS
Berliner Musikzeitung	1878; 1883	ANNO
Berliner Politisches Wochenblatt	1831–181	ANNO
Berliner Tageblatt und Handels-Zeitung	1877–1939	ZEFYS
Berliner Tageblatt und Handels-Zeitung	1932–1933	CRL
Berliner Vereinsbote	1896–1897	CompMem

Title	Dates	Key
Berliner Volkszeitung	1890–1891; 1894–1895; 1904–1930	ZEFYS
Berliner Volks-Zeitung	1919–1920	CRL
Berliner Zeitung	1945–1993 (special login)	ZEFYS
Berlinische Nachrichten von Staats- und gelehrten Sachen	1812–1814	Hathi
Berlinische privilegierte Zeitung	1740	ZEFYS
Berlinisches litterarisches Wochenblatt	1776	Hathi
Berlinisches litterarisches Wochenblatt	1860–1865	GooNews
Berner Schulfreund	1861–1867	UZRCH
Bernisches Freytags-Blätlein	1722–1724	DiFMOE
Besinnung und Aufbruch	1929–1932	Anarch
Betrieb und Front	1940	ANNO
Betriebsgemeinschaft Renner	1944	DHM
Betriebsräte-Zeitschrift des DMV	1920–1931	FES
Beylage zum Münchner Policey-Anzeiger	1824	GooBook
Beylage zur Münchner Politische Zeitung	1820	GooBook
Bialystoker Zeitung	1916–1917; 1919	Euro
Bienen-Zeitung	1860; 1883	GooBook
Bitburger Kreis- und Intelligenzblatt	1854–1867	UBONN
Blätter für das Volk zunächst in Bayern	1848	DigiPress

Title	Dates	Key
Blätter für literarische Unterhaltung	1826–1873	ANNO
Blätter für Literatur und bildende Kunst	1836–1843	SLUB
Blätter für Polizei und Kultur	1801–1803	UBIEL
Blätter für Religion und Erziehung	1870–1871	Bethel
Blätter für religiöse Erziehung	1913–1914	UJENA
Blätter für Theater, Musik und Kunst	1855–1873	ANNO
Blätter von der Saale	1850–1858	UJENA
Blau-Weiß-Blätter	1913–1919	CompMem
Blau-Weiß-Blätter (Neue Folge)	1923–1925	CompMem
Blau-Weiß-Blätter Führerheft	1917–1923	CompMem
Bludenzer Anzeiger	1885–1941; 1946–1947	ANNO
Blumen-Zeitung	1837–1848 6 y; gaps	Bio
Bochumer Kreisblatt	1842–1874	UMST
Bockenheimer Anzeiger	1914	UFFM
Bohemia	1846–1914	Kram
Bohemia, ein Unterhaltungsblatt	1832–1845	Kram
Bohemia, oder Unterhaltungsblätter für gebildete Stände	1830–1832	Kram
Böhmerwald Volksbote	1909–1919	ANNO
Böhmerwald-Volksbote	1915–1917	ANNO

Title	Dates	Key
Bonner Anzeiger	1850	UBONN
Bonner Chronik	1890–1891	UBONN
Bonner Dekadenschrift	1794–1795	UBONN
Bonner Tageblatt	1883–1890	UBONN
Bonner Volksblatt	1862	UBONN
Bonner Volkszeitung	1882–1906	UBONN
Bonner Wochenblatt	1808–1891	NRW
Bonner Zeitung	1848	UBONN
Bonner Zeitung	1851–1919	UBONN
Bonner Zeitung	1892–1932	NRW
Bonner Zeitung (Thormann)	1824–1830	UBONN
Bönnischer Sitten, Staats- und Geschichtslehrer	1772	UBONN
Bönnisches Wochenblatt	1785–1788	UBONN
Bönnisches Wochenblatt	1814–1815	UBONN
Börsenblatt für den deutschen Buchhandel	1872	GooBook
Börsen-Halle: Hamburgische Abendzeitung für Handel, Schiffahrt und Politik	1833	GooBook
Börsen-Nachrichten der Ost-See	1838; 1847	UGREI
Botanische Zeitung	1844–1910	Bio
Bote vom Untersee und Rhein	1900–2016	Switz

Title	Dates	Key
Bozner Nachrichten	1894–1925	Tessmann
Bozner Tagblatt	1943–1945	Tessmann
Bozner Zeitung	1842–1918	Tessmann
Brand Aus	1960–present	ANNO
Brauereiarbeiterzeitung	1906–1910	FES
Brauerzeitung	1893–1906	FES
Braunschweigische landwirtschaftliche Zeitung	1882–1899 coming	UBRAU
Braunschweigisches Journal	1790–1791	BBF
Bregenzer Wochenblatt	1793–1863 67 y; gaps	ANNO
Bregenzer/Vorarlberger Tagblatt	1889–1915; 1919–1944	ANNO
Breisgauer Zeitung	1896	Baden
Bremer Handelsblatt	1856	DigiPress
Bremer Zeitung	1817–1818; 1820	GooBook
Breslauer jüdisches Gemeindeblatt	1924–1937	DiFMOE
Breslauer Zeitung	1848	ZEFYS
Breslauer Zeitung	1886 Aug	UHEID
Brieger Zeitung	1914 Oct 1; 1943 Mar 16	ZEFYS
Briesetal-Bote	1902–1923	ZEFYS
Brioni Insel-Zeitung	1910–1913	ANNO

Title	Dates	Key
Brixener Chronik	1888–1925	Tessmann
Brixner Diözesanblatt	1877–1925	ANNO
Bromberger Tageblatt	1886 Aug	UHEID
Bromberger Wochenblatt	1846–1861	Pol Byd
Brünner Hebammen-Zeitung	1910–1918	ANNO
Brünner Tagesbote	1851–1944	DiFMOE
Brünner Zeitung der k. K. Priv. Mähr. Lehenbank	1779–1848	ANNO
Buch- und Kunst-Anzeiger	1836–1842	SLUB
Buchbinder-Zeitung	1874; 1885–1909	FES
Buckower Lokal-Anzeiger	1933–1934	ZEFYS
Budissener Nachrichten	1828–1868	UDRES
Buffalo Volksfreund	1891 annotated	Archivaria
Bukowinaer Fortuna	1902–1904	ANNO
Bukowinaer Landwirtschaftliche Blätter	1897–1912; 1914	ANNO
Bukowinaer Nachrichten	1888–1892; 1913–1914	ANNO
Bukowinaer Post	1893–1914	ANNO
Bukowinaer Rundschau	1883–1907	ANNO
Bukowinaer Volks-Zeitung	1907–1908	ANNO
Bukowiner Pädogigische Blätter	1885; 1901–1902	ANNO

Title	Dates	Key
Bukowiner Schule	1904–1914	ANNO
Bukowiner Volksblatt	1908–1912	ANNO
Bukowiner Zeitung	1892–1892	ANNO
Bulletin des Parteitags der KPD	1925	SLUB
Bundesblatt	1849–1990	CH
Bündner Landbote	1845–1847	RERO
Bündner Nachrichten	1885–1892	RERO
Burgenländische Freiheit	1921–1934; 1946–2007	BF-Archiv
Bürger- und Beamten-Zeitung	1910	Euro
Bürger-Blatt für die Kreise Rees, Borken und Cleve	1852–1866	NRW
Bürger-Zeitung	1867–1868	GooBook
Bütower Anzeiger	1916–1918	ZEFYS
Cameralistische Zeitung	1836	GooBook
Carinthia	1842	AustLit
Carinthia I	1891–1944	ANNO
Carinthia II	1934	ANNO
Carinthia: Zeitschrift für Vaterlandskunde, Belehrung und Unterhaltung	1811–1877	ANNO
Casselische Polizey- und Commerzien-Zeitung	1735–1821	UKASL
Castellauner Zeitung	1924	DiLibri

Title	Dates	Key
Central- und Bezirks-Amtsblatt für Elsass-Lothringen	1883–1907 25 y; gaps	Hathi
Central-Anzeiger für jüdische Literatur	1890	CompMem
Centralblatt der Bauverwaltung	1889	GooBook
Centralblatt der Land- und Forstwirtschaft in Böhmen	1850–1870	ANNO
Centralblatt des Landwirthschaftlichen Vereins	1836–1840	Hathi
Central-Blatt für das deutsche Reich	1873; 1875–1876; 1878	GooBook
Central-Blatt für das deutsche Reich	1880–1918	Hathi
Centralblatt für Eisenbahnen und Dampfschiffahrt in Oesterreich	1862–1877	ANNO
Central-Verein Zeitung	1922–1938	CompMem
Cetinjer Zeitung	1916–1918	ANNO
Champagne-Kriegs-Zeitung	1915–1917	France
Champagner Kriegs-Zeitung	1917–1918; scattered	UHEID
Charis	1821–1824	UHEID
Charlottenburger Zeitung	1880	ZEFYS
Chemische Zeitung	1879; 1881	GooBook
Cholera-Zeitung	1831	GooBook
Christliche Frauenzeitung	1930–1948	ANNO
Christlicher Gemeinde-Kalender	1892–1970	Bethel
Christlicher Textilarbeiter	1899–1905	FES

Title	Dates	Key
Christlich-soziale Arbeiter-Zeitung	1902–1934	ANNO
Churbaierisches Intelligenzblatt	1766–1776	BavLib
Churbaierisches Intelligenzblatt	1770; 1773	GooBook
Churpfalzbaierisches Regierungsblatt	1802–1805	Hathi
Cincinnati Volksblatt	1910–1918	Chron
Cincinnati Volksfreund	1863–1904	GB
Clevisches Volksblatt	1855–1866	NRW
Coblenzer Tageblatt	1863–1865	UBONN
Coburger Nationalzeitung	1930–1934; 1940–1945	DigiPress
Coburger Regierungs-Blatt	1919–1920	DigiPress
Coburger Regierungs-Blatt / Bezirksamt Coburg	1921–1922	DigiPress
Coburger Tagblatt	1848–1849	GooBook
Coburger Zeitung	1854–1935 74 y; gaps	BavLib
Coburgische wöchentliche Anzeige	1777–1782	Hathi
Cochemer Anzeiger	1851–1867	NRW
Colorado Post	1874–1880	Colo
Columbus Westbote	1843–1862	Ohio Mem
Conivn- und Avgirte Wöchentliche Avisen	1630	UBREM
Conservative Provinzial-Zeitung für Rheinland und Westphalen	1866	UBONN

Title	Dates	Key
Constitutionelle Zeitung	1848	Euro
Conversationsblatt für München und Bayern	1834	GooBook
Cook's-Welt-Reise-Zeitung	1890–1891; 1894–1916	ANNO
Correspondenz	1867–1869	Kram
Correspondenzblatt der Generalkommission der Gewerkschaften Deutschlands	1891–1919	FES
Courier	1901–1916	FES
Cur- und Fremden-Liste des Badeortes Aussee	1894–1913	ANNO
Cur-Liste Bad Ischl	1842–1938 89 y; gaps	ANNO
Curliste von Abbazia	1895–1897; 1902–1906	ANNO
Cur-Liste von Teplitz-Schönau	1894–1897	ANNO
Czernowitzer Allgemeine Zeitung	1904–1914; 1917–1918	ANNO
Czernowitzer Gemeinde-Bote	1885	ANNO
Czernowitzer Presse	1887–1907	ANNO
Czernowitzer Tagblatt	1903–1916; 1918–1919	ANNO
Daheim	1914–1918	UHEID
Danzers Armee-Zeitung	1924–1938	ANNO
Danziger Allgemeine Zeitung	1922–1928; 1930–1934	Pom
Danziger Dampfboot	1834–1852	ZEFYS
Danziger Volksstimme	1920–1932; 1936	FES

Title	Dates	Key
Danziger Volks-Zeitung	1934–1937	GDAN
Danziger Zeitung	1808–1809; 1812–1813; 1819	GDAN
Danziger Zeitung	1886 Aug	UHEID
Darmstädter Freie Presse	1887	UDARM
Darmstädter Tageblatt	1886 Aug	UHEID
Darmstädter Zeitung	1872–1920	UDARM
Das Abendland	1864–1868	DiFMOE
Das Bozner Kriegsblättchen	1796	Tessmann
Das deutsche Echo	1938	ANNO
Das Echo	1890; 1893	GooBook
Das freie Wort	1848	DigiPress
Das illustrierte Blatt	1914	UFFM
Das Inland	1836–1863	ANNO
Das Inland	1836–1863	UTART
Das Interessante Blatt	1914–1944	ANNO
Das jüdische Echo	1917	Hathi
Das Kleine Blatt	1927–1944	ANNO
Das Kleine Journal	1927	DHM
Das kleine Volksblatt	1938–1941	ANNO

Title	Dates	Key
Das Luxemburger Land	1882–1886	Lux
Das Lycker gemeinnützige Unterhaltungsblatt	1843	Poland
Das Motorrad	1925–1939	ANNO
Das neue Reich	1919; 1925; 1929–1932	DHM
Das Neue Wiener Tagblatt	1867–1943; 1891–1924; 1938–1945	ANNO
Das Painier des Fortschrittes	1848 Nov 9	DHM
Das Posthörnchen	1838–1845	Aargau Dig
Das Recht der Feder	1901–1902	ZEFYS
Das Riesengebirge in Wort und Bild	1881–1898	DiFMOE
Das rote Berlin	1932	DHM
Das Vaterland	1854–1916	ANNO
Das Vaterland	1869–1870	Lux
Das Volk: Thüringer Zeitung	1921–1926 (more coming)	UJENA
Das Wienerblättchen	1783–1785; 1788; 1792	ANNO
Das Wittenbergsche Wochenblatt	1768–1785	ANNO
Das Wort der Frau	1932	Euro
Das Zelt	1924	CompMem
Das Ziel	1930–1932	ANNO
Deborah	1866	CompMem

Title	Dates	Key
Deggendorfer Donaubote	1871–1873	GooBook
Dein Reich Komme	1920–1921; 1937	Bethel
Deister- und Weser-Zeitung	1886	UHEID
Demminer Tageblatt	1899–1919	UGREI
Der Aargauer Volks-Bote	1840–1842	Aargau Dig
Der Adler	1838–1844	ANNO
Der Alpenfreund	1895–1896; 1921–1943	ANNO
Der Anzeiger	1799–1802	ZEFYS
Der Arbeitersturm	1938	ANNO
Der Architekt	1895–1921 25 y; gaps	ANNO
Der arme Teufel aus der Oberlausitz	1927–1928	SLUB
Der Armierer	1917–1918	USTR
Der ärztliche Hausfreund	1896	ZEFYS
Der aufrichtige und wohlerfahrene Schweizer-Bote ... see Der Schweizerbote		
Der Bauernbündler	1906–1938	ANNO
Der Bautechniker	1880–1921	ANNO
Der Bay City Demokrat	1856	Sandusky
Der bayerische Beobachter	1864	GooBook
Der bayerische Landwehrmann	1914–1918	USTR

Title	Dates	Key
Der Bayerische Volksfreund	1826–1847 9yr; gaps	GooBook
Der Baystadt Demokrat	1906	Sandusky
Der Bazar	1904–1913; 1931–1937	ANNO
Der Beobachter	1902	Brazil
Der Beobachter an der Saar	1798–1799	DiLibri
Der Beobachter an der Weichsel	1806	ZEFYS
Der Berg	1934–1940	Bethel
Der Bergfreund	1839	ZEFYS
Der Berggeist	1856–1873	GooBook
Der Böhmiche Bierbrauer	1891–1902; 1909; 1911–1912; 1915	ANNO
Der Bote an der Ems	1867	UMST
Der Bote aus dem Riesen-Gebirge	1813–1914 7 y; gaps	Euro
Der Bote aus Thüringen	1788–1816	UJENA
Der Bote aus Thüringen	1789–1809 10 y; gaps	GooBook
Der Bote für Tirol	1813–1819	Tessmann
Der Breslauer Erzähler	1835	GooBook
Der Brummbär	1933	ZEFYS
Der Bureauangestellte	1906–1919	FES
Der Burggräfler	1883–1926	Tessmann

Title	Dates	Key
Der Calculator an der Elbe	1872–1844	UDRES
Der Champagne-Kamerad	1915–1918	UHEID
Der christliche Botschafter	1840–1849	Hathi
Der Communist	1854–1855	France
Der Correspondent	1863–1869; 1933	FES
Der Demokrat	1848	Euro
Der Demokrat	1862–1865	Chron
Der Deutsche Beobachter	1894–1910	Chron
Der deutsche Correspondent	1841–1918	Chron
Der deutsche Holzarbeiter	1903–1908	FES
Der deutsche Krieger	1862	Gale
Der deutsche Metallarbeiter	1903–1933	FES
Der deutsche Patriot	1803–1804; 1831	UJENA
Der deutsche Pionier	1869–1887	NAUSA
Der deutsche Volksbote	1832	GooBook
Der Deutsche: Sondershäuser Zeitung	1860–1908 39 y; gaps	UJENA
Der deutsch-österreichische Photograph	1922–1925	ANNO
Der Drahtverhau	1915–1918	UHEID
Der Eilbote	1837–1866	GooBook

Title	Dates	Key
Der Eilbote aus dem Bezirk	1833–1836	GooBook
Der Erzähler	1806–1865	Switz
Der Erzähler	1849–1851	UBONN
Der Fortschritt (Bolzano)	1966–1979	Tessmann
Der Fortschritt (New Ulm)	1891–1915	Chron
Der freie Angestellte	1919–1933	FES
Der freie Arbeiter	1904; 1907	Anarch
Der freie Rhätier	1843	RERO
Der freie Staatsbürger	1848–1850	DigiPress
Der Freiheitskampf	1945	Euro
Der Freund der Wahrheit und des Volkes	1848–1849	DigiPress
Der Frieden	1914–1915	UFFM
Der Friedens- und Kriegs-Kurier	1822–1839	GooBook
Der Front-Kamerad	1942–1944	ANNO
Der Führer	1933–1941 (editions)	Baden
Der Funke	1932–1933	FES
Der Gebirgsfreund	1890–1941	ANNO
Der Gemeindearbeiter	1913–1922	FES
Der Genealogische Archivarius	1731–1736; 1738–1770; 1937	ANNO

Title	Dates	Key
Der gerade Weg	1932–1933	DigiPress
Der Gewerkverein	1869–1870; 1905–1919	FES
Der Grundstein	1888–1933 40 y; gaps	FES
Der gute Film	1934–1937	ANNO
Der Hahn	1875	NRW
Der Halleiner Bothe	1805–1806	ANNO
Der Hausbesitzer/Hausherren Zeitung	1892–1916; 1922–1937	ANNO
Der Hausfreund	1839	GooBook
Der Hausfreund	1838–1841	Bavarica
Der Hausfreund (Pustertal)	1879; 1895–1896; 1917–1918	Tessmann
Der Heideboden	1919 Sep 10; 17; 24	DiFMOE
Der Heidelberger Student	1929–1938	UHEID
Der Heinsberger Bote	1851–1857	UBONN
Der helvetische Volksfreund	1799–1801	Switz
Der Herold	1848 Aug 16	Lpzg
Der Holzarbeiter	1909–1933	FES
Der Horchposten	1916	France
Der Horchposten des Kgl. Württembergischen Gebirgsbattaillions	1917–1918	UHEID
Der Humorist	1837–1862	ANNO

Title	Dates	Key
Der Hunsrücken	1839–1842	UBONN
Der Internationale Klassenkampf	1936	DHM
Der Israelit	1860–1938	CompMem
Der Israelit des neunzehnten Jahrhunderts	1840–1848	CompMem
Der israelitische Volkslehrer	1851–1860	CompMem
Der Jude	1768–1772	CompMem
Der Jude	1832–1833; 1835	CompMem
Der Jude	1916–1928	CompMem
Der Judenkenner	1935	DHM
Der jüdische Arbeiter	1927–1934	CompMem
Der jüdische Student	1902–1903	CompMem
Der jüdische Student (Neue Folge)	1904–1933	CompMem
Der jüdische Wille (Alte Folge)	1918–1920	CompMem
Der jüdische Wille (Neue Folge)	1933–1937	CompMem
Der junge Jude	1927–1931	CompMem
Der Kamerad	1918	France
Der Kämpfer	1920 Jun 26	DHM
Der Kampfruf	1929	DHM
Der Katholik	1821–1823	UTUB

Title	Dates	Key
Der katholische Christ	1854–1862	ANNO
Der Kinderfreund	1778–1781	UGOT
Der Kinobesitzer	1917–1919	ANNO
Der Klassenkampf	1931 May 3	DHM
Der Kolonist	1851–1857	Aargau Dig
Der Korrespondent von und für Deutschland	1813	GooBook
Der Kroatische Korrespondent	1789	Croat
Der Krüppel	1927–1929	ANNO
Der Kuckuck	1929–1934	ANNO
Der Kyffhäuser	1892	ANNO
Der Ladiner	1908 May 15	Tessmann
Der Landbote	1938–1944	ANNO
Der Landbote des freiburgischen Seebezirks	1909–1914	RERO
Der Landsturm	1915–1916	UHEID
Der Landsturm-Bote von Briey	1914 Oct–Nov	France
Der Laubaner Bote	1849–1869	SLUB
Der Lecha Patriot	1839–1959	Chron
Der Lecha Patriot und Northampton Demokrat	1839–1840; 1841–1847	Chron
Der Lechbote	1848–1851	OPACPlus

Title	Dates	Key
Der Lehrerbote	1870–1876	ANNO
Der letzte Appell	1920	DHM
Der Leuchtturm	1848–1850	ZEFYS
Der Liberale Alpenbote	1847–1860	RERO
Der Liberale Beobachter und Berks, Montgomery und Schuylkill Counties Anzeiger	1839–1851	Chron
Der Liberale Beobachter und Northampton Caunty Wöchentlicher Anzeiger	1838–1839	Chron
Der Lindenbuck	1896	Baden
Der Maler	1924–1933	FES
Der Mennonit	1948–1954	Bethel
Der Montag	1910 May 2–30	ZEFYS
Der Montag	1912–1923; 1938–1940	ANNO
Der Morgen	1925–1938	CompMem
Der Morgen, Wiener Montagblatt	1910–1938	ANNO
Der Morgenstern	1841–1842	RERO
Der Münchner Gevattersmann	1848	BavLib
Der Naabthal-Bote	1868	GooBook
Der Nationalsozialist	1921–1935 5 y; gaps	DHM
Der neue Anfang	1919	CompMem
Der neue Mahnruf	1948–2008	ANNO

Title	Dates	Key
Der neue Tag	1919–1920	ANNO
Der Neue Teutsche Merkur	1790–1810	UBIEL
Der niederschlesische Anzeiger	1821–1826	ZEFYS
Der Nordstern	1877–1884	Chron
Der Oberschlesische Wanderer	1833–1936 23 y; gaps	ZEFYS
Der Odenwälder	1846–1852	UDARM
Der Oklahoma Courier	1894	OK Hist
Der Oldenburgische Volksfreund	1949–1952	UOLD
Der Omnibus	1848	GooBook
Der Orient	1840–1851	CompMem
Der Orientfrontkaempfer	1932–1934	France
Der Ostafrikanische Pflanzer	1909–1916	UFFM
Der österreichische Zuschauer	1836–1846	ANNO
Der Papierfabrikant	1914–1920	Hathi
Der Pilger	1842–1849	GooBook
Der Postbote aus Franken: eine Würzburger politische Zeitung	1832	GooBook
Der preußische Postfreund für Norddeutschland	1867–1868	GooBook
Der preußische Staatsanzeiger	1806	Bavarica
Der Proletarier	1924 Jul 30	DHM

Title	Dates	Key
Der Proletarier (Hannover)	1892–1933	FES
Der Proletarier (Oedenburg)	1919 Jul	DiFMOE
Der Radikale	1849 Nov 4	DHM
Der Reichsbanner	1932	DHM
Der Reichsbote	1848–1849	DigiPress
Der Reporter	1872–1875	ANNO
Der Rheinbayer	1833–1835	GooBook
Der Rotthaler Bote	1872–1873	GooBook
Der Schatzgräber	1926	UFFM
Der Schuhmacher (Gotha)	1884–1885	FES
Der Schuhmacher (Nürnberg)	1922–1933	FES
Der Schützengruben	1915–1916	France
Der Schweizer-Bote	1807	Bavarica
Der Schweizer-Bote	1798, 1836–1842	GooBook
Der Schweizer-Bote	1798–1835 few issues 5 yrs	DDB
Der schweizerische Auswanderer	1850	Aargau Dig
Der schweizerische Republikaner	1801–1802	GooBook
Der Siebenbürger Bote	1785–1862	ANNO
Der Siebenbürger Bote	1842–1848; 1878	DiFMOE

217

Title	Dates	Key
Der Sion	1865–1869; 1872–1873	ANNO
Der Sonntag	1940 Apr 8	DHM
Der Sozialist	1910	Anarch
Der Spiegel	1947–present (latest year $)	Spiegel
Der St. Pöltner Bote	1861–1868; 1877	ANNO
Der Stahlhelm	1931 Sep 6	DHM
Der Standpunkt	1947–1957	Tessmann
Der Steinarbeiter	1899–1933	FES
Der Stoßtrupp	1917–1918	France
Der Sturm	1910–1919	ANNO
Der Stürmer	1937	DHM
Der Syndikalist	1924–1926	Anarch
Der Tabakarbeiter	1899–1933	FES
Der Tag	1931	CRL
Der Tagesbote aus Böhmen	1853–1857	GooBook
Der Tagesspiegel	1948–1950	CRL
Der Tägliche Demokrat	1915–1918	Geneanet
Der Tägliche Demokrat	1917–1918	Chron

Title	Dates	Key
Der Telegraph	1836–1838	ANNO
Der teutsche Reichs-Herold	1727	GooBook
Der Textilarbeiter	1901–1902; 1904–1928; 1930–1933	FES
Der Tiroler	1900–1925	Tessmann
Der Traunbote	1868–1869	UMUN
Der treue Zions-Wächter	1845–1854	CompMem
Der Umbruch	1940–1944	Liecht
Der ungarische Israelit	1874–1908	DiFMOE
Der Unpartheyische	1848	GooBook
Der unpartheyische Correspondent am Rhein	1794	UBONN
Der Vaterlandsfreund und Westliche Beobachter	1836–1837	Chron
Der Völkische Beobachter	1940–1944	ANNO
Der Volksbote	1894–1908; 1910–1933	FES
Der Volksfreund (Chur)	1879–1885	RERO
Der Volksfreund (Czernovitz)	1913–1914	ANNO
Der Volksfreund (Karlsruhe)	1881–1913	Baden
Der Volksfreund (Wesel)	1848–1868	NRW
Der Vorarlberger	1881–1892; 1917 –1927	ANNO
Der Vorarlberger Volksbote	1933–1939; 1941–1942; 1944	ANNO

Title	Dates	Key
Der Vorarlberger Volksfreund	1893–1918 22 y; gaps	ANNO
Der Wächter am Rhein	1848–1849	UDUS
Der Wächter: Polizeiblatt für Mecklenburg	1838–1933 coming	Berlin
Der Wächter: Polizeiblatt für Mecklenburg	1871–1872	GooBook
Der Wähler	1896–1897	ANNO
Der Wahrheitsfreund (Chicago)	1838–1922 23 y; gaps	Hathi
Der Wahrheitsfreund (St. Gallen)	1835–1863	Switz
Der Wanderer	1814–1873	ANNO
Der Weckruf	1911–1914	ANNO
Der Weltbothe und wahre Republikaner von Berks, Montgomery und Schuylkill Counties	1814–1827	Newspapers
Der Westbote	1843–1892	OhioMem
Der Zeitgeist	1920 May 19	SLUB
Der Zeitungs-Bote	1862–1905	NRW
Der Zeitungs-Verlag	1906–1942 17 y; gaps	ANNO
Der Zimmerer	1894–1933	FES
Der Zugerbieter	1865–1868	Switz
Detroiter Abend-Post	1914–1918	GB

Title	Dates	Key
Deutsch-amerikanische Buchdrucker-Zeitung	1899–1928 9 y; gaps	GooBook
Deutsch-Amerikanischer Jugendfreund	1890 (title page, contents)	Ablit
Deutsch-chinesische Nachrichten	1930–1939	ZEFYS
Deutsche allgemeine Zeitung	1918–1931	ZEFYS
Deutsche Auswanderer-Zeitung	1867	GooBook
Deutsche Bäcker- und Konditoren-Zeitung	1908–1923	FES
Deutsche Bäckerzeitung	1895–1907	FES
Deutsche Bau-Zeitung	1867–1923	UCOT
Deutsche Berg- und Hüttenarbeiterzeitung	1892–1900	FES
Deutsche Blätter aus Thüringen	1848–1851	UJENA
Deutsche Brauerzeitung	1892	FES
Deutsche Brüsseler Zeitung	1847–1848	BelgLib
Deutsche Buchbinderzeitung	1880–1885	FES
Deutsche constitutionelle Zeitung	1848–1849	DigiPress
Deutsche demokratische Zeitung	1918–1921	UBONN
Deutsche Fleischbeschauer-Zeitung	1906	OpenLib
Deutsche Gemeinde-Zeitung	1870	GooBook
Deutsche Industri-Zeitung	1866	GooBook
Deutsche Israelitische Zeitung	1900–1938	Baeck

Title	Dates	Key
Deutsche Kolonialzeitung	1884–1922	UFFM
Deutsche Kolonialzeitung	1885–1902; 1905–1919	Hathi
Deutsche Kolonialzeitung	1887–1908 10 y; gaps	GooBook
Deutsche Kolonialzeitung	1932–1941	Poland
Deutsche Kriegszeitung	1914–1918	UHEID
Deutsche Kriegszeitung von Brunowitschi	1916–1917	France
Deutsche Levante-Zeitung	1912–1920	UHBG
Deutsche Marokko-Zeitung	1907–1913	Humboldt
Deutsche Metall-Arbeiter-Zeitung	1883–1933	FES
Deutsche Musik-Zeitung	1902	ANNO
Deutsche Post (Curitiba)	1892	Brazil
Deutsche Post (Lodz)	1915–1918	DiFMOE
Deutsche Post (São Leopoldo)	1893	Brazil
Deutsche Reichs- und Gesetz-Zeitung	1797–1799	GooBook
Deutsche Reichs-Bremse	1849–1850	ZEFYS
Deutsche Reichszeitung	1871–1939	NRW
Deutsche Schriftsteller-Zeitung	1910–1911	ZEFYS
Deutsche Soldatenpost	1914–1916	France

222

Title	Dates	Key
Deutsche Uhrmacher-Zeitung	1879–1880; 1882–1942	UDRES
Deutsche Volkszeitung	1891	Brazil
Deutsche Volks-Zeitung	1867–1877	ANNO
Deutsche Wacht	1883–1919	Slovenia
Deutsche Weinzeitung	1864–1865, 1867, 1872–1895	DiLibri
Deutsche Zeitung	1918	Euro
Deutsche Zeitung	1929–1937	Slovenia
Deutsche Zeitung	1847–1850	GooBook
Deutsche Zeitung	1896–1898	CRL
Deutsche Zeitung (Curitiba)	1895–1897	Brazil
Deutsche Zeitung (Porto Alegre)	1893	Brazil
Deutsche Zeitung / Heimat	1934–1935, 1939	ANNO
Deutsche Zeitung Bohemia	1914–1938	Kram
Deutsche Zeitung für die Krim und Taurien	1918	UBERL
Deutsche Zeitung für Ost-Taurien	1918	UBERL
Deutsche Zeitung in Nordchina	1939–1941	ZEFYS
Deutsche Zeitung von Mexiko	1913 Feb 22; Mar 1	ZEFYS
Deutsche Zinngießer-Zeitung	1893–1904	UKLN
Deutscher Beobachter oder Hanseatische privilegirte Zeitung	1816	GooBook

Title	Dates	Key
Deutscher Herold	1907–1918	Chron
Deutscher Reichs-Anzeiger	1872–1873	GooBook
Deutscher Verkehrsbund	1924–1929	FES
Deutsches Bauernblatt	1919 March 1	DiFMOE
Deutsches Kolonialblatt	1901	GooBook
Deutsches Kunstblatt	1850–1858	UHEID
Deutsches Nachrichtenbüro	1936–1940	ZEFYS
Deutsches Nordmährerblatt	1902–1916	ANNO
Deutsches Südmährisches Blatt	1911	ANNO
Deutsches Tageblatt	1886 Aug	UHEID
Deutsches Tageblatt	1919 Feb March	DiFMOE
Deutsches Tageblatt (Rio de Janeiro)	1915	Brazil
Deutsches Volksblatt	1889–1922	ANNO
Deutsches Volksblatt (Porto Alegre)	1893	Brazil
Deutsches Volksecho	1937–1939	ZEFYS
Deutsches Wochenblatt	1917–1919	Hathi
Deutsches Wochenblatt (Curitiba)	1883	Brazil
Deutsches Wochenblatt für constitutionelle Monarchie	1849–1851	DigiPress
Deutsch-Kroner Zeitung	1886 Aug	UHEID

Title	Dates	Key
Deutsch-Ostafrikanische Zeitung	1899–1916	ZEFYS
Diarium Hebdomadale, oder wöchentliche auiso	1620	UBREM
Dibre Emeth	1845–1906	CompMem
Didaskalia: Blätter für Geist, Gemüth und Publizität	1830; 1839	GooBook
Didaskalien	1830	SLUB
Die Ameise	1876–1926 40 y; gaps	FES
Die Angelegenheiten und Ereignisse Westfalens und der Rheinlande	1829–1831	NRW
Die Arbeit	1885–1886	ANNO
Die Arbeit	1894–1921	ANNO
Die Arbeit	1924–1933	FES
Die Arbeiterin	1928–1931	ANNO
Die Arbeiterinnenzeitung	1913; 1915–1916	ANNO
Die Archäologische Zeitung	1845–1873	ANNO
Die Armierer	1917	France
Die Aurora	1876 Jun	UGOT
Die Autonomie	1886	A-Bib
Die Baugewerkschaft	1906–1917; 1920–1933	FES
Die bayerische Landwehr	1916–1918	USTR

Title	Dates	Key
Die Bergbau-Industrie	1929–1932	FES
Die Berner Woche	1938–1948	UZRCH
Die Betriebsgemeinschaft der Leipziger Funkgerätebau	1940–1941; 1944	DHM
Die Bewegung	1936; 1942–1944	UHEID
Die Biene	1849*	Baden
Die Bombe	1871–1925	ANNO
Die Botschaft	1856	Aargau Dig
Die braune Sonntagszeitung	1933–1934 limited	DigiPress
Die Brennessel	1877	DiLibri
Die Bühne	1929–1938; 1945–1947	ANNO
Die Debatte und Wiener Lloyd	1864–1869	Euro
Die Deborah	1901–1902	Hathi
Die Deutsche Zucker-Industrie: Wochenblatt	1907	Hathi
Die Donau	1940–1944	DiFMOE
Die Drogisten-Zeitung	1886–1943	ANNO
Die Eiche	1898–1902; 1905; 1912–1933	FES
Die Energie	1928	SLUB
Die evangelische Kirchen-Zeitung für Österreich	1884–1918	ANNO

Title	Dates	Key
Die Fackel	1914–1918	UFFM
Die Fackel	1898–1917	AAS
Die Feder	1898–1917	ZEFYS
Die Film-Welt	1919; 1921–1925	ANNO
Die fränkischen Zuschauer	1772–1773	DigiPress
Die Frauen-Zeitung	1851–1852	SLUB
Die Freie Generation	1906–1908	Anarch
Die freie Meinung	1919–1932	Poland
Die Freie Zeitung	1917	Hathi
Die Freistatt	1913–1914	CompMem
Die G. K B. Zeitung für Eisenbahn und Bergbau	1938–1940	ANNO
Die Gegenwart	1897–1906	UKLN
Die Geissel. Tagblatt aller Tagblätter	1848–1849	ANNO
Die Gemeinde	1914	UFFM
Die Gerechtigkeit	1933–1938	ANNO
Die Gewerkschaft	1897–1933	FES
Die Grenzboten	1841–1848	GooBook
Die Grüne	1950–1980 (search only)	Hathi
Die Handels-Marine der Provinzen Pommern, Ost- und Westpreussen	1883–1914	Meck

Title	Dates	Key
Die Internationale	1924–1926	Anarch
Die Judenfrage	1886 Aug	UHEID
Die jüdische Presse	1906; 1909	GooBook
Die Kahlberger Woche	in process	Poland
Die Kämpferin	1932	DHM
Die Kämpferin	1907–1914	DiFMOE
Die Karpathen	1907–1914	DiFMOE
Die Karpathen-Post	1880–1942	DiFMOE
Die katholische Lehrerin	1926–1937	ANNO
Die Kauwenhowen	1926	Bethel
Die Kino-Woche	1919–1921	ANNO
Die Kommunistin	1919	DHM
Die KPD	1923	DHM
Die Kreatur	1926–1930	CompMem
Die Laterne	1848 Jan–Mar	ZEFYS
Die Leipziger Zeitung	1848	ANNO
Die literarische Praxis	1901–1910	ZEFYS
Die Lokomotive	1904–1943	ANNO
Die Maabrick	1919	UFFM

Title	Dates	Key
Die Mährisch–Schlesische Presse	1892–1917	ANNO
Die Mauer	1917	UHEID
Die Muskete	1905–1941	ANNO
Die Neue Freie Presse	1879	ANNO
Die Neue Illustrirte Zeitung	1876–1892	ANNO
Die neue Mainzer Zeitung	1793	GooBook
Die neue Welt	1901–1912	FES
Die neue Welt	1927–1938	CompMem
Die neue Zeit	1849	Euro
Die Neue Zeit: Olmüzer politische Zeitung	1849; 1854–1877	ANNO
Die neue Zeitung	1907–1934	ANNO
Die Neuzeit	1861–1903 37 y; gaps	ANNO
Die Nürnberger Estaffette	1835	OPACPlus
Die Nutz- und Lust-erweckende Gesellschafft Der Vertrauten Nachbarn am Isarstrom	1868–1869	BavLib
Die Oberösterreichischen Nachrichten	1945	ANNO
Die Ostschweiz	1874–1900	Switz
Die Patrulle	1916	USTR
Die Pilsener Abendpost	1877–1879	ANNO
Die Post aus Deutschland	1925–1927	ZEFYS

Title	Dates	Key
Die Presse	1848–1896	Euro
Die Pyramide	1916–1937	Baden
Die Redaktion	1902–1916	ZEFYS
Die Rheinische Volks-Halle	1848 Dec 16	Euro
Die Rheinpfalz	1869	GooBook
Die rote Fahne	1918–1921; 1928–1933	ZEFYS
Die rote Fahne	1918–1939	ANNO
Die Rote Front	1927	DHM
Die Sappe	1915–1918	USTR
Die Schwarze Fahne	1925	DHM
Die Schwarze Front	1932 May	DHM
Die Slovenin, Das Organ der slovenischen Frauenwelt	1897–1902	ANNO
Die Somme Wacht	1917–1918	France
Die Somme-Wacht	1917	UHEID
Die Sonntags-Zeitung	1932	DHM
Die Soziale Revolution	1937	Anarch
Die Spinnmaschine	1938; 1940	DHM
Die Stimme [Alte Folge]	1928–1938	CompMem
Die Stimme [Neue Folge]	1947–1966	CompMem

Title	Dates	Key
Die Tat	1935–1976	RERO
Die Uhrmacher-Woche	1914–1942	UDRES
Die Union	1866–1867	TX Hist
Die Vedette	1871	ANNO
Die Volksblätter aus Salzburg	1848	ANNO
Die Volkspost	1926–1934	ANNO
Die Voss	1921–1922	CRL
Die Voss	1921–1925	ZEFYS
Die Wacht im Osten	1916–1918	France
Die Wacht im Westen	1915–1918	France
Die Wage	1848–1852	Lippe
Die Wahrheit	1871–1872	DiFMOE
Die Wahrheit	1899–1938	CompMem
Die Wahrheit	1907–1912; 1914	ANNO
Die Wartburg	1850	ZEFYS
Die Welt	1963	CRL
Die Welt	1897–1914	CompMem
Die Zeit	1894–1919	ANNO
Die Zeit	1946–present	CompMem

Title	Dates	Key
Die Zukunft	1880–1884	Anarch
Dinkelsbühlisches Intelligenzblatt	1797–1799	GooBook
Dolomiten	1923–2000	Tessmann
Dolomiten Landausgabe	1942–1943	Tessmann
Donau-Armee-Zeitung	1917	UBERL
Donau-Zeitung	1851–1852; 1858; 1862	GooBook
Dornaer Curblatt	1898	ANNO
Dörptsche Zeitung	1791, 1804–1864	Euro
Dortmunder Zeitung	coming	NRW
Dr. Blochs Österreichische Wochenschrift	1891–1920	CompMem
Dramaturgisches Wochenblatt	1815–1817	UMST
Dresden	1843–1845	SLUB
Dresdner Anzeiger	1886 Aug	UHEID
Dresdner fliegende Blätter	1893–1907 5y; gaps	SLUB
Dresdner Journal	1886 Aug	UHEID
Dresdner Journal	1906 Jan 1–2	WikiS
Dresdner Morgenzeitung	1827	GooBook
Dresdner Nachrichten	1886 Aug	UHEID
Dresdner neueste Nachrichten	1903–1930	SLUB

Title	Dates	Key
Dresdner Volks-Zeitung	1908–1933	SLUB
Dresdner Zeitung	1945	Euro
Dresdner Zeitung	1838; 1840–1843	ANNO
Dresdner Zeitung	1886 Aug	UHEID
Drey wahrhafftige erbärmliche newe Zeitungen	1611	ANNO
Drey wahrhafftige newe Zeitungen	1593	ANNO
Duisburger Intelligenz-Zeitung	1739–1768	Blank
Düna-Zeitung	1916–1918	France
Dürener Anzeiger und Unterhaltungsblatt	1855–1856	UBONN
Dürener Zeitung	1886–1919	NRW
Düsseldorfer Erzähler	1818; 1822	UDUS
Düsseldorfer Intelligenz- und Adreß-Blatt	1824–1825	UDUS
Düsseldorfer Literarisch-Merkantilisches Intelligenz- und Adreß-Blatt	1825–1826	UDUS
Düsseldorfer Sonntagsblatt	1884–1915 19 y; gaps in process	UDUS
Düsseldorfer Volksblatt	1871–1882; in process	UDUS
Düsseldorfer Zeitung	1814–1836 17 y; gaps	UDUS
Düsseldorfer Zeitung	1886 Aug	UHEID
Echo	1911–1920	Chron
Echo aus Pilsen und Westböhmen	1899–1902	ANNO

Title	Dates	Key
Echo der Gegenwart	1851–1935	NRW
Echo der Gegenwart	1886 Aug	UHEID
Echo des Siebengebirges	1873–1941	NRW
Egerer Anzeiger	1847–1868	Kram
Egerer Anzeiger	1847–1868	Portafont
Egerer Zeitung	1868–1900	Portafont
Egerer Zeitung	1868–1910	Kram
Eggenburger Zeitung	1914–1919	ANNO
Ehrenbreitsteiner Intelligenzblatt	1838	UBONN
Eichsfelder Generalanzeiger	coming	HIgnst
Eichsfelder Tageblatt	coming	HIgnst
Eichsfelder Volksblätter	1864– coming	HIgnst
Eichsfeldia	1884–1924 coming	HIgnst
Eichstätter Intelligenzblatt	1810–1812; 1823; 1828	GooBook
Eichstätter Tagblatt	1864	GooBook
Eidgenössische Zeitung	1845–1848	Hathi
Einheimisches	1826–1827	SLUB
Eisenbahn und Industrie	1929–1933	ANNO
Eisenbahn-Zeitung	1832–1850 12 y; gaps	GooBook

Title	Dates	Key
Eisenbergisches Nachrichtsblatt	1821–1906	UJENA
Eiserne Front	1932	DHM
el	1844–1846	ZEFYS
Elberfelder Intelligenzblatt	1827–1828; 1838–1840	UBONN
Elberfelder Zeitung	1886 Aug	UHEID
Elbinger Anzeiger	1918–1945	Elblag
Elbinger Volksblatt	1870	Euro
Elsässer Kurier	1897; 1914–1917	France
Elsässer Tagblatt	1889; 1913–1918	France
Elsäss-Lothringisches Schulblatt	1871; 1914–1918	France
Entomologische Zeitung	1842–1911	Bio
Erdöl-Zeitung	1950–1955	Sweden
Erfa, Kreis-Intelligenzblatt für Euskirchen, Rheinbach und Ahrweiler	1840–1847	UBONN
Erfurtisches Intelligenz-Blatt	1769–1771; 1773	GooBook
Erinnerungsblätter der 211. Infanterie-Division	1918	France
Erkenntnis und Befreiung	1919–1921; 1924	Anarch
Erlanger Mittwochs-Blatt	1835	GooBook
Erlanger Real-Zeitung	1820	GooBook
Erlanger Tagblatt	1863–1865	GooBook

Title	Dates	Key
Erlanger Zeitung	1827–1829	GooBook
Ermländische Zeitung	1844–1850; 1902–1905	ZEFYS
Erschreckliche Zeitunge von Zwayen Mördern	1570	ANNO
Erste Allgemeine Nachrichten	1940–1943	ANNO
Es muß Tag werden	1848–1849	DigiPress
Esra	1919–1920	CompMem
Etwas von gelehrten Rostockschen Sachen	1737–1748	UROS
Eureka Post	coming 2017	Chron
Europe Speaks	1940–1947	FES
Evangelisches Gemeindeblatt für Galizien und die Bukowina	1904–1911; 1913–1918	ANNO
Extract der eingelauffenen Nouvellen	1742–1744, 1746, 1748	ZEFYS
Fechenheimer Anzeiger	1910	UFFM
Fehrbelliner Zeitung	1925–1941	ZEFYS
Feierabend	1903–1914; 1916; 1918	SLUB
Feldkircher Anzeiger	1866–1947 72 y; gaps	ANNO
Feldkircher Wochenblatt	1810–1857	ANNO
Feldpostbrief der 56er	1942–1944	ANNO
Feldpostbrief Niederdonau	1940–1942	ANNO
Feldzeitung der Armee-Abteilung Scheffer	1918	UHEID

Title	Dates	Key
Fest-Zeitung	1890	UBONN
Feuilles d'affiches annonces et avis divers de Bonn	1812–1814	UBONN
Feuilleton zum Pfälzischer Kurier	1868–1871; 1873	Bavarica
Fliegende Blätter	1844–1944	UHEID
Flora	1818–1902	UREG
Flora	1837–1862 19 y; gaps	ANNO
Floridsdorfer Zeitung	1895–1903; 1907–1918; 1925	ANNO
Flörsheimer Zeitung	1906–1932	RheinMain
Flugblatt	1849	UBONN
Flugzeug und Yacht	1923–1934	ANNO
Franckfurtische gelehrte Zeitungen	1738; 1756	UFFM
Frankensteiner Kreisblatt	1877–1896	ZEFYS
Frankensteiner Wochenblatt	1836–1842	ZEFYS
Frankenthaler Wochen-Blatt	1823–1828	GooBook
Frankenzeitung	1863	GooBook
Frankfurt-Bockenheimer Anzeige-Blatt	1914	UFFM
Frankfurter Aerzte-Correspondenz	1913–1918	UFFM
Frankfurter Bürgerzeitung Sonne	1914	UFFM
Frankfurter Illustrierte	1942	UDARM

Title	Dates	Key
Frankfurter Israelitisches Familienblatt	1902–1923	CompMem
Frankfurter Journal	1886 Aug	UHEID
Frankfurter Konversationsblatt	1834; 1840–1852	GooBook
Frankfurter Krebbel-Zeitung	1859–1914 14 y; gaps	UFFM
Frankfurter Leben	1908–1909; 1914	UFFM
Frankfurter Nachrichten	1857–1865 7 y; gaps	Hathi
Frankfurter Nachrichten und Intelligenzblatt	1914	UFFM
Frankfurter Oberpostamts-Zeitung	1814–1849 26 y; gaps	GooBook
Frankfurter Reform	1862–1866	UFFM
Frankfurter Universitäts-Zeitung	1914–1919	UFFM
Frankfurter Volksfreund	1876	UFFM
Frankfurter Wohlfahrtsblätter	1919–1933	UFFM
Frankfurter Zeitung	1886 Aug	UHEID
Frankfurter Zeitung und Handelsblatt	1914	UFFM
Frankfurter Zeitung und Handelsblatt	1909–1910	CRL
Fränkische Provinzialblätter	1802–1804	GooBook
Fränkische Zeitung	1863	GooBook
Fränkischer Anzeiger	1870–1873	GooBook
Fränkischer Kurier	1852–1873	GooBook

Title	Dates	Key
Fränkischer Merkur	1814; 1838–1839; 1843	GooBook
Fränkischer Wald	1859; 1871; 1907–1936	GooBook
Fränkisches Bürgerblatt	1848	DigiPress
Franzensbader Curliste	1894–1913	ANNO
Frauen-Beilage der Leipziger Volkszeitung	1917–1918	SLUB
Freiburger Nachrichten	1904–2006	RERO
Freiburger Pfennigblatt	1896	Baden
Freiburger Wochenblatt	1818	GooBook
Freiburger Zeitung	1784; 1788–1798; 1800–1943	UFRBG
Freiburger Zeitung und Anzeiger für die westliche Schweiz	1864–1903	Switz
Freiburger Zeitung und Anzeiger für die westliche Schweiz	1869–1920	RERO
Freie Lehrer-Zeitung	1901–1902	ANNO
Freie Presse für Elsaß-Lothringen	1898; 1914–1918	BNF
Freie Stimmen	1882; 1918–1938	ANNO
Freie Tribüne	1919–1921	CompMem
Freies Deutschland	1848 Apr 12	DHM
Freiheit!	1927–1932	ANNO
Freiheitsbothe	1810 Feb 14	NewsBank
Freimaurer-Zeitung	1876	GooBook

Title	Dates	Key
Freimunds Kirchlich-Politisches Wochenblatt für Stadt und Land	1839; 1857	GooBook
Freisinger Tagblatt	1868–1942; 1949–1968	UMUN
Freisinger Tagblatt	1871–1873	GooBook
Fremden-Blatt	1847–1875; 1902; 1913–1919	ANNO
Freymaurer-Zeitung	1786	UBONN
Freysinger Wochenblatt	1849	GooBook
Frischmanns Berichte = see under Bericht … and Zeitung …	1617–1625	ZEFYS
Front und Heimat	1940–1941; 1943	ANNO
Frontpost	1944	ZEFYS
Frontzeitung	1940–1944	ANNO
Front-Zeitung Wiener-Neustadt	1940–1944	ANNO
Füe unsere Frauen	1893; 1896–1898	SLUB
Fuldaisches Intelligenz-Blatt	1804–1815	UFULD
Funken-Zeitung der Leichten Funken-Station 1	1916	Europeana
Fürstenfeldbrucker Zeitung	1928–1939; 1942; 1944–1945	DigiPress
Fürstlich Reuß-plauisches Amts-und Verordnungsblatt	1836–1842	GooBook
Fürstlich Waldeckisches Regierungsblatt	1837	BavLib
Fürstlich Waldeckisches Regierungsblatt, -blätter	1853–1869, 1880–1908	Hathi
Fürstlich Waldeckisches Regierungsblätter	1853–1908 37 y; gaps	Hathi

Title	Dates	Key
Fürstlich-Lippisches Regierungs- und Anzeigeblatt	1843–1871	NRW Lib
Fürstlich-Oranien-Nassau-Fuldaische Polizei-, Kommerz- unnd Zeitungsanzeigen	1802–1803	UFULD
Fürther Abendzeitung	1845	GooBook
Fürther Tagblatt	1838–1934	OPACPlus
Fürther Tagblatt	1849	GooBook
Fürther Tagblatt/Erzähler	1918	DHM
Fürther Tagblatt/Erzähler	1851–1896	OPACPlus
Fussball-Zeitung	1937–1940	ANNO
Gambrinus, Brauerei- und Hopfen-Zeitung	1886–1920	ANNO
Garde-Feld-Post	1917–1918	France
Garten-Zeitung	1883–1885	Bio
Gazette des Ardennes	1914–1918	UHEID
Gebweilerer Wochenblatt	1870–1871	Hathi
Gefolgschaft Pittler	1943	DHM
Gemeindeblatt der Israelitischen Gemeinde Frankfurt am Main	1922–1938	CompMem
Gemeindeblatt der Mennoniten	1871–1953	Bethel
Gemeindebrief der Mennonitengemeinde zu Hamburg und Altona	1937	Bethel
Gemeinde-Zeitung; unabhängiges politisches Journal	1862–1877	ANNO
Gemeinnütziges Anclammer Wochenblatt für alle Stände	1839–1843	Meck

Title	Dates	Key
Gemeinnütziges Hausarchiv	1807–1808	UMST
Gemeinnütziges Justiz- und Polizeiblatt der Teutschen	1810	UJENA
Gemeinnütziges Volksblatt	in process	Poland
Gemeinnütziges Wochenblatt für Geilenkirchen und Umgegend	1836–1837	UBONN
Gemeinnütziges Wochenblatt für Geilenkirchen, Heinsberg und Umgegend	1838–1866 16 y; gaps	UBONN
General Staatsbothe	1811 Dec 27	NewsBank
General-Anzeiger	1886 Aug	UHEID
General-Anzeiger für Berlinchen, Bernstein und Umgegend	1923	GooBook
General-Anzeiger für Bonn und Umgegend	1889–1945; 1949–1950	UBONN
General-Anzeiger für Deutschland	1872	GooBook
General-Anzeiger für Stadt und Kreis Düren	1891–1895	UBONN
General-Gouvernements-Blatt fur Sachsen	1813–1815	Berlin
General-Gouvernements-Blatt fur das Königlich Preussische Herzogthum Sachsen	1815–1816	Berlin
Genossenschafts- und Vereins-Zeitung	1891–1901	ANNO
Gerdauener Zeitung	1896	ARCOR
Gerichts-Halle	1871	ANNO
Germania	1886 Aug	UHEID
Geschäfts- und Unterhaltungsblatt für den Kreis Grevenbroich und dessen Umgebung	1863, 1865–1866	UBONN
Gesetzblatt für das Königreich Bayern	1818–1872 35 y; gaps	Hathi

Title	Dates	Key
Gesetzes- und Verordnungsblatt für das Großherzogthum Baden	1901–1903; 1909, 1911	Hathi
Gewerkschaftliche Rundschau	1923–1933	FES
Gewissen	1919–1929	ZEFYS
Gießener Anzeiger	1886 Aug	UHEID
Glaube und Heimat	1924–1935; 1937–1941	UJENA
Glück-Auf!	1889	FES
Gnädigst privilegirtes Altenburgisches Intelligenz-Blatt	1818–1819	GooBook
Gnädigst privilegirtes Bönnisches Intelligenz-Blatt	1772–1796	NRW
Godesberger Volkszeitung	1913–1941	NRW
Goldaper Kreisblatt	1908–1914; 1916–1929	ZEFYS
Goldingenscher Anzeiger	1911–1915; 1929–1930	Latvia
Görlitzer Anzeiger	1808–1849; 1859–1860; 1867–1868	ZEFYS
Görlitzer Fama	1842–1849	ZEFYS
Gothaische gelehrte Zeitungen	1781	ANNO
Göttingische gelehrte Anzeigen	1772–1845 10 y; gaps	GooBook
Göttingische Zeitung von gelehrten Sachen	1739–1752	UCLAU
Göttingsche Anzeigen von gelehrten Sachen	1771–1850	ANNO
Göttingsche Policey-Amts Nachrichten	1765–1767	UBIEL
Götz von Berlichingen	1919; 1923–1934	ANNO

Title	Dates	Key
Gradaus mein deutsches Volk!	1848–1849	DigiPress
Grafinger Zeitung	1923–1949 22 y; gaps	DigiPress
Graphische Presse	1889–1917	FES
Graphische Stimmen	1905–1917; 1924–1933	FES
Grätzer Zeitung	1845	GooBook
Grazer Mittags-Zeitung	1914–1921	ANNO
Grazer Tagblatt	1891–1923	ANNO
Grazer Volksblatt	1868–1915	ANNO
Grazer Zeitung	1775–1877 56 y; gaps	ANNO
Greifenhagener Kreisblatt	1844–1850	ZEFYS
Greifenhagener Kreiszeitung	1915–1921	ZEFYS
Greifswalder gemeinnütziges Wochenblatt	1794–1795	Meck
Greifswalder Zeitung	1896–1920	UGREI
Greifswaldisches Wochen-Blatt von allerhand gelehrten und nützlichen Sachen	1743	UGOT
Grevenbroicher Kreisblatt	1855–1869 8 y; gaps	UBONN
Grevenbroicher Kreisblatt und landwirthschaftlicher Anzeiger für das Jülicher Land	1861–1863	UBONN
Grevenbroicher Kreisblatt und Organ für die Gilbach	1858–1859	UBONN
Grevesmühlener Wochenblatt	1851–1868	UROS
Grönenbacher Wochenblatt	1859	GooBook

Title	Dates	Key
Großenhainer Unterhaltungs- und Anzeigeblatt	1847–1859	UDRES
Großherzoglich badische Staats-Zeitung	1811–1816	Baden
Großherzoglich badisches Amts- und Regierungsblatt für den Oberrhein-Kreis	1839–1855	GooBook
Großherzoglich badisches Anzeigeblatt für den Seekreis	1848	GooBook
Großherzoglich Badisches niederrheinisches Provinzialblatt	1808–1810	UHEID
Großherzoglich frankfurtisches Regierungsblatt	1810–1813	UFFM
Großherzoglich Hessisches Regierungsblatt	1820–1895 17y; gaps	DigiBib
Großherzoglich Mecklenburgisch-Strelitzer officieler Anzeiter für Gesetzgebung und Staatsverwaltung	1870–1873	GooBook
Großherzoglich Sachsen-Weimar-Eisenachisches Regierungs-Blatt	1817–1836	UJENA
Großherzoglich-Badisches Regierungs-Blatt	1831–1868	Hathi
Großherzoglich-Badisches Staats- und Regierungs-Blatt	1803–1844	Hathi
Gross-Strehlitzer Kreisblatt	1915–1926	ZEFYS
Gross-Wartenberger Kreisblatt	1908–1925	ZEFYS
Grottkauer Stadt- und Kreisblatt	1841–1845	Poland
Grottkauer Zeitung	1883–1939 46 y; gaps	Poland
Grünberger Wochenblatt	1825–1933 38 y; gaps	ZielG
Grünberger Wochenblatt	1848;1875	Euro
Grünberger Wochenblatt	1857–1863	ZEFYS

Title	Dates	Key
Gründliche und warhafftige newe Zeitung	1586	ANNO
Gründliche Warhafftige Newe Zeitung	1626	BavLib
Grütlianer	1851–1925	RERO
Gubener Kriegs-Zeitung	30-Mar-05	France
Guhrauer Anzeiger	1914–1917	ZEFYS
Gülich und bergische wöchentliche Nachrichten	1769–1802	UDUS
Gumbinner Allgemeine Zeitung	1843–1844	ZEFYS
Gumbinner Kreisblatt	1907–1914; 1925–1930	ZEFYS
Gummersbacher Kreisblatt	1835–1852	NRW
Günser Zeitung	1883–1935	Hungary
Güssinger Zeitung	1921–1938	Hungary
Guttentager Stadtblatt	1907–1921	Poland
Haaner Zeitung	1896–1941	NRW
Habelschwerdter Kreisblatt	1843–1909	Berlin
Hagenauer Zeitung	1882; 1912–1918	France
Hallisches patriotisches Wochenblatt	1828–1845; 1847	GooBook
Hallisches Tageblatt	1828–1845; 1847	Hathi
Hallisches Wochenblatt	1828–1847	Hathi
Hamburger Abendblatt	1948–present	Abendblatt

Title	Dates	Key
Hamburger Anzeiger	1888–1945	Euro
Hamburger Börsenhalle	1805–1904	Euro
Hamburger Fremdenblatt	1886 Aug	UHEID
Hamburger Garten- und Blumenzeitung	1852–1890 17 y; gaps	Bio
Hamburger Musikalische Zeitung	1837–1838	GooBook
Hamburger Nachrichten	1792–1939	Euro
Hamburger neueste Nachrichten	1939–1941	Euro
Hamburger Zeitung	1943; 1944–1945	Euro
Hamburgischer Correspondent	1886 Aug	UHEID
Hamburgischer Correspondent (coming)	1721–1934	Euro
Hamburgisches Gesetz- und Verordnungsblatt	1906–1920	Hathi
Hamburgisches Gesetz- und Verordnungsblatt	1921–1922	Hathi
Hamechaker	1877–1879	DiFMOE
Hammsches Wochenblatt	1824	UMST
Hanauer neue europäische Zeitung	1797	GooBook
Handels-, Geschäfts- Verkehrs- und Intelligenzblatt	1868–1871	Tessmann
Handels-Zeitung für die gesamte Uhren-Industrie	1898	UDRES
Handlungsgehilfen-Zeitung	1909–1919	FES
Handlungsgehülfen-Blatt	1897–1918	FES

Title	Dates	Key
Hannoverscher Courier	1867–1869	ZEFYS
Hannoverscher Courier	1886 Aug	UHEID
Hannoversches Polizeiblatt	1846–1856; 1858–1870	Berlin Lib
Hannoversches Tagblatt	1886 Aug	UHEID
Haus und Herd	1893; 1896–1904	SLUB
Hausangestellten-Zeitung	1909–1932	FES
Hebammenzeitschrift	1907–1912	ANNO
Hebammen-Zeitung	1887–1912; 1915–1934	ANNO
Heidelberger Neueste Nachrichten	1936	UHEID
Heidelberger Tagblatt	1848–1860	UHEID
Heidelberger Zeitung	1861–1867; 1903–1905; 1919	UHEID
Heimat	1918	ANNO
Heimat (Greiz)	1925–1936	UJENA
Heimat und Ferne	1932–1935	ZEFYS
Heimat und Welt	1932–1939	Poznan
Heinsberger Kreisblatt	1851–1868	NRW
Helios	1922–1925; 1928–1930	ANNO
Helmstedter Kreisblatt	1934 May 1	GooBook
Henneberger Zeitung	1872–1877; 1880–1883; 1885–1913	UJENA

Title	Dates	Key
Herforder oeffentlicher Anzeiger	1824	NRW
Hermanner Zeitung	1875–1922	Chron
Herold des Glaubens	1838–1841	GooBook
Herzogl. Sachsen-Coburgisches Regierungs- und Intelligenzblatt	1826–1839	DigiPress
Herzogl. Sachsen-Coburg-Saalfeldisches Regierungs- und Intelligenzblatt	1807–1825	GooBook
Herzoglich Mecklenburg-Schwerinisches officieles Wochenblatt	1812–1815	Hathi
Herzoglich Mecklenburg-Schwerinisches officieles Wochenblatt	1814; 1829	GooBook
Herzoglich nassauisches allgemeines Intelligenzblatt	1819	DigiPress
Herzoglich nassauisches allgemeines Intelligenzblatt	1819	GooBook
Hessische Gemeindebeamten-Zeitung	1923	UDARM
Hessische landwirtschaftliche Zeitschrift	1845–1865	Hathi
Hessische Morgenzeitung	1886 Aug	UHEID
Hessisch-Nassauischer Volksbote	1914–1919	UFFM
Hildener Rundschau	1924–1936	NRW
HJ im Vormarsch	1934	ZEFYS
Hochheimer Stadtanzeiger	1911–1932	RheinMain
Hochobrigkeitlich privilegirtes Aargauischen Intelligenz-Blatt	1811–1833	Aargau
Hochzeits-Zeitung	1902	Euro
Hofer Zeitung	1868	GooBook

Title	Dates	Key
Holsteinische Stände-Zeitung	1857	GooBook
Holzarbeiterzeitung	1893–1933	FES
Holzmindisches Wochenblatt	1785–1792	ZEFYS
Honnefer Volkszeitung	1889–1942	NRW
Honnefer Volkszeitung	1892–1939 42 y; gaps	Honnef
Hüben und drüben	1942–1946	ZEFYS
Hunsrücker Erzähler	1905; 1907	DiLibri
Illustrirtes Familien-Journal	1855–1856	AustLit
Illustrierte Frauen-Zeitung	1924–1938	ANNO
Illustrierte Garten-Zeitung	1861–1875	Bio
Illustrierte Kronen-Zeitung	1905–1944	ANNO
Illustrierte Sonntags-Zeitung	1895–1917	UBONN
Illustrierte Wochenbeilage der Schlesischen Zeitung	1924–1934	Poland
Illustrierter Sonntag	1929–1931	DigiPress
Illustriertes Familienblatt	1912	DiFMOE
Illustriertes Familienblatt	1913; 1925–1938	ANNO
Illustriertes Österreichisches Journal	1874–1876	ANNO
Illustriertes Österreichisches Sportblatt	1924–1926	ANNO

Title	Dates	Key
Illustriertes Sonntags-Blatt	1899–1916	UFFM
Illustriertes Unterhaltungs-Blatt	1875–1899; 1901–1917	UDARM
Illustriertes Wiener Extrablatt	1902–1903	ANNO
Illustrirte Monatshefte	1865–1866	CompMem
Illustrirte Zeitung	1841–1873	GooBook
Illustrirte Zeitung	1843–1877	ANNO
Illustrirtes Sonntagsblatt	1884	Brazil
Im Deutschen Reich	1895–1922	CompMem
Im Schützengraben in den Vogesen	1915–1916	USTR
Indiana Tribüne	1900–1907	IndHS
Ingolstädter Anzeiger	1920; 1922–1933	DigiPress
Ingolstädter Tagblatt	1873	GooBook
Ingolstädter Wochen-Blatt	1839–1868 26 ; gaps	GooBook
Ingolstädter Zeitung	1920, 1922–1933	DigiPress
Innsbrucker Nachrichten	1854–1945	ANNO
Innsbrucker Nachrichten	1860–1903	Euro
Innsbrucker Zeitung	1809; 1954–1919	ANNO
Innviertler Heimatblatt	1939–1944	ANNO
Innzeitung	1862–1866	Tessmann

Title	Dates	Key
Intelligenz-Blatt	1856	Sandusky
Intelligenz-Blatt der freien Stadt Frankfurt	1864	ArchOrg
Intelligenz-Blatt der freien Stadt Frankfurt	1750–1864 71 y; gaps	Hathi
Intelligenz-Blatt der freien Stadt Frankfurt	1750–1865 41 y; major gaps	GooBook
Intelligenzblatt der Jenaischen allgemeinen Literatur-Zeitung	1803–1842	ArchOrg
Intelligenzblatt der königlich baierischen Stadt Kempten	1827	GooBook
Intelligenzblatt der Königlich bayerischen Stadt Nördlingen	1816; 1818–1819	GooBook
Intelligenzblatt der Königlichen Bayerischen Stadt Nördlingen	1815–1841	GooBook
Intelligenz-Blatt der königlichen Regierung von Oberbayern	1841–1874	DigiPress
Intelligenz-Blatt der königlichen Regierung von Schwaben und Neuburg	1838	GooBook
Intelligenzblatt der Reichsstadt Lindau	1783–1787	GooBook
Intelligenzblatt des königlich baierischen Iller-Kreises	1811–1816	GooBook
Intelligenz-Blatt des Königlichen Bayerischen Rheinkreises	1827–1829	GooBook
Intelligenzblatt des pharmaceutischen Vereins in Baiern	1827	GooBook
Intelligenzblatt des Rezat-Kreises	1817; 1825; 1835	GooBook
Intelligenz-Blatt des Rheinkreises	1818–1830	GooBook
Intelligenz-Blatt für das Königreich Bayern	1819–1820; 1825	GooBook
Intelligenzblatt für den Kreis Bingen	1837	UDARM
Intelligenz-Blatt für den Kreis Simmern	1843–1846	UBONN

Title	Dates	Key
Intelligenz-Blatt für den Kreis Simmern und dessen Umgegend	1839–1862	NRW
Intelligenz-Blatt für den Unter-Mainkreis des Königreichs Bayern	1818	GooBook
Intelligenz-Blatt für die Kreise Prüm, Bitburg, Daun und den ehemaligen Kreis St. Vith	1841–1866	UBONN
Intelligenzblatt für die Provinz Oberhessen	1833–1934	UDARM
Intelligenzblatt für die Stadt Bern	1834–1922	U BERN
Intelligenzblatt für die Städte Oels, Bernstadt, Juliusburg, Hundsfeld und Festenberg	1856–1859	ZEFYS
Intelligenzblatt für Kunst und Literatur	1808; 1823–1824	Bavarica
Intelligenzblatt für Nassau	1868	GooBook
Intelligenzblatt für Ungarn	1798–1809; 1811–1813	DiFMOE
Intelligenzblatt für Unterfranken und Aschaffenburg	1851; 1855–1856	GooBook
Intelligenz-Blatt und wöchentlicher Anzeiger der königlich bairischen Stadt Augsburg	1819–1872 7 y; major gaps	GooBook
Intelligenzblatt von Salzburg	1800–1806	GooBook
Intelligenzblatt von täglichen Vorkommenheiten in Pommern und Rügen	1753–1757	UGRF
Intelligenzblatt von Unterfranken und Aschaffenburg	1838–1839; 1841; 1851; 1861	GooBook
Intelligenzblatt zur deutschen Zeitung	1789–1790	SPO
Iris	1850–1855; 1859–1864	ANNO
Ischler Bade-Liste	1861	ANNO
Ischler Fremden-Salon	1855	ANNO
ISIS, oder, Enzyclopaedische Zeitung von Oken	1817–1848	ANNO

Title	Dates	Key
ISIS, oder, Enzyclopaedische Zeitung von Oken	1818–1819	Bio
Israelitische Annalen	1849–1841	CompMem
Israelitische Gemeinde-Zeitung	1897; 1899; 1901	DiFMOE
Israelitische Religionsgesellschaft Frankfurt a.M.	1864–1929 58 y; gaps	CompMem
Israelitische Rundschau	1901–1902	CompMem
Israelitischer Lehrerbote	1875–1877	DiFMOE
Israels Herold	1849	Hathi
ITF	1929–1933	FES
Jagd-Zeitung	1858–1877	ANNO
Jahrbuch der Gesellschaft der Geschichte der Juden in der ...echoslowakischen Republik	1929–1938	CompMem
Jahrbuch der Jüdisch–Literarischen Gesellschaft	1903–1932	CompMem
Jahrbuch für die Geschichte der Juden und des Judenthums	1860–1862; 1869	CompMem
Jahrbuch für jüdische Geschichte und Literatur	1898–1937 33 y; gaps	CompMem
Jahrbücher für jüdische Geschichte und Literatur	1874–1890 9 y; gaps	CompMem
Jahresbericht	1872	GooBook
Jahresbericht der höheren Bildungsschule (Mittelschule) für Mädchen, am Wiener Frauen-Erwerb Verein, Wien (VI.)	1881–1916	ANNO
Jahresbericht der K. Studienanstalt zu Kaiserslautern	1824	GooBook

Title	Dates	Key
Jahresbericht der Konferenz der süddeutschen Mennoniten	1904–1920 5 y; gaps	Bethel
Jahresbericht der königlichen Bewerbschule in Wunsiedel	1867; 1869–1870; 1873	GooBook
Jahresbericht der Königlichen Gewerb- und Handelsschule zu Fürth	1853; 1864; 1870	GooBook
Jahresbericht der königlichen Gewerbschule zu Kissingen	1873	GooBook
Jahresbericht der Königlichen Kreisackerbauschule	1861	GooBook
Jahresbericht der Königlichen Landwirthschafts- und Gewerbsschule zu Schweinfurt	1853–1855; 1869	GooBook
Jahresbericht der königlichen Studienschule zu Memmingen	1823	GooBook
Jahresbericht der lateinischen Vorbereitungsschulen zu Erlangen	1824	GooBook
Jahresbericht der Lateinschule zu Thurnau	1864	GooBook
Jahresbericht der Niederösterreichischen Ober-Realschule	1869–1870; 1906	GooBook
Jahresbericht der Realanstalt am Donnersberg	1900–1904	Bethel
Jahresbericht der Realschule erster Ordnung zu Siegen	1865	GooBook
Jahresbericht der Schulen des Frauenerwerb-Vereins	1907–1918	ANNO
Jahresbericht der Taufgesinnten Missionsgesellschaft	1912; 1917	Bethel
Jahres-Bericht der Vereinigung der Mennoniten-Gemeinden im deutschen Reich	1886–1932 48 y; gaps	Bethel
Jahresbericht des deutschen Wohltätigkeits-Vereins St. Petersburg	1872	GooBook
Jahresbericht des Entomologischen Vereins von Stettin	1839	Bio
Jahresbericht des Gymnasiums zu Zwickau	1872	GooBook

Title	Dates	Key
Jahresbericht des K. K. Gymnasiums zu Pilsen	1863–1865; 1867–1868	GooBook
Jahresbericht des K. K. Ober-Gymnasiums in Görz	1856	GooBook
Jahresbericht des Königl. kath. Gymnasiums zu Neisse	1873	GooBook
Jahresbericht des Königl. Katholischen Gymnasiums zu Glatz	1840; 1843	GooBook
Jahresbericht des Königlichen Gymnasiums und des Realgymnasiums zu Hamm	1908	GooBook
Jahresbericht des Königlichen Gymnasiums zu Lyck	1901	GooBook
Jahresbericht des Königlichen Gymnasiums zu Wongrowitz	1874	GooBook
Jahresbericht des Königlichen Katholischen Gymnasium zu Groß-Glogau	1843–1907 9 y; gaps	GooBook
Jahresbericht des königlichen katholischen Gymnasiums an Marzellen zu Cöln	1863	GooBook
Jahresbericht des königlichen katholischen Gymnasiums zu Oppeln	1902	GooBook
Jahresbericht des Lyceums 1 zu Hannover	1874	GooBook
Jahresbericht des Mädchen-Lyzeums am Kohlmarkt	1902–1913	ANNO
Jahresbericht des Mädchen-Lyzeums der Stadt Znaim	1906–1919	ANNO
Jahresbericht des N. ö. Landes-Realgymnasiums in Klosterneuburg	1936	GooBook
Jahresbericht des städtischen Gymnasiums zu Neustadt Ob.-Schl.	1873	GooBook
Jahresbericht des Vereins für erweiterte Frauenbildung in Wien	1888–1914	ANNO
Jahresbericht für die Landwirthschafts- und Gewerbsschule zu Schwabach	1838	GooBook
Jahresbericht über das grossh. Lyceum zu Heidelberg	1867	GooBook
Jahresbericht über das Gymnasium Celle	1888; 1893; 1897	GooBook

Title	Dates	Key
Jahresbericht über das Gymnasium Dionysianum zu Rheine	1868;1873	GooBook
Jahresbericht über das Gymnasium und die Lateinische Schule zu Speyer	1838; 1869	GooBook
Jahresbericht über das Gymnasium zu Prenzlau	1831	GooBook
Jahresbericht über das Gymnasium zu Sorau	1864; 1868; 1873	GooBook
Jahresbericht über das Königlich Katholische Gymnasium zu Braunsberg	1859	GooBook
Jahresbericht über das Königliche Gymnasium und die Vorschule zu Saarbrücken	1874	GooBook
Jahresbericht über das Königliche Gymnasium zu Duisburg	1850–1851; 1873	GooBook
Jahresbericht über das Königliche Gymnasium zu Rinteln	1847	GooBook
Jahresbericht über das Königliche katholische Gymnasium zu Leobschütz	1883	GooBook
Jahresbericht über das Königliche Progymnasium zu Rothenburg	1854; 1870	GooBook
Jahresbericht über das Kurfürstliche Gymnasium zu Hanau	1849	GooBook
Jahresbericht über das Schuljahr 1873–1874	1874; 1901	GooBook
Jahresbericht über das Schuljahr von Ostern 1878–Ostern 1879	1879	GooBook
Jahresbericht über das Schwarzburgische Gymnasium zu Sondershausen	1845–1846	GooBook
Jahresbericht über die Gewerbschule Amberg	1865	GooBook
Jahresbericht über die höhere Knaben-Schule	1870	GooBook
Jahresbericht über die K. Bayer. Lateinschule zu Hassfurt	1859–1860	GooBook
Jahresbericht über die Kgl. Bayerische Katholische Lateinschule zu Kitzingen	1864	GooBook
Jahresbericht über die kgl. Bayerische Studienanstalt in Burghausen	1873	GooBook

257

Title	Dates	Key
Jahresbericht über die kgl. Bayerische Studienanstalt in Edenkoben	1837–1858	GooBook
Jahresbericht über die Königl. Bayer. Lateinische Schule zu Kirchheimbolanden	1895	GooBook
Jahresbericht über die Königl. Bayer. Lateinschule zu Miltenberg a. M.	1854	GooBook
Jahresbericht über die Königlich Bayerische Lateinschule in Günzburg	1863	GooBook
Jahresbericht über die königlich Bayerische Lateinschule in Hammelburg	1872	GooBook
Jahresbericht über die Königlich Bayerische Lateinschule zu Homburg in der Pfalz	1842	GooBook
Jahresbericht über die Königliche Bayerische Lateinische Schule ... Frankenthal	1869	GooBook
Jahresbericht über die Königliche Bayerische Lateinische Schule ... Germersheim	1860–1873 10 y; gaps	GooBook
Jahresbericht über die königliche Gewerbschule in Traunstein	1873	GooBook
Jahresbericht über die königliche Gewerbschule zu Straubing	1870; 1873; 1876–1877	GooBook
Jahresbericht über die Königliche lateinschule zu Nördlingen	1848	GooBook
Jahresbericht über die Königliche Realschule zu Weißenburg a. Sd.	1872	GooBook
Jahresbericht über die Königliche Studien-Anstalt in Münnerstadt	1861	GooBook
Jahresbericht über die lateinische Schule Blieskastel	1840	GooBook
Jahresbericht über die lateinische Schule im Benediktiner-Stifte Metten	1844	GooBook
Jahresbericht über die Lateinische Schule zu Cusel	1841	GooBook
Jahresbericht über die Lateinische Schule zu Dürkheim	1838	GooBook
Jahresbericht über die Lateinische Schule zu Hersbruck	1873	GooBook
Jahresbericht über die Lateinische Schule zu Kaufbeuren	1867	GooBook

Title	Dates	Key
Jahresbericht über die nied. Österr. Landes-Oberrealschule in Krems	1865	GooBook
Jahresbericht über die Realschule Barmen	1872	GooBook
Jahresbericht von dem Königlichen Progymnasium zu Grünstadt im Rheinkreise	1820–1824	GooBook
Jahresbericht von der Königlichen Studien-Anstalt zu Dillingen	1820; 1822; 1827	GooBook
Jahresbericht von der Lateinischen Stadtschule in Landsberg im Isarkreis	1832	GooBook
Jahresbericht von der lateinischen Vorbereitungsschule in Neustadt a. d. Haardt	1827	GooBook
Jahresbericht von Ostern 1863 bis dahin 1864 (Gymnasium Eisleben)	1864	GooBook
Jahresbericht. Evangelisches Städtisches Gymnasium zu Lauban	1896	GooBook
Jahresbericht. Josephstädter Obergymnasium	1830–1881 23y; gaps	ANNO
Jahresberichte der Jacobson-Schule	1867–1928; 1930–1931	CompMem
Jahresberichte der Landes-Rabinnerschule in Budapest	1878–1918	CompMem
Jahresberichte der Verwaltungsbehörigen der freien Stadt Hamburg	1906	Hathi
Jahresberichte des jüdisch-theologischen Seminars Fraenkelische Stiftung	1854; 1856–1937	CompMem
Jedem Etwas	1891–1893	Tessmann
Jenaer Literaturzeitung	1874–1876	UJENA
Jenaer Volksblatt	1890–1941	UJENA
Jenaische Allgemeine Literaturzeitung	1804–1841	UJENA
Jenaische Beyträge zur neuesten gelehrten Gechichte	1757	UJENA
Jenaische gelehrte Anzeigen	1787	UJENA

259

Title	Dates	Key
Jenaische gelehrte Zeitungen	1749–1786	UCLAU
Jenaische Nachrichten von Gelehrten und andere Sachen	1747	UJENA
Jenaische Zeitung	1872–1919; 1929; 1937	UJENA
Jeschurun (Alte Folge)	1854–1869; 1883–1887	CompMem
Jeschurun (Neue Folge)	1901–1902	DiFMOE
Jeschurun (Neue Folge)	1914–1930	CompMem
Jocusstädtische Carnevals-Zeitung	1828–1829	DiLibri
Journal des Nieder- und Mittelrheins	1814–1816	UDUS
Journal des österreichischen Lloyd	1836–1846; 1848–1849	ANNO
Journal für Ornithologie	1853–1921	Bio
Journal für Prediger	1770–1802	GooBook
Journal von und für Deutschland	1784–1792	UBIEL
Judaica	1934–1937	CompMem
Jüdische Allgemeine	1946– ?	Jud Allg
Jüdische Arbeits- und Wanderfürsorge	1927–1929	CompMem
Jüdische Gemeinde- und Schulzeitung	1873–1874	DiFMOE
Jüdische Korrespondenz	1915–1920	CompMem
Jüdische Pester Zeitung	1870–1871; 1874–1888	DiFMOE
Jüdische Presse	1920–1938	CompMem

Title	Dates	Key
Jüdische Rundschau	1902–1938	CompMem
Jüdische Schulzeitung	1925–1938	CompMem
Jüdische Volksstimme	1912–1920	CompMem
Jüdische Welt-Rundschau	1939–1940	CompMem
Jüdische Woche	1932	DiFMOE
Jüdische Zeitschrift für Wissenschaft und Leben	1862–1872; 1875	CompMem
Jüdische Zeitung	1807–1920	CompMem
Jüdische Zeitung	1932–1937	DiFMOE
Jüdische Zeitung für Ostdeutschland	1924–1931	DiFMOE
Jüdischer Pester Lloyd	1875	DiFMOE
Jüdisches Gefühl	1900–1901; 1912	ANNO
Jüdisches Jahrbuch für die Schweiz	1916–1922	CompMem
Jüdisches Jahrbuch für Sachsen	1931–1932	CompMem
Jüdisches Volksblatt	1913	DiFMOE
Jüdisches Volksblatt	1899–1905	CompMem
Jüdisches Wochenblatt	1920–1940	DiFMOE
Jüdisch-liberale Zeitung	1920–1938	CompMem
Jugend	1896–1940	UHEID
Jugendbewegung	1921	SLUB

Title	Dates	Key
Jugend-Post	1888–1889; 1894–1895	Hathi
Jülicher Kreis-, Correspondenz und Wochenblatt	1850–1866	NRW
Junge Gemeinde	1948–1953	Bethel
Jung–Juda	1900–1935	DiFMOE
Juristische Zeitung für das Königreich Hannover	1828; 1836–1837; 1847–1849	GooBook
KAIN	1919	DHM
KAIN	1911–1914; 1918–1919	Anarch
Kais. Kön. privilegiertes Prager Intelligenzblatt	1797	GooBook
Kais. Königl. Schlesische Troppauer Zeitung	1816–1848	ANNO
Kaiserlich auch k. k. priv. prager Intelligenz-Blatt	1805–1806	GooBook
Kaiserlich privilegirter Reichs-Anzeiger	1793–1806	GooBook
Kaiserlich und kurpfalzbairische privilegirte allgemeine Zeitung	1806	GooBook
Kaiserliche Reichs-Ober-Post-Amts-Zeitung zu Köln	1763–1794	UKLN
Kaiserlich-Königlich privilegirter Bothe von und für Tirol und Vorarlberg	1848	ALO
Kaiserlich-Königlich privilegirtes Bürgerblatt		UFFM
Kalender und Jahrbuch für Israeliten	1842–1851	CompMem
Kalender und Jahrbuch für Israeliten [II. Folge]	1854–1855	CompMem
Kalender und Jahrbuch für Israeliten [III. Folge]	1865–1868	CompMem
Kameralistische Zeitung	1836	GooBook

Title	Dates	Key
Kampf	1912–1914	Anarch
Kampfsignal	1932	DHM
Kanal-Zeitung	1888–1920	Dithm
Karlsruher Tagblatt	1843–1937	Baden
Karlsruher Unterhaltungsblatt	1850*	Baden
Karlsruher Zeitung	1784–1810; 1817–1933	Baden
Kärntner Nachrichten	1945	ANNO
Karpathen-Edelweiss	1880	Slovakia
Karpathen-Post	1881–1942	DiFMOE
Kartell-Convent Blätter	1910–1933	CompMem
Kartell-Mitteilungen	1924–1930	CompMem
Kaschau-Eperieser Kundschaftsblatt	1847–1870 18 y; gaps	DiFMOE
Kaschauer Zeitung	1872–1914	DiFMOE
Kasselsches Journal	1847	Euro
Kattowitzer Zeitung	1930	SBC
Kattowitzer Zeitung	1875–1927 7 y; gaps	Euro
Kaufmännische Zeitschrift	1877–1904	ANNO
Kaukasische Post	1906–1914	DiFMOE
Kemptner Zeitung	1841–1857; 1859–1873	Bavarica

263

Title	Dates	Key
Keramischer Bund	1927–1933	FES
Kikiriki	1861–1933	ANNO
Kinematographische Rundschau	1907–1911	ANNO
Kino-Journal	1922–1939	ANNO
Kirchenblatt für Sachsen-Weimar-Eisenach	1920	UJENA
Kirchlicher Anzeiger für Thüringen	1921	UJENA
Kirchlicher Gemeindeblatt für Reuss	1905–1919	UJENA
Kirchliches Amtsblatt für die Erzdiözesen Gnesen und Posen	1889	Poland
Kirchliches Verordnungsblatt für die Diözese Gurk	1945–1947	ANNO
Kirchliches Verordnungsblatt für Sachsen-Weimar-Eisenach	1880–1921	UJENA
Kissinger Tagblatt	1870	GooBook
Kladderadatsch	1848–1944	UHEID
Kladderadatsch	1918 Nov 29	DHM
Klagenfurter Zeitung	1815–1875; 1906–1909	ANNO
Kleine Presse	1914–1918	UFFM
Kleine Volks-Zeitung	1920–1933; 1938–1944;	ANNO
Kleine Wiener Kriegszeitung	1944	ANNO
Kleiner Gasthof- und Geschäftsanzeiger	1898–1899	Tessmann
Kolmarer Kreisblatt	1885–1888;1891–1894; 1897	ZEFYS

Title	Dates	Key
Kolmarer Kreiszeitung	1911; 1913; 1916–1918	ZEFYS
Köln-Bergheimer Zeitung	1880–1889	NRW
Kölner Arbeiterzeitung	1888–1892	NRW
Kölner Local-Anzeiger	1887–1944	NRW
Kölner Sonntags-Anzeiger	1877–1897	NRW
Kölnische Zeitung	1857–1858	ZEFYS
Kölnische Zeitung	1886 Aug	UHEID
Kölnischer Anzeiger	1859–1863	NRW
Kommunist: Organ der Vereinigten Kommunistischen Partei für Südwestdeutschland	1921–1922	UFFM
Königlich Baierische Staats-Zeitung von München	1806	GooBook
Königlich baierisches Intelligenzblatt des Salzach-Kreises	1810	GooBook
Königlich baierisches Intelligenzblatt für den Innkreis	1814	GooBook
Königlich baierisches Salzach-Blatt-Kreis	1811–1815	GooBook
Königlich bairisches Intelligenzblatt für den Regen-Kreis	1830–1837	GooBook
Königlich Bayerischer Polizey-Anzeiger für München	1820–1823	GooBook
Königlich bayerisches Amts- und Intelligenzblatt für die Pfalz	1838–1853	Bavarica
Königlich Bayerisches Intelligenzblatt für den Isar-Kreis	1825	GooBook
Königlich Bayerisches Intelligenz-Blatt für den Ober-Donau Kreis	1817–1837 (?)	GooBook

Title	Dates	Key
Königlich Bayerisches Intelligenzblatt für Mittelfranken	1839; 1854	GooBook
Königlich bayerisches Intelligenzblatt für Niederbayern	1838–1839	GooBook
Königlich bayerisches Intelligenz-Blatt für Oberfranken	1838–1852 10 y; gaps	GooBook
Königlich Bayerisches Kreis-Amts-Blatt der Oberpfalz und von Regensburg	1868	GooBook
Königlich Bayerisches Kreis-Amtsblatt für Oberbayern	1838	GooBook
Königlich Bayerisches Kreis-Amtsblatt von Unterfranken und Aschaffenburg	1873	GooBook
Königlich preußische Staats-Anzeiger	1868	GooBook
Königlich preußisches Central-Polizei-Blatt	1855; 1857–1865	GooBook
Königlich preußisch-pommersches Intelligenz-Blatt	1811	Meck
Königlich privilegirte Berlinische Zeitung von Staats- und gelehrten Sachen	1839; 1848–1849; 1857	GooBook
Königlich privilegirte Berlinische Zeitung von Staats- und gelehrten Sachen	1839–1918 8 y; many gaps	ZEFYS
Königlich Württembergisches Allgemeines Amts- und Intelligenz-Blatt für den Jaxt-Kreis	1826; 1831–1839	GooBook
Königlich-bayerisches Kreisamtsblatt der Pfalz	1854–1856	GooBook
Königlich-Bayerisches Kreis-Amtsblatt der Pfalz	1854–1872	Bavarica
Königlich-Bayerisches Kreis-Amtsblatt für Niederbayern	1854–1859	GooBook
Königlich-Bayerisches Kreis-Amtsblatt von Schwaben und Neuburg	1854–1869 12 y; gaps	GooBook
Königliches Düsseldorfer Intelligenzblatt	1819–1820	UDUS
Königsberger allgemeine Zeitung	1942	ZEFYS
Königsberger Gelehrte und Politische Zeitungen	in process	Poland

Title	Dates	Key
Königsberger Hartungsche Zeitung	1896	Baden
Königsberger Hartungsche Zeitung	1886 Aug	UHEID
Königsberger Hartungsche Zeitung	1912–1919	ZEFYS
Königswinterer Zeitung	1902–1905	NRW
Konstitutionelle Volks-Zeitung	1865–1974	ANNO
Kornblumen	1880	ZEFYS
Korrespondent für Deutschlands Buchdrucker und Schriftgießer	1870–1877; 1880–1897; 1900–1901	FES
Korrespondent Leipzig	1863–1869	FES
Korrespondenzblatt des Vereins zur Gründung und Erhaltung einer Akademie für die Wissenschaft des Judentums	1920–1930	CompMem
Korrespondenzblatt für Deutschlands Buchdrucker und Schriftgießer	1870–1933	FES
Koschminer Zeitung und Anzeiger für die Städte Borek und Pogorzela	1909–1911; 1914–1918	ZEFYS
Kösliner Volksblatt	1919	Euro
Kösliner Zeitung	1919; 1942	Euro
Kourier an der Donau: Zeitung für Niederbayern	1813–1847 9 y; gaps	GooBook
Krakauer Jüdische Zeitung	1898–1900	JDL
Kreis- und Intelligenzblatt zunächst für Rheydt, Gladbach, Odenkirchen, Giesenkirchen, Wickrath und Dahlen	1852–1862	NRW
Kreis- und Volksblatt für den Kreis Anclam	1849	Meck
Kreis-Anzeiger für den Kreis Greifswald	1877–1895	UGRF

Title	Dates	Key
Kreisblatt (Fulda)	1869–1870	UFULD
Kreis-Blatt der Kreisverwaltung Fellin	1918	Est
Kreisblatt des vorhinnigen Regierungsbezirkes Fulda	1852–1860	NRW
Kreisblatt für den Kreis Bublitz	1889–1993	Meck
Kreis-Blatt für den Kreis Geldern	1889–1993	UBONN
Kreisblatt für den Kreis Malmedy	1866–1905	BelgArch
Kreisblatt für den Kreis Rees	1848	UBONN
Kreisblatt für den Neustädter Kreis	1845–1847	ZEFYS
Kreisblatt für die Kreisstadt Greifenhagen und Umgegend	1836	ZEFYS
Kreisblatt für Mülheim, Sieg und Landkreis Köln	1849–1855	NRW
Kreisblatt-Repertorium der Oberpfalz und von Regensburg	1872	GooBook
Kreis-Intelligenzblatt für Euskirchen und Rheinbach	1811–1814	NRW
Kreis-Wochenblatt für den Kreis Adenau und Umgegend	1853–1854	UBONN
Kremser Wochenblatt	1856–1877	ANNO
Kriegs-Zeitung	1914	Meck
Kriegs-Zeitung	1915	Euro
Kriegszeitung der 4ten Armee	1914–1918	France
Kriegszeitung der 7. Armee	1916–1918	UHEID
Kriegs-Zeitung der Elften Armee	1915–1916	France

Title	Dates	Key
Kriegs-Zeitung des Korps-Marschall	1915–1916	France
Kriegs-Zeitung des Nationalen Studentendienstes	1916–1917	wartime paper
Kriegs-Zeitung für das XV. Armee-Korps	1914–1916	France
Kriegs-Zeitung Heeresgruppe von Scholtz	1917	France
Kritische Blätter der Börsen-Halle	1831	GooBook
Kroatischer Korrespondent	1789	CompMem
Kronstädter Zeitung	1848–1944	ANNO
Kujawisches Wochenblatt	1863–1868	Poland
Kunst und Volk	1924–1932	Poland
Kunstchronik	1866–1918	UHEID
Kurfürstlich gnädigst privilegirte Münchner Zeitung	1787	GooBook
Kurier fur Niederbayern	1856–1873	GooBook
Kurier von der Mosel und den belgischen und französischen Gränzen	1792	DiLibri
Kyffhäuser	1936	DHM
La Semaine (French and German)	1858–1916	NRW
La Tribune Juive (multilingual)	1923–1939	France
Lager-Echo	1916–1917	BritLib
Lähner Anzeiger	1906–1911; 1918–1919	ZEFYS
Laibacher Tagblatt	1868–1877	ANNO

Title	Dates	Key
Laibacher Tagblatt	1868–1880	Slovenia
Laibacher Wochenblatt	1816; 1818; 1880–1893	Slovenia
Laibacher Zeitung	1784–1918	Slovenia
Landauer Wochenblatt	1823–1828	GooBook
Landesgesetzblatt für das Herzogtum Krain	1849–1914 47 y; gaps	Hathi
Landes-Gesetzblatt für das Königreich Böhmen	1848–1907 58 y; gaps	Hathi
Landes-Regierungsblatt für das Herzogthum Salz burg	1853	GooBook
Landes-Regierungsblatt für das Königreich Böhmen	1854–1857; 1859	Hathi
Landes-Zeitung für das Fürstenthum Reuß	1885–1902	UJENA
Landpost	1938	ANNO
Landshuter Wochenblatt	1823–1828	GooBook
Landshuter Zeitung	1860; 1869; 1872–1873	GooBook
Landsturm	1914–1915	France
Landsturm	1915–1916	UHEID
Landsturm's Krieg's Bote	1914	France
Landwirthschaftliches Centralblatt	1853; 1855–1856; 1858–1859	GooBook
Landwirthschaftliches Wochenblatt für das Großherzogthum Baden	1833–1851 13 y; gaps	Hathi
Landwirthschaftliches Wochenblatt für Schleswig-Holstein	1891–1894	Hathi
Landwirtschaftliche Beilage der Greifswalder Zeitung	1921–1922	Meck

Title	Dates	Key
Landwirtschaftliche Beilage zur Deutschen Post	1916–1917	DiFMOE
Langenberger Zeitung	1865–1866	NRW
Langensalzaer Kreis- und Nachrichtenblatt	1853–1863	UJENA
Langensalzaer Kreisblatt	1831–1860; 1863–1911	UJENA
Langensalzaer Kreis-Wochenblatt	1824–1830	UJENA
Langensalzaer Tageblatt	1911–1916	UJENA
Langensalzaer Wochenblatt	1801–1818	UJENA
Langensalzaisches Wochenblatt	1760–1770; 1776–1798	UJENA
Langensalzer Wochenblatt	1801–1813; 1817–1818	UJENA
Lappland-Kurier	1945	DHM
Lausizisches Wochenblatt	1790–1792	UBIEL
Lauterbacher Anzeiger	1859–1860	UDARM
Lavantthaler Bote	1887–1938	ANNO
Le Juif (bilingual)	1923	France
Leipzig	1807–1810	SLUB
Leipziger Illustrirte Zeitung	1861–1940 39 y; gaps	Hathi
Leipziger Intelligenz-Blatt	1765	ArchOrg
Leipziger Intelligenz-Blatt	1760–1804	GooBook
Leipziger Intelligenz-Blatt	1766–1807 19 y; gaps	Hathi

Title	Dates	Key
Leipziger jüdische Wochenschau	1928–1933	SLUB
Leipziger jüdische Zeitung	1922–1926	SLUB
Leipziger Lokomotive	1843 Feb 1	Lpzg
Leipziger Mieter-Zeitung	1923	DHM
Leipziger Neueste Nachrichten	1935	DHM
Leipziger Tageblatt	1810–1816	SLUB
Leipziger Tageblatt	1812–1813	Hathi
Leipziger Tageblatt und Anzeiger	1833–1834	SLUB
Leipziger Tageblatt und Anzeiger	1886 Aug	UHEID
Leipziger Tageszeitung	1933	DHM
Leipziger Uhrmacher-Zeitung	1900	UDRES
Leipziger Völkisches-Echo	1924 Nov 22	DHM
Leipziger Volkszeitung	1927	DHM
Leipziger Volkszeitung	1894–1933	SLUB
Leipziger Westend-Zeitung	1906	ZEFYS
Leipziger Zeitungen	1739–1749	ZEFYS
Leipzig's roter Straßenbahner	1933	DHM
Leitmeritzer Zeitung	1908–1911	ANNO
Lemberger Zeitung	1812–1866	ANNO

Title	Dates	Key
Liberales Judentum	1908–1922	CompMem
Liechtensteiner Heimatdienst	1933–1935	Liecht
Liechtensteiner Landeszeitung	1863–1867	Liecht
Liechtensteiner Nachrichten	1924–1935	Liecht
Liechtensteiner Vaterland	1936–2005	Liecht
Liechtensteiner Volkblatt	1878–2005	Liecht
Liechtensteiniche Wochenzeitung	1873–1877	Liecht
Lienzer Zeitung	1886–1915; 1919; 1938–1945	Tessmann
Liller Kriegszeitung	1914–1918	UHEID
Lindauer Tagblatt für Stadt und Land	1870–1873	GooBook
Linnaea	1826–1882	Bio
Linzer Abendbote	1855–1856; 1864–1868	ANNO
Linzer Tagespost	1865–1944	ANNO
Linzer Volksblatt	1870–1875	Euro
Linzer Volksblatt	1870–1938	ANNO
Linzer Zeitung	1844	GooBook
Linzer Zeitung	1816–1818; 1835–1846	ANNO
Lippische Intelligenzblätter	1767–1808	NRW Lib
Lippische Landes-Zeitung	1886 Aug	UHEID

Title	Dates	Key
Lippische Tages-Zeitung / Sonderausgabe	1914–1917	Lippe
Lippisches Intelligenzblatt	1809–1842	NRW Lib
Lippisches Volksblatt	1848–1852	Lippe
Literarisches Centralblatt für Deutschland	1850–1919	GooBook
Literarisches Conversationsblatt	1822–1823	GooBook
Literarisches Notizenblatt	1832–1835	SLUB
Literatur- und Kunstblatt	1843–1845	SLUB
Literaturblatt der Abendzeitung	1854–1855	SLUB
Literaturblatt des Deutschen Kunstblattes	1854–1858	UHEID
Livländische Gouvernements-Zeitung	1852–1917	Est
Livländische Gouvernements-Zeitung	1860–1914; 1930–1940	Latvia
Local-Anzeiger für Mähr.-Ostrau und Umgebung	1875–1878	ANNO
Lochner's Geschäfts-Zeitung über landwirthschaftliche Producte, diverse Fabrikate und Waaren	1860–1865; 1867; 1876–1877	ANNO
Locomotive	1848	ZEFYS
Lodzer Rundschau (und Handelsblatt)	1911–1912	DiFMOE
Lokomotive an der Oder	1862–1883 9 y many gaps	ZEFYS
Louisville Anzeiger	1861 Dec 3	KDL
Lüderitzbuchter Zeitung	1909–1937	Newsbank

274

Title	Dates	Key
Lüneburger Landeszeitung	1946–1949	CRL
Luxemburger Illustrierte	1924–1931	Lux
Luxemburger Wochenblatt	1821–1826	Lux
Luxemburger Wort	1848–1950	Lux
M (just M, not a misprint)	1836–1839	ZEFYS
Magazin für die Wissenschaft des Judentums	1876–1893	CompMem
Magdeburgische Zeitung	1848–1862 6 y; gaps	GooBook
Magdeburgische Zeitung	1886 Aug	UHEID
Mährischer Correspondent	1862–1865	ANNO
Mährisches Tagblatt	1880–1915	ANNO
Mainzer Carneval-Zeitung Narrhalla	1903	DiLibri
Mainzer Eulenspiegel	1875	DiLibri
Mainzer Fastnachts-Zeitung	1886–1890	DiLibri
Mainzer Journal	1871	GooBook
Mainzer Schwewwel	1876–1877	DiLibri
Mainzer Witz-Raketen	1898	DiLibri
Maiser Wochenblatt	1903–1915	Tessmann
Mallersdorfer Anzeiger	1902–1926 (coming)	BavLib
Malmedy-St. Vither Volkszeitung	1905–1934	BelgArch

275

Title	Dates	Key
Mannheimer Intelligenzblatt	1790–1792	GooBook
Marburger Zeitung	1860; 1872; 1882–1891; 1893–1918	ANNO
Marburger Zeitung	1862–1945 80 y; gaps	DiFMOE
Mayener Volkszeitung	1876–1919 29 y; gaps	UBONN
Mecklenburgische gemeinnützige Blätter	1790–1793	UBIEL
Mecklenburgische Anzeigen	1886 Aug	UHEID
Medicinisch-chirurgische Zeitung	1815	GooBook
Medicinisch-chirurgische Zeitung	1790–1842	ANNO
Medizinische Zeitung	1852–1853	Hathi
Medizinisches Wochenblatt	1783–1789; 1792–1793	UGOT
Meenzer Klepper-Buwe-Zeitung	1859	DiLibri
Mein Film	1926–1939; 1946–1947	ANNO
Meininger Tageblatt	1849–1956 (coming)	UJENA
Meldereiter im Sundgau	1915–1918	UHEID
Memeler Dampfboot	1857–2010 84 y; gaps	Memel
Memminger Bezirksamtsblatt	1863–1869	GooBook
Mennoblatt	1930–1945	Bethel
Mennonitenbrief aus Göttingen	1866–1870	Bethel
Mennonitische Blätter	1854–1925; 1927–1941; 1974	Bethel

Title	Dates	Key
Mennonitische Geschichtsblätter	1936–1940	Bethel
Mennonitische Jugendwarte	1920–1938?	Bethel
Mennonitische Volkswarte	1935–1936	Bethel
Mennonitische Warte	1937–1938	Bethel
Mennonitische Welt	1950–1952	Bethel
Menorah	1923–1932	CompMem
Meraner Zeitung	1855; 1867–1920; 1923–1926	Tessmann
Metallarbeiter Jugend	1920–1933 6 y; gaps	FES
Mettmanner Kreisblatt	1869–1870	NRW
Mettmanner Zeitung	1919–1950	NRW
Milchwirtschaftliches Zentralblatt	1887	GooBook
Militär-Wochenblatt	1816–1919 92 y; gaps	Hathi
Militär-Zeitung	1857–1868	GooBook
Militär-Zeitung	1872–1896 19 y; gaps	Hathi
Miltenberger Tagblatt	1863–1865	GooBook
Milwaukie Flugblätter	1852–1855	Kram
Minnesota Staats-Zeitung	1858–1872	Chron
Mitausche Zeitung	1905–1906	Latvia

Title	Dates	Key
Mitteilungen aus dem Gebiete der Flora und Pomona	1829	SLUB
Mitteilungen aus dem Verband der Vereine für jüdische Geschichte und Literatur in Deutschland	1895–1921	CompMem
Mitteilungen der Arbeitsgemeinschaft jüdisch-liberale Jugendvereine Deutschlands	1919–1922	CompMem
Mitteilungen der Gesellschaft für jüdische Volkskunde [Alte Folge]	1898–1904	CompMem
Mitteilungen der Gesellschaft für jüdische Volkskunde [Neue Folge]	1905–1929	CompMem
Mitteilungen des Gesamtarchivs der deutschen Juden	1909–1914: 1926	CompMem
Mitteilungen des Sippenverbandes der Danziger Mennoniten-Familien	1935–1944	Bethel
Mitteilungsblatt der Arbeitsgemeinschaft freier Angestelltenverbände	1919–1920	FES
Mitteilungsblatt der Berliner Mennoniten-Gemeinde	1936–1945	Bethel
Mitteilungsblatt des Ortskommittes der RGO Leipzig	1933 Feb 12	DHM
Mittelbayerische Zeitung	1945–1950	DigiPress
Mitteldeutsche Rundschau	1914–1918	UFFM
Mittelrheinische Landeszeitung	1935–1939	UBONN
Mittelrheinische Sportzeitung	1920–1925	UDARM
Mittheilungen aus dem Religiösen Leben	1848	Bethel
Mittheilungen aus Oldenburg	1835–1848	UOLD
Mittheilungen der K. K. Mährisch-Schlesischen Gesellschaft zur Beförderung des Ackerbaues, der Natur- und Landeskunde in Brünn	1821–1843	ANNO
Mode und Heim	1902	ZEFYS

Title	Dates	Key
Moh†cser Wochenblatt	1879–1880	OSZK
Molkerei-Zeitung	1887–1913 9 y; gaps	GooBook
Möllers deutsche Gärtner-Zeitung	1886; 1895; 1897	GooBook
Monatsblätter der Mennonitengemeinde Crefeld	1905–1907	Bethel
Monatshefte der Comenius Gesellschaft	1892–1893	Bethel
Monatsschrift für die evangelischen Mennoniten	1846–1848	Bethel
Monatsschrift für Geschichte und Wissenschaft des Judentums	1851–1939	CompMem
Montagspost	1940	DHM
Montags-Zeitung	1898–1922	ANNO
Montjoiér Volksblatt	1880–1936	UKLN
Morgenblatt für gebildete Stände	1807–1849; 1853–1860; 1865	ANNO
Morgenblatt für gebildete Stände	1809; 1811; 1814	Hathi
Morgenblatt für gebildete Stände	1816–1849	UHEID
Morgenpost	1854–1859; 1865–1886	BavLib
Moskauer Deutsche Zeitung	1870	ZEFYS
Moskauer Rundschau	1932 Jul 24	DHM
Mülhauser Frauenzeitung	1901–1929 19 y; gaps	France
Mülhauser Tagblatt	1914–1918; 1944	France
Mülheimer Volkszeitung	1908–1919	NRW

Title	Dates	Key
Mülheimer Zeitung	1894–1912	NRW
Münchener Amtsblatt	1793–18??	Bavarica
Münchener Conversations-Blatt	1831–1832; 1844	GooBook
Münchener Guckkasten	1888–1891	DigiPress
Münchener Herold	1851–1853	GooBook
Münchener Omnibus	1862	GooBook
Münchener Post	1930; 1932–1933	DHM
Münchener Ratsch-Kathl	1889–1907	DigiPress
Münchener Stadtanzeiger	1915–1920	DigiPress
Münchener Stadtanzeiger und Münchener Ratsch-Kathl	1908–1914	DigiPress
Münchener Wochenblatt für das katholische Volk	1868–1869	DigiPress
Münchener Zeitung	1848	Euro
Münchner Intelligenzblatt	1779; 1789	GooBook
Münchner Intelligenzblatt	1796–1799	DigiPress
Münchner Staats-, gelehrte und vermischte Nachrichten	1782	GooBook
Münchner Zeitung	1786	GooBook
Münsterberger Kreisblatt	1888–1931 17 y; gaps	ZEFYS
Münsterberger Wochenblatt	1840–1848	ZEFYS
Münsterische Universitäts-Zeitung	1907–1914	UMST

Title	Dates	Key
Münsterisches gemeinnütziges Wochenblatt	1785–1803	UMST
Münsterisches gemeinnütziges Wochenblatt	1785–1804	NRW
Münsterisches Intelligenzblatt	1765–1849 81 y; gaps	UMST
Musikalische Real-Zeitung	1789	GooBook
Musikalisches Wochenblatt	1870–1893, 1907–1910	ANNO
Musikalisches Wochenblatt	1892–1910	UJENA
Muskauer Wochenblatt	1821–1822, 1824	ZEFYS
Nachalath Zewi	1930–1938	CompMem
Nachrichtendienst	1922–1928	CompMem
Nahe-Blies-Zeitung	1861–1867	UBONN
Nationalzeitung	1906–1907	CompMem
National-Zeitung	1857	ZEFYS
National-Zeitung	1886 Aug	UHEID
Naturwissenschaftliche Rundschau	1887–1912	Bio
Naumburger Briefe	1919 Apr 20	DHM
Naumburger Kreisblatt	1911	UHAL
Naumburger Kreis-Blatt	1845	GooBook
Naumburger Kreis-Blatt	1821–1899 66 y; gaps	UJENA
Nawe Zeitung	1595	ANNO

Title	Dates	Key
Neckar-Zeitung	1822–1823; 1825–1828	GooBook
Neu Braunfelser Zeitung	1852–1853	TX Hist
Neu-ankommender Currier Auß Wienn	1622–1639	UBREM
Neubau und Siedlung	1931	DHM
Neuburger Wochenblatt	1862–1863; 1866–1868; 1871–1873	GooBook
Neue Allgemeine Schweizerische Auswanderungszeitung	1850–1851	Aargau Dig
Neue Allgemeine Wiener Handlungs- und Industrie-Zeitung	1827–1828	ANNO
Neue Aschaffenburger Zeitung und Aschaffenburger Anzeiger	1865–1866	GooBook
Neue Augsburger Zeitung	1830	GooBook
Neue Bonner Zeitung	1796–1895 8 y; major gaps	UBONN
Neue Bonner Zeitung	1892–1895	NRW
Neue Bonner Zeitung (Kinkel)	1848–1850	NRW
Neue Breslauer Zeitung	1821	GooBook
Neue critische Nachrichten	1766–1774	Meck
Neue Didaskalia	1856–1873	GooBook
Neue Folge der Gesundheits-Zeitung	1840–1850	ANNO
Neue Fränkische Zeitung	1848–1850	DigiPress
Neue Freie Presse	1864–1939	ANNO
Neue Hamburger Zeitung	1896–1922	Euro

Title	Dates	Key
Neue Illustrirte Zeitung	1873–1875	ANNO
Neue jenaische allgemeine Literatur-Zeitung	1804–1812; 1838–1848	ANNO
Neue jenaische allgemeine Literatur-Zeitung	1804–1841	UJENA
Neue jüdische Monatshefte	1916–1920	CompMem
Neue jüdische Pester Zeitung	1884–1888	DiFMOE
Neue jüdische Rundschau	1926–1930	DiFMOE
Neue jüdische Zeitung	1881–1884	DiFMOE
Neue kielische gelehrte Zeitung	1797	UKIEL
Neue Kino Rundschau	1917–1921	ANNO
Neue Klosterneuburger Zeitung	1929–1938	ANNO
Neue Leipziger Zeitung	1940–1941	DHM
Neue Lodzer Zeitung	1908 Jul–Dec	DiFMOE
Neue Mannigfaltigkeiten	1774–1777	UBIEL
Neue Militär-Zeitung	1856–1858; 1859–1860	GooBook
Neue Mülhauser Zeitung	1914–1918	France
Neue Münchener Zeitung	1860–1861	GooBook
Neue Nationalzeitung	1907–1916	CompMem
Neue Nürnbergische gelehrte Zeitung	1791	GooBook
Neue Passauer Zeitung	1849–1854	GooBook

283

Title	Dates	Key
Neue Pommersche Provinzialblätter	1826	Meck
Neue Post	1918–1919	DiFMOE
Neue Preußische Zeitung	1848 Sep 23	DHM
Neue preußische Zeitung	1857–1859, 1867–1868; 1892–1893	ZEFYS
Neue preußische Zeitung	1886 Aug	UHEID
Neue Rheinische Zeitung	1953	Euro
Neue Salzburger Zeitung	1854–1858	ANNO
Neue Speyerer Zeitung	1817–1853 30 y; gaps	Bavarica
Neue Tiroler Stimmen	1868–1877	ANNO
Neue Tischlerzeitung	1881–1890; 1892–1893	FES
Neue Vetschauer Zeitung	1902–1944 12 y; many gaps	ZEFYS
Neue Warte am Inn	1881–1944	ANNO
Neue wöchentliche Rostock'sche Nachrichten und Anzeigen	1842 Feb 17	WikiS
Neue Wogen der Zeit	1870; 1878	ZEFYS
Neue Würzburger Zeitung	1842–1872 10 y; gaps	GooBook
Neue Zeit	1945–1994 (special login)	ZEFYS
Neue Zeitung	1906–1907	CompMem
Neue Zeitungen von gelehrten Sachen	1715–1770; 1773–1774; 1776–1784	UJENA
Neue Zeitungen von gelehrten Sachen	1715–1772	ANNO

Title	Dates	Key
Neue Zuger Zeitung	1846–1891	Switz
Neue Zürcher Zeitung	1780–present	NZZ
Neue Zürcher Zeitung	1886 Aug	UHEID
Neuer Anzeiger	1885	UDARM
Neuer Bayerischer Kurier für Stadt und Land	1864–1868	GooBook
Neuer Elbinger Anzeiger	1849–1852; 1854–1872	Poland
Neuer Görlitzer Anzeiger	1803–1808	ZEFYS
Neuer Rheinischer Merkur	1819	GooBook
Neuer Rheinischer Merkur	1817–1818	UJENA
Neues 8-Uhr Blatt	1914–1925	ANNO
Neues Budapester Abendblatt	1919	DiFMOE
Neues Bürgerblatt: eine Wochenschrift	1811–1812; 1814	UFFM
Neues Deutschland	1946–1990 (special login)	ZEFYS
Neues Deutschland	1948–1949	CRL
Neues Fremdenblatt	1865–1876	ANNO
Neues Journal für die Botanik	1806–1810	Bio
Neues Münchener Tagblatt	1848–1849	DigiPress
Neues Österreich	1945	ANNO
Neues Schweizerisches Auswanderungsblatt	1857	Aargau Dig

Title	Dates	Key
Neues St. Petersburgisches Journal	1783–1784	GooBook
Neues Tagblatt aus der östlichen Schweiz	1856–1873	Switz
Neues Tagblatt für München und Bayern	1839	GooBook
Neues Volksblatt	1851	GooBook
Neues Wiener Journal	1893–1939	ANNO
Neues Wiener Tagblatt	1883–1948 42 y; gaps	ANNO
Neueste Bürser Funken-Zeitung	1939	ANNO
Neueste critische Nachrichten	1775–1804	Meck
Neueste Mittheilungen	1882–1894	ZEFYS
Neueste Nachrichten	1893–1903	SLUB
Neueste preußische Zeitung	1849	UFFM
Neueste Weltbegebenheiten	1823–1831; 1833–1840	Bavarica
Neueste Zeitung	1931–1936; 1938–1942	UFFM
Neuhauser Allgemeiner Anzeiger	1844–1848	Kram
Neuhauser Wochenblatt	1848	Kram
Neuhauser Wochenpost	1854–1855	Kram
Neu-Helvetia-Amerika-Zeitung	1850–1851	Aargau Dig
Neuigkeiten	1854–1857	ANNO
Neuigkeiten	1912–1916	OK Hist

Title	Dates	Key
Neulengbacher Zeitung (Wienerwald-Bote)	1900–1943	ANNO
Neu-ostpreußisches Intelligenzblatt	1805	Polona
Neustädter Kreisblatt	1832–1844; 1846–1848	GooBook
Neustädter Kreisblatt	1852–1911 27 y; gaps	ZEFYS
Neustädter Kreisbote	1818–1819; 1822–1831; 1833–1905	UJENA
Neustadter Wochenblatt	1838	GooBook
Neustettiner Kreisblatt	1862–1869	ZEFYS
Neustrelitzer Zeitung	1886 Aug	UHEID
Neüwe Zeitung, Wie die Ritterschafft, mitsampt der Landtschafft vnd Burgerschafft zu Wien in Österreich seind Eingeritten	1527	ANNO
Neuwieder Intelligenz- und Kreis-Blatt	1843–1855	NRW
Neuwiedische Nachrichten	1846–1855	UBONN
New Orleanser Deutsche Zeitung	1876–1906	GooNews
New Yorker Presse	1876	GB
New Yorker Volkszeitung	1889–1932	NewsArch
Newe Zeittung. Des Türkischen Keisers Absagbrieff	1556	ANNO
Newe Zeitung	1857	UBREM
Newe Zeitung und eigentlicher Bericht …	1620	DiLibri
Newe Zeitung von den Widertauffern zu Münster	1535	ANNO

Title	Dates	Key
Newe Zeitung von Kaiserlicher Maiestat Kriegsrüstung	1535	ANNO
Newe Zeitung. Ware vnnd gründtliche anzaygung vnd bericht	1547	ANNO
Newe Zeitung. Wie der Türck Die Statt Nicosiam...	1571	ANNO
Newe zeytung des erschrocklichen grossen Wassers	1530	ANNO
Newe Zeytung. Die Widerteuffer zu Münster belangende	1535	ANNO
Newe Zeytung: Oder Kurtzer Discurs von dem jetzigen	1591	ANNO
Newe Zeytunge. Von einem Manne Hans Vader genannt	1562	ANNO
Niederlausitzisher Anzeiger	1816	ZEFYS
Niederösterreichischer Grenzbote	1912–1918; 1920–1944	ANNO
Niederrheinische Musik-Zeitung für Kunstfreunde und Künstler	1853	GooBook
Niederrheinischer Kurier	1831	GooBook
Niederschlesisches Tageblatt	1883–1913 ? y; gaps	ZielG
Nikolsburger Kreisblatt	1939–1940	Kram
Nikolsburger Wochenschrift	1879–1939	Kram
Nikolsburger Wochenschrift für landwirtschaftliche, gemeinnützige Interessen und Unterhaltung	1860–1878	Kram
Nordböhmischer Gebirgsbote	1857–1867	ANNO
Nordböhmisches Volksblatt	1873; 1883	ANNO
Norddeutsche Allgemeine Zeitung	1884	CRL
Norddeutsche Allgemeine Zeitung	1878–1918	ZEFYS

Title	Dates	Key
Norddeutsche Allgemeine Zeitung	1886 Aug	UHEID
Norddeutsche Nachrichten (coming)	1879–1943	Euro
Nordenburger Anzeiger	1876	ARCOR
Nördlinger Wochenblatt	1849–1850	GooBook
Nördlingisches Intelligenz- und Wochenblatt	1811–1814	GooBook
Nördlingsche wöchentliche Nachrichten	1766–1768	Bavarica
Nordmährische Rundschau	1913–1919	ANNO
Nordwestzeitung Oldenburg	1946–2018	NWZ
Notariatsblatt für das Großherzogthum Baden	1852–1870	ZEFYS
Notariats-Blatt für das Großherzogthum Baden	1852–1870	Hathi
Notiz-Blatt des Architekten- und Ingenieur-Verein für das Königreich Hannover	1853	GooBook
NS-Telegraf	1938	ANNO
Numismatische Zeitung	1842	GooBook
Nürnberger Abendblatt	1844–1845	GooBook
Nürnberger Stadtzeitung	1873	GooBook
Nürnberger Tagblatt	1848–1850	DigiPress
Oberbergischer Bote	1933–1942	NRW
Oberdeutsche Staatszeitung	1787	GooBook
Oberelsässische Landes-Zeitung	1815; 1914–1918	France

Title	Dates	Key
Ober-Elsäßischer Volksfreund: Anzeiger für Hüningen, Sierenz und die angrenzenden Kantone	1914–1918	France
Oberhessissche Volkszeitung	1911–1916	UDARM
Oberhessische Zeitung	1914	Hes
Oberkasseler Zeitung	1912–1973	UBONN
Oberkircher Bote	1896	Baden
Oberlausitzische Fama	1824–1827; 1831	ZEFYS
Oberrheinische Nachrichten	1914–1924	Liecht
Oberschlesische Zeitung	1908; 1922–1924	ZEFYS
Oberschlesisches Wochenblatt	1920	SilDlg
Oberwarther Sonntags-Zeitung	1938–1944	ANNO
Octoberfest-Zeitung	1905	BavLib
Oderberger Zeitung und Wochenblatt	1929, 1932–1933	ZEFYS
Oedenburger Arbeiterrat	1919	DiFMOE
Oedenburger Proletarier	1919 Jul–Aug	DiFMOE
Oedenburger Zeitung	1888–1919 25 y; gaps	DiFMOE
Oesterreichische Jugend-Zeitschrift	1849; 1851	ANNO
Oesterreichisches Bürgerblatt	1831	GooBook
Oesterreichisches pädagogisches Wochenblatt	1842–1865	ANNO

Title	Dates	Key
Oettingisches Wochenblatt	1788–1823 31 y; gaps	Bavarica
Offenbacher Abendblatt	1914	UDARM
Offenbacher Zeitung	1912	UDARM
Offenburger Nachrichten	1887*	Baden
Öffentlicher Anzeiger der königlich preussischen Regierung zu Cleve	1816–1821	UDUS
Öffentlicher Anzeiger der königlichen Regierung zu Posen	1818; 1827	Poznan
Öffentlicher Anzeiger: Amtsblatt für den Stadtkreis Frankfurt a. M.	1914–1918	UFFM
Officielle Beilage für amtliche Bekanntmachungen	1863	Hathi
Ohio	1873–1874	Chron
Ohio Staats-Bote	1846–1851	Chron
Ohio Waisenfreund	1874–1875; 1940–1953	Chron
Oklahoma Neuigkeiten	1912–1916	OK Hist
Olympiade-Pressedienst	1925	UFFM
Oppositions-Blatt oder Weimarische Zeitung	1816–1820	GooBook
Ordentliche wöchentliche Franckfurter Frag- und Anzeigungs-Nachrichten	1750–1864 66 y; major gaps	GooBook
Ordinari Sontags-Zeitung, aus Deutschland, Polen Schweden …	1657	UBREM
Ordinari-Münchner-Zeitungen	1760	GooBook
Organe de Malmedy (French and German)	1893–1901	UBONN
Osnabrücker Zeitung	1919 Jun 1	Euro

Title	Dates	Key
Ost und West	1901–1923	CompMem
Ost und West, Blätter für Kunst, Literatur und geselliges Leben	1837–1847	ANNO
Ostdeutsche Morgenpost	1920	Silesia
Österreichische Auto-Rundschau	1923–1939	ANNO
Österreichische Buchhändler-Korrespondenz	1860–1875	Euro
Österreichische Fahrrad- und Auromobil-Zeitung	1905–1914; 1925	ANNO
Österreichische Illustrirte-Zeitung	1894–1938	ANNO
Österreichische Land-Zeitung	1903–1918	ANNO
Österreichische Lehrerinnen-Zeitung	1893–1901	ANNO
Österreichische Nähmaschinen- und Fahrrad-Zeitung	1904–1938	ANNO
Österreichische Volkszeitung	1907	ANNO
Österreichische Volks-Zeitung	1914–1918; 1920–1926; 1938–1944	ANNO
Österreichischer Beobachter	1810–1847 27 y; gaps	Hathi
Österreichisches Abendblatt	1933	ANNO
Österreichisches entomologisches Wochenblatt	1851–1857	Bio
Österreichisches pädagogisches Wochenblatt	1842–1865	Euro
Österreichisch-ungarisches Cantoren-Zeitung	1881–1897	CompMem
Ostfriesen Zeitung	1957; 1968	Ostfr

Title	Dates	Key
Ostfriesische Anzeigen und Nachrichten von allerhand zum gemeinen Besten überhaupt auch zur Beförderung Handels und Wandels dienenden Sachen	1747–1782	UGOT
Ostfriesische Nachrichten	1884–1913; 1915; 1940	Ostfr
Osthavelländisches Kreisblatt	1849–1859; 1890–1892	ZEFYS
Ostholsteinischer Anzeiger	1802–2006 (needs login)	Eutin
Ostjüdische Zeitung	1919–1937	DiFMOE
Ostpreußische Zeitung	1886 Aug	UHEID
Ostsee-Zeitung	1852–1891 21 y; gaps	UGREI
Ostsee-Zeitung	1886 Aug	UHEID
Paderborner Anzeiger	1827–1848	NRW
Paderbornsches Intelligenzblatt	1772–1849 71 y; gaps	UMST
Paderbornsches Intelligenzblatt für den Appellationsgerichts-Bezirk	1820–1843 11 y; gaps	GooBook
Palästina	1902–1938	CompMem
Palästina Nachrichten	1934–1936	CompMem
Palatina	1859–1862; 1869–1873	GooBook
Pannonia	1837–1900 16 y; gaps	DiFMOE
Passauer Neue Presse	1946–1965	DigiPress
Passauer Neue Presse	1946–1965	PNP
Passauer Tagblatt	1873	GooBook
Passavia	1829; 1840–1843; 1845–1846	GooBook

Title	Dates	Key
Pastoralblatt	1870–1908	Hathi
Patrouillen-Zeitung	1915–1918	SLUB
Pekinger Deutsche Zeitung	1901	Boxer
Pennsylvanischer Staatsbote	1776 Jul 4	Germpuls
Permanente Revolution	1932	DHM
Pernausches Wochenblatt	1823	DIGAR
Pester Lloyd	1888; 1891–1922	ANNO
Pester Lloyd	1908–1910	ANLib
Pesther Tageblatt	1841	GooBook
Pesth-Ofner Localblatt und Landbote	1854–1860	ANNO
Pettauer Zeitung	1890–1904	Slovenia
Pfälzer Demokrat und Sonntags-Blatt	1870–1871	GooBook
Pfälzer Sonntagsblatt	1867–1869	GooBook
Pfälzer Unterhaltungsblatt	1865–1866	GooBook
Pfälzer Zeitung	1850–1858	Bavarica
Pfälzer-Bote für das Glantal und Anzeige-Blatt für den Bezirk Kusel	1857–1873	Bavarica
Pfälzische Blätter	1853–1873	Bavarica
Pfälzische Post	1871; 1873	GooBook
Pfälzische Volkszeitung	1865–1871	GooBook

Title	Dates	Key
Pfälzischer Kurier	1865–1868; 1870–1871; 1873	Bavarica
Pfälzischer Zeitung	1859–1872	Bavarica
Pfälzisches Sonntags-Blatt	1867–1869	GooBook
Pfalz-Neuburgische Provinzialblätter	1803; 1805–1806; 1808	GooBook
Philadelphischer Wochenblat	1790–?	Newspapers
Philanthropin	1869–1915	CompMem
Pillauer Merkur	1870–1913 24 y; gaps	ZEFYS
Pilsener Zeitung	1867–1876	ANNO
Pilsner Fremdenblatt	1874–1876	ANNO
Pilsner Tagblatt	1900–1918; 1923–1938	ANNO
Pittsburger Volksblatt	1859–1900	GooNews
Plauderstübchen	1848; 1850–1851; 1866–1868	GooBook
Pola	1883–1885	UPULA
Polaer Tagblatt	1905–1918	UPULA
Politische Frauen-Zeitung	1869–1871	ANNO
Politische Zeitung im Saar-Departement	1798–1799	DiLibri
Politischer Gevattersmann	1848	DigiPress
Polizei-Blatt für das Herzogthum Salzburg	1872	GooBook
Polyhymnia	1832–1833	Bavarica

Title	Dates	Key
Polytechnisches Journal	1820–1871	ANNO
Pommersche Zeitung	1860	Euro
Pommersche Zeitung	1875–1937 8 y; gaps	CRL
Pommersche Zeitung	1935, 1937–1939	ZEFYS
Pommersches Volks- und Anzeigeblatt	1847–1848	Meck
Pommersche-Zeitung	1886 Aug	UHEID
Populäre österreichische Gesundheits-Zeitung	1830–1840	ANNO
Populär-wissenschaftliche Monatsblätter zur Belehrung über das Judentum für Gebilldete aller Confessionen	1881–1908	CompMem
Posener Tagesblatt	1895–1939	Poznan
Posener-Zeitung	1886 Aug	UHEID
PostZeitung	1636	UBREM
Prager Abendblatt	1872–1875	ANNO
Prager land- und volkswirtthschaftliches Wochenblatt	1873–1877	ANNO
Praktische Mitteilungen	1899–1918	Tessmann
Preßburger jüdische Zeitung	1908–1911	DiFMOE
Preßburger Zeitung	1766–1965 160 y; gaps	DiFMOE
Preßburger Zeitung	1767–1848 44 y; gaps	ANNO
Preßburgisches Wochenblatt	1771–1773	DiFMOE

Title	Dates	Key
Pressedienst des Generalgouvernements	1940–1943	ZEFYS
Preußische Provinzial-Blätter	1834–1860 9 y; gaps	GooBook
Preußische Zeitung	1944	ZEFYS
Preußisches Zentral-Polizei-Blatt	1855; 1857–1865	BavLib
Privilegirte jenaische Wochenblätter	1839–1840; 1842; 1848	UJENA
Privilegirte jenaische wöchentliche Anzeiger	1816; 1819–1826; 1833–1836	UJENA
Prossnitzer Wochenblatt	1871–1875	Kram
Protestantische Kirchenzeitung	1886 Aug	UHEID
Protokoll der Sitzung des Kuratoriums der Vereinigung der Mennoniten-Gemeinden im Deutschen Reich	1893; 1895–1897; 1899–1914	Bethel
Provinzialblatt	1848–1849	GateBay
Provinzial-Blatt für das Großherzogthum Fulda	1815–1821	UFULD
Provinzial-Correspondenz	1863–1884	ZEFYS
Provinzialnachrichten aus den kaiserl. Königl. Staaten	1782–1789	ANNO
Punch	1849–1850	GooBook
Pustertaler Bote	1850–1927	Tessmann
Pustertaler Bote	1858–1863; 1872–1877	ANNO
Putna-Zeitung	1918	SLUB
Radfahrer-Zeitung	1908–1911; 1913–1914	ANNO

Title	Dates	Key
Ragniter Kreis-Anzeiger	1882–1885; 1887; 1893–1895	ZEFYS
Ragniter Kreisblatt	1882–1883; 1885–1886	ZEFYS
Raketen	1881	DiLibri
Ranglisten der k. k. Landwehr und der k. k. Gendarmerie	1916–1918	Kram
Ranglisten des kaiserlichen und königlichen Heeres	1916–1918	Kram
Regensburger Anzeiger	1867	GooBook
Regensburger Conversations-Blatt	1840–1842	GooBook
Regensburger Intelligenzblatt	1810–1812; 1814	GooBook
Regensburger Morgenblatt	1861–1867; 1869–1872	GooBook
Regensburger Neueste Nachrichten	1911–1925 (coming)	BavLib
Regensburger Wochenblatt	1837; 1870	GooBook
Regensburger Zeitung	1843; 1854–1855; 1858–1859	GooBook
Regensburgisches Diarium	1770–1779	GooBook
Regierungs- und Gesetzblatt für das Königreich Bayern	1819	GooBook
Regierungs- und Gesetzblatt für das Königreich Bayern	1821–1825	Hathi
Regierungs- und Intelligenzblatt	1807–1809	GooBook
Regierungs- und Intelligenzblatt für das Herzogtum Coburg	1840–1964	DigiPress
Regierungs- und Nachrichtenblatt für Sachsen-Weimar-Eisenach	1919–1921	UJENA
Regierungsblatt der Fürstlich-Wiedischen Regierung in Wied	1827–1848	NRW

Title	Dates	Key
Regierungsblatt der Militär-Regierung Württemberg-Baden	1946–1952	Baden
Regierungsblatt des Königreichs Griechenland	1835	GooBook
Regierungsblatt für das Großherzogthum Sachsen	1817–1820; 1822–1823	Hathi
Regierungsblatt für das Großherzogthum Sachsen-Weimar-Eisenach	1893–1912	Hathi
Regierungs-Blatt für das Herzogtum Coburg	1865–1918	DigiPress
Regierungsblatt für das Königreich Bayern	1826–1872	Hathi
Regierungsblatt für das Königreich Württemberg	1806–1922 81 y; gaps	Hathi
Regierungsblatt für das Land Thüringen	1945–1949	UJENA
Regierungsblatt für das Markgrafthum Mähren	1855–1859	GooBook
Regierungsblatt für Mecklenburg	1842–1922 48 y; gaps (*–1930)	Hathi
Regierungsblatt für Mecklenburg-Schwerin Amtliche Beilage	1873–1919 27 y; gaps	Hathi
Regierungsblatt für Sachsen-Weimar-Eisenach	1837–1918	UJENA
Regierungsblatt für Thüringen	1952	UJENA
Regierungsblatt für Württemberg	1920–1922 (*–1927)	Hathi
Reichenberger Zeitung	1860–1938	Kram
Reichenhaller Badeblatt	1914	ANNO
Reichs-Gesetz-Blatt für das Kaiserthum Österreich	1854–1864; 1866	GooBook
Reichspost	1894–1938	ANNO
Reichswart	1920–1936	ZEFYS

Title	Dates	Key
Relation aller Fuernemmen und gedenckwuerdigen Historien	1609	UHEID
Rendsburger Tagespost	coming	Rndsbg
Resolution, Welche etliche Obristen, mit dem Fürsten von Friedland...	1634	UBREM
Revalsche Post-Zeitung	1709 Oct 18	Est
Rhein- und Mosel-Bote	1853–1855	UBONN
Rhein- und Nahe-Zeitung	1910–1941	UDARM
Rheinbacher Anzeiger	1850–1910	NRW
Rheinbacher Kreisblatt	1850–1864	UBONN
Rheinberger Wochenblatt	1859–1861	NRW
Rheinhessischer Beobachter	1856–1873	UDARM
Rheinisch Westfälische Zeitung	1886 Aug	UHEID
Rheinisch-Bergische Zeitung	1830–1945	UBONN
Rheinische Allgemeine Zeitung	1840–1842	UKLN
Rheinische Allgemeine Zeitung	1869–1870	UBONN
Rheinische Blätter	1816–1820	GooBook
Rheinischer Humorist	1860	DiLibri
Rheinischer Merkur	1814–1816	UDUS
Rheinisches conservatives Volksblatt	1864–1866	NRW
Rheinisches Land	1926–1928	FES

Title	Dates	Key
Rheinisches Volksblatt	1863–1941	NRW
Rheinisches Wochenblatt	1838	UBONN
Rheinisches Wochenblatt für Stadt und Land	1834–1837	UBONN
Rheinsberger Zeitung	1912; 1922; 1925–1942	ZEFYS
Rheinsberger Zeitung: Illustrirte Beilage	1926–1931	ZEFYS
Rheinsberger Zeitung: Illustrirte Unterhaltungsbeilage	1925–1926	ZEFYS
Rhön-Zeitung	1892–1941 41 y; gaps	UJENA
Rieder Intelligenzblatt	1810	GooBook
Rigaische Rundschau	1908–1920	Euro
Rigasche Hausfrauen-Zeitung	1887	URIGA
Rigasche Industrie-Zeitung	1854	Hathi
Rigasche Stadtblätter	1858	GooBook
Rigasche Zeitung	1869–1918	Latvia
Rigische Novellen	1681–1699	UBREM
Rio Negrische Zeitung	1910–1943 9 y; gaps	Brazil
Rohö Zeitung	1921 Feb	Euro
Rosenheimer Anzeiger	1864–1925 59 y; gaps	BavLib
Rosenheimer Tagblatt Wendelstein	1877–1912 22 y; gaps	BavLib
Rosenheimer Wochenblatt	1833–1834; 1851; 1855–1863	BavLib

Title	Dates	Key
Rostocker Zeitung	1886 Aug	UHEID
Rote Frauenpost	1933	ANNO
Ruhestands Schematismus der Österreich-Ungarischen Armee	1906–1914 6 y; gaps	Kram
Rummelsburger Zeitung	1930	Euro
Rundschau der Frau	1930–1933	FES
Rundschreiben des Präfekten von Bozen	1944–1945	Tessmann
Russische Blätter	1929	Bethel
Rybniker Kreisblatt	1842–1846; 1914	ZEFYS
SA im Feldgrau	1940–1943	ANNO
Saar- und Mosel-Zeitung	1886 Aug	UHEID
Sachsenpost	1934	DHM
Sachsenstimme	1904–1905	Dres
Sachsenstimme	1904–1905	SLUB
Sachsenzeitung	1830–1834	Dres
Sächsische Arbeiter-Zeitung	1890–1908	SLUB
Sächsische Volkszeitung	1902–1930	SLUB
Salzburger Chronik für Stadt und Land	1865–1889; 1891–1938	ANNO
Salzburger Constitutionelle Zeitung	1848–1850	ANNO
Salzburger Fremden-Zeitung	1889	ANNO

Title	Dates	Key
Salzburger Intelligenzblatt	1794–1810 15 y; gaps	GooBook
Salzburger Montags-Zeitung	1899	ANNO
Salzburger Sportblatt	1926	ANNO
Salzburger Tagblatt	1945–1947	ANNO
Salzburger Volksblatt	1872–1942	ANNO
Salzburger Zeitung	1853–1877; 1945	ANNO
Sammlung der Administrativ-Verordnungen und Bekanntmachungen für den Oberrhein-Kreis	1837–1838	GooBook
Samoanische Zeitung	1903–1904; 1907; 1910–1915	NZ
San Antonio Zeitung	1854 Jul 14	TX Hist
Sanct-Paulinus-Blatt für das deutsche Volk	1875	DiLibri
Sangerhäuser Kreisblatt	1855–1857	UHAL
Sankt Pöltener Diözesanblatt	1914–1939 19 y; gaps	ANNO
Sattler- und Portefeuiller Zeitung	1909–1920	FES
Sattler- und Tapezierer Zeitung	1899–1900	FES
Sattler-Tapezierer- und Portefeuiller Zeitung	1923–1933	FES
Sattler-Zeitung	1900–1902; 1908–1909	FES
Sauerländischer Anzeiger	1851–1904	NRW
Schaffhauser Nachrichen	1861–2014	Schaffhsn

Title	Dates	Key
Scharfschützen-Warte	1917–1918	France
Schematismus der k. k. Armee	1804–1808	Kram
Schematismus der k. k. Landwehr und der k. k. Gendarmerie	1877; 1880; 1882–1913	Kram
Schematismus der Oesterreich-Kaiserlichen Armee	1810–1814	Kram
Schematismus für das kaiserliche und königliche Heer und die kaiserlieche und königliche Kriegs-Marine	1890–1914	Kram
Schild und Schwert	1848	GooBook
Schlesische Landarbeiter	1919–1922	Poland
Schlesische privilegirte Staats-, Kriegs- und Friedens-Zeitung	1742–1779 16 y; gaps	Poland
Schlesische Provinzialblätter	1862; 1864–1867	Hathi
Schlesische Zeitung	1886 Aug	UHEID
Schlesisches Pastoralblatt	1880–1929	Poland
Schlesisische Arbeiterzeitung	1919–1926	FES
Schleswig-Holsteinische Blätter	1835–1840	GooBook
Schleswig-Holsteinische Provinzialblätter	1787–1798	UKIEL
Schleswig-Holsteinische Tageszeitung	coming	Rndsbg
Schlettstadter Tageblatt	1914–1918	France
Schneider-Zeitung	1904–1920	FES
Schrattenthals Frauenzeitung	1893–1894	DiFMOE

Title	Dates	Key
Schuhmacherfachblatt	1900–1903; 1911; 1914–1922	FES
Schützengrabenzeitung	1915–1916	UHEID
Schützengruben in den Vogesen	1915–1916	France
Schwäbischer Merkur	1801–1872 12 y; gaps	GooBook
Schwarzburger Bote	1926–1934	UJENA
Schwedisches ökonomisches Wochenblatt	1765	Meck
Schwedter Tageblatt	1925–1941 14 y; gaps	ZEFYS
Schweinfurter Anzeiger	1869–1875	GooBook
Schweinfurter Tagblatt	1863; 1865–1873; 1875	GooBook
Schweinfurter Tagblatt	1863–1873	BavLib
Schweizer Schule	1893–2000 coming	e-lib.ch
Schweizerische Bienen-Zeitung	1898	GooBook
Schweizerische Tagblätter	1798	Switz
Schweizerische Volks-Zeitung	1851–1857	Aargau Dig
Schwerter Zeitung	1869–1950	NRW
Scranton Wochenblatt	1869–1918	Chron
Sechseläuten Tagblatt	1851	GooBook
Seelower Tageblatt	1943	ZEFYS
Seguiner Zeitung	1900–1932	TX Hist

Title	Dates	Key
Seifenblasen	1896	ZEFYS
Seille-Bote	1915–1916	France
Selbst-Emancipation	1885–1893	CompMem
Selbstwehr	1907–1938	Kram
Shanghai Echo	1947	DNB
Sichel und Hammer	1925	DHM
Sickinger Bote	1862–1863	Bavarica
Siebenbürger Bote	1842–1848	DiFMOE
Siebenbürger Wochenblatt	1861	GooBook
Siebenbürger Wochenblatt	1843–1844	Hungary
Siebenbürgisch-Amerikanisches Volksblatt	1939–1954	Chron
Siebenbürgisch-Deutsches Tageblatt	1874–1941 34 y; gaps	DiFMOE
Siebenbürgisch-Deutsches Tageblatt	1886 Aug	UHEID
Siebenbürgische Provinzialblätter	1808	GooBook
Siebenbürgische Zeitung	1950–present	SbgZ
Siebenbürgisches Bürgerblatt	1838–1839	GooBook
Siebenbürgisches Wochenblatt	1869–1870	Hathi
Sieg-Bote	1886–1915	NRW
Siegburger Kreisblatt	1862–1866	UBONN

Title	Dates	Key
Signale für die Musikalische Welt	1876–1881; 1913–1941	ANNO
Simplicissimus	1896–1944	Simplic
Sinai	1846	Hathi
Sinziger Volksfreund	1894	DiLibri
Sion. Eine Stimme in der Kirche für unsere Zeit	1846–1873	ANNO
Sobernheim-Kirner Intelligenz-Blatt	1864–1867	UBONN
Solidarität	1900–1932	FES
Solinger Kreis-Intelligenzblatt	1835–1912	NRW
Solothurnisches Wochenblatt	1810–1834	Hathi
Sonntagsblatt	1787	GooBook
Sonntagsblatt	1831–1849; 1851–1853	Bavarica
Sonntagsblatt (Pustertal)	1880–1917 29 y; gaps	Tessmann
Sonntagsblatt: hrgb. zur Hebung u Stärkung d. evangel. Glaubens	1914–1918	UFFM
Sonntagsblätter	1845	GooBook
Sonntagsgruss unserer Heimatkirche	1928–1930	UJENA
Sonntagsgruß: Kirchlicher Anzeiger für Frankfurt a.M. und Umgebung	1914–1918	UFFM
Sonntagsgruß: Reußisches Kirchenblatt für Stadt und Land	1925–1928	UJENA
Sonntagspost	1914	CRL
Sonntagsruhe	1932–1934	ZEFYS

Title	Dates	Key
Sorauer Kreisblatt	1843–1847	ZEFYS
Sorauer Tageblatt	1923–1944 15 y; gaps	ZEFYS
Sorauer Wochenblatt für Unterhaltung, Belehrung und Ereignisse der Gegenwart	1817–1846 9 y; gaps	ZEFYS
Sozialistische Arbeiter-Zeitung	1931–1933	FES
Spandauer Zeitung	1925; 1931; 1933	ZEFYS
Spartacus	1849	UBONN
Spartakus	1929	DHM
Speyerer Tagblatt	1870	GooBook
Speyerer wöchentliches Anzeige-Blatt	1823; 1825; 1828	GooBook
Sport im Bild	1928–1931	ANNO
Sportblatt: Centralblatt für die Interessen der Pferdezucht und des Sports	1870–1877	ANNO
Sprottauer Wochenblatt	1839–1840; 1845–1846	ZEFYS
St. Galler Volksblatt	1856–1900	Switz
St. Galler Zeitung	1831–1881	Switz
St. Goarer Kreisblatt	1839–1850	UBONN
St. Vither Volkszeitung	1834–1941; 1955–1964	BelgArch
St.-Benno-Blatt	19227–1931	SLUB
Staats- und Gelehrte-Zeitung des hamburgischen unpartheyischen Correspondenten	1819–1831; 10 y gaps	GooBook
Staats- und Gelehrte-Zeitung des unpartheyischen Correspondenten	1731; 1795; 1814	Hathi

308

Title	Dates	Key
Staats- und Gelehrte-Zeitung des unpartheyischen Correspondenten	1795–1826	Gale
Staats- und Gelehrte-Zeitung des unpartheyischen Correspondenten	1806–1812	Hathi
Staats- und Regierungsblatt für Baiern	1806–1817	Hathi
Staats- und Regierungsblatt für Hamburg	1890–1920	Hathi
Staats-Anzeiger für das Grossherzogtum Baden	1869–1873; 1908	Hathi
Stadt- und Landbote	1855–1936	NRW
Stadt- und Landbote	1867–1936	UKLN
Stadt- und Wochenblatt	1848–1849	ZEFYS
Staufener Volksblatt	1878–1978	UFBRG
Staufener Wochenblatt	1875–1876; 1880–1938; 1949–1978	UFBRG
Steirerland	1940–1944	ANNO
Steirische Grenzwacht	1938–1944	ANNO
Stenographische Protokolle der Verhandlungen der Zionisten-Kongresse	1897–1937 19 y; gaps	CompMem
Sterne und Blumen	1901–1925	Baden
Sterzinger Bezirks-Anzeiger	1907–1908	Tessmann
Stettiner Entomologische Zeitung	1912	Bio
Stettiner General-Anzeiger	1936–1937	ZEFYS
Stettiner illustrierte Zeitung	1918; 1920; 1926–1930	Meck
Stettiner Intelligenz-Blatt	1817–1829; 1831–1849	Meck

Title	Dates	Key
Stettiner Zeitung	1886 Aug	UHEID
Steyermärkische Intelligenz-Blätter der Grätzer Zeitung	1824	GooBook
Steyermärkisches Amtsblatt zur Grätzer Zeitung	1826–1848 17 y; gaps	ANNO
Stimme der Kirche	1871–1876	UJENA
Stobsiade: Stobser Zeitung	1914	Swarth
Stolper Neueste Nachrichten	1901–1918	Euro
Stolper Wochenblatt	1858– 1938 6 y; gaps	Poland
Stralsundische Zeitung	1772–1806	SLUB
Stralsundische Zeitung	1772–1926 147 y; gaps	Meck
Stralsundischer RelationsCourier	1796	Meck
Strassburger Bürger-Zeitung	1616; 1892–1893; 1914–1918	France
Strassburger Diözesanblatt	1899; 1914–1918	France
Straßburger Handelsblatt	1873	GooBook
Straßburger Neue Zeitung	1909; 1914–1919	France
Strassburger neueste Nachrichten: General-Anzeiger für Strassburg und Elsass-Lothringen	1914–1918	Baden
Strassburger neueste Nachrichten: General-Anzeiger für Strassburg und Elsass-Lothringen	1914–1918	France
Strassburger Post	1914–1918	France
Strassburger privilegierte Zeitung	1788–1791; 1793–1794	France

Title	Dates	Key
Strassburgisches Wochenblatt (bilingual)	1788–1789	France
Straubinger Tagblatt	1861–1875	GooBook
Strehlener Stadtblatt	1835–1843	ZEFYS
Süd Australische Zeitung	1860–1874	Trove
Süd Dakota Nachrichten	1896–1900	Chron
Süd Dakota Nachrichten und Herold	1900–1907	Chron
Südaustralische Zeitung	1850–1851	Trove
Südböhmische Volkszeitung	1936–1938	DiFMOE
Süddeutsche Blätter für Leben, Wissenschaft und Kunst	1831; 1837–1838; 1841–1845	GooBook
Süddeutscher Anzeiger	1863–1865	GooBook
Süddeutscher Geschäftsanzeiger	1864–1865	GooBook
Sudetendeutsche Zeitung	1951–1955	DigiPress
Sudetenland	1951	BavLib
Südösterreichische Nachrichten	1910	UPULA
Südsteirische Post	1881	ANNO
Südtiroler Heimat	1923–1938	Tessmann
Südtiroler Landeszeitung	1920–1922	Tessmann
Südtiroler Nachrichten	1963–1974	Tessmann
Südtiroler Ruf	1956–1984	Tessmann

Title	Dates	Key
Südtiroler Volksblatt	1862–1925	Tessmann
Suhler Zeitung	1919–1931	UJENA
Sulamith	1806–1848 37 y; gaps	CompMem
Sulzbacher Wochenblatt	1870–1871	GooBook
Sundine	1840	GooBook
Swakopmunder Echo	1916	CRL
Swakopmunder Zeitung	1911–1912	CRL
Szatmarer allgemeine jüdische Zeitung	1902–1903	Hungary
Tag-Blatt der Stadt Bamberg	1834	OPACPlus
Tagblatt für die Kreishauptstadt Augsburg	1830	GooBook
Tagblatt für die Städte Dillingen, Lauingen, Höchstadt, Wertingen und Gundelfingen	1856	GooBook
Tagblatt für Landshut und Umgegend	1848	GooBook
Tagesbote	1851–1945	DiFMOE
Tagespost	1837; 1856–1877	ANNO
Tageszeitung für die deutsche Bevölkerung	1945	Dres
Tageszeitung für die deutsche Bevölkerung	1945	SLUB
Tägliche Rundschau	1886 Aug	UHEID
Täglicher Anzeiger der Stadt Aarau und Umgebung	1854–1857	Aargau Dig
Täglicher Anzeiger für Berg und Mark	1850–1868; 1872–1873	UBONN

Title	Dates	Key
Täglicher Buffalo Volksblatt	1876	GB
Tägliches Cincinnatier Volksblatt	1910–1918	Chron
Tags-Blatt für München	1827	GooBook
Teltower Kreisblatt	1856–1896	ZEFYS
Teplitz-Schönauer Anzeiger	1861–1919	ANNO
Teschner Zeitung	1919–1932 10 y; gaps	Cieszyn
Teutsches Volksblatt	1848–1849	DigiPress
Textilarbeiterzeitung	1914–1933	FES
Textilarbeiterzeitung für die Interessen der Textilarbeiter und -Arbeiterinnen aller Branchen	1906–1913	FES
Theater-Zeitung	1846	UMST
Theatralisches Wochenblatt	1802	UMST
Thorner Freiheit	1939–1945	Poland
Thorner Intelligenzblatt	1858	Poland
Thorner Wochenblatt	1816–1868	Poland
Thorner Zeitung	1796–1842 17 y; gaps	Euro
Thüringer Kirchenblatt	1849–1851	UJENA
Thüringer Kirchenblatt und Kirchlicher Anzeiger	1922–1943; 1945–1947; 1949	UJENA
Thüringer Kirchenblatt: Gesetz- und Verordnungsblatt	1920–1921	UJENA

Title	Dates	Key
Thüringer Lehrerzeitung	1912–1921	UJENA
Thüringer Volk	1946–1950	UJENA
Thüringer Volksfreund	1829–1831	UJENA
Tilsiter allgemeine Zeitung	1914; 1916–1917	ZEFYS
Tilsiter Zeitung	1894, 1914	ZEFYS
Tiroler Schützenzeitung	1846–1847; 1857–1872	ANNO
Tiroler Volksblatt	1869–1877	ANNO
Tiroler Volksbote	1892–1919	Tessmann
Tiroler Zeitung	1794; 1850–1853	Tessmann
Transsilvania (Beiblatt zum Siebenbürger Boten)	1842–1844; 1863	ANNO
Traun-Alz Bote	1869–1872	GooBook
Traun-Alz-Salzach Bote	1873	GooBook
Treffurter Wochenblatt	1849	ZEFYS
Treviris	1834–1836	GooBook
Tribunal	1932	DHM
Trierische Staats- und gelehrte Zeitungen	1744–1745	DiLibri
Trierisches Wochen-Blättgen	1768–1819 5 y; wide gaps	DiLibri
Triestingtaler und Priestingtaler Wochenblatt	1925–1939	ANNO
Tsingtauer neueste Nachrichten	1918	ZEFYS

Title	Dates	Key
Tübinger Blätter	1901	UTUB
Tübingische gelehrte Anzeigen	1790–1792	UGOT
Türkische Post	1926–1943	ZEFYS
Türkische Post Halbmonatliche Wirtschaftsausgabe	1938; 1940–1941	ZEFYS
Turner-Schnaken	1891	UFFM
Über Land und Meer	1896	Baden
Überetscher Gemeindeblatt für Eppan und Kaltern	1908–1935; 1949–1974	Tessmann
Ulk	1914–1930	UHEID
Ungarisch-jüdische Wochenschrift	1871–1872	DiFMOE
Ungarländische jüdische Zeitung	1910–1915	DiFMOE
Union	1872–1874	Euro
Unser Landsturm im Hennegau	1916–1917	UHEID
Unser Blatt	1947–1950	Bethel
Unser Egerland	1897	Kram
Unser Landsturm im Hennegau	1916–1917	France
Unser Teltow	1835–1839	Brandenburg
Unsere Tribüne	1924–1926	CompMem
Unsere Zeitung	1923–1934	UpAust
Unterhaltung, Wissen und Heimat	1938	ZEFYS

Title	Dates	Key
Unterhaltungen	1836	UBONN
Unterhaltungs- und Anzeiger für den Kreis Schleiden	1911–1927	Eusk
Unterhaltungs- und Anzeigerblatt für den Kreis Schleiden	1849–1866	UBONN
Unterhaltungs-Beilage der Lodzer Rundschau	1911–1912	DiFMOE
Unterhaltungsblatt der Neustadter Zeitung	1853–1867	GooBook
Unterhaltungsblatt zum Pilsner Fremdenblatt	1874	ANNO
Unterhaltungsblätter	1828–1829	Kram
Unterkärntnerische Nachrichten see Lavanttaler Bote		
Unterländer Kurier	1908; 1914–1918	France
Urwähler-Zeitung	1849–1850	CompMem
Vaterländische Blätter für den österreichischen Kaiserstaat	1808–1820	ANNO
Vaterlandsfreund	1834–1836; 1845–1846	Chron
Vaterlandsfreund und Geist der Zeit	1837–1845	Chron
Velberter Morgen-Zeitung	1921–1949	NRW
Velberter Zeitung	1880–1960	NRW
Velocipedista	1888–1890	ANNO
Verbands-Bote	1919	Tex Cult
Verbandszeitung Verband der Brauerei- und Mühlenarbeiter und Verwandter Berufsgenossen	1910–1915; 1917–1920	FES

Title	Dates	Key
Verbandszeitung Verband der Lebensmittel- und Getränkearbeiter Deutschlands	1922–1928	FES
Vereinigte Laibacher Zeitung	1815–1817; 1822–1849; 1853–1876	ANNO
Vereinigte Ofner-Pester Zeitung	1814; 1832–1845	DiFMOE
Vereinsanzeiger Vereinigung der Maler, Lackierer, Anstreicher und Verwandter Berufsgenossen Deutschlands	1900–1923 20 y; gaps	FES
Verhandlungen des Landraths im Ober-Donau Kreis	1817–1837 (?)	GooBook
Verkündiger für den Kreis Düren	1856–1858	UBONN
Verlustliste	1914–1919	ANNO
Verlustliste	1914–1919	Kram
Verlustliste Alphabetisches Verzeichnis	1914–1919	ANNO
Verordnungs- und Anzeigeblatt der königl. Bayerischern Verkehrs-Anstalten	1867	GooBook
Verordnungs- und Anzeigeblatt für die königlich Bayerischen Posten	1845–1847	Bavarica
Verordnungs-Anzeigeblatt für den Kreis Heppenheim	1929	UDARM
Verordnungsblatt für das Gebiet der Apostolischen Administratur Feldkirch-Innsbruck	1941	ANNO
Verordnungsblatt für die Beamten und Angestellten der Steuerverwaltung	1842	GooBook
Vogesenwacht	1916–1918	USTR
Vogtländischer Anzeiger und Tageblatt	1886 Aug	UHEID
Volk	1950	UJENA
Volk und Land	1919	CompMem

Title	Dates	Key
Volksblatt	1862–1925	Tessmann
Volksblatt für Berg und Mark	1856–1864	NRW
Volksblatt für Bergisch-Gladbach und Umgegend	1890–1906	UBONN
Volksblatt für die Kreise Bonn und Sieg	1849	UBONN
Volksblatt und Freiheits-Freund	1901–1995	GooNews
Volksbote	1919–1995	Tessmann
Volksfreund	1881–1933	Baden
Volksmund	1906–1921	NRW
Volksrecht	1920–1923	Tessmann
Volksstimme	1848	Euro
Volksstimme	1895–1932	FES
Volksstimme (Budapest)	1919 Apr–Aug	DiFMOE
Volkswacht	1912–1919	GDAN
Volkswacht (Freiburg)	1911	Baden
Volkswacht für Schlesien	1891–1928; 1930–1933	FES
Volkswirtschaftliche Blätter	1872–1883	Tessmann
Volkswirtschaftliche Wochenschrift	1883–1908	ANNO
Volks-Zeitung	1853–1854	Hathi
Volks-Zeitung	1856–1858; 1890–1904	ZEFYS

Title	Dates	Key
Volkszeitung für Sachsen-Weimar-Eisenach	1919–1920	UJENA
Volkszeitung Großherzogtum Sachsen-Weimar-Eisenach	1916–1918	UJENA
Vom Nordkap bis nach Afrika	1941–1944	ANNO
Vorarlberger Landes-Zeitung	1863–1931	Euro
Vorarlberger Landes-Zeitung	1863–1931 66 y; gaps	ANNO
Vorarlberger Volksblatt	1866–1938; 1946–1947	ANNO
Vorarlberger Wacht	1910–1920; 1923–1938	ANNO
Vorwärts	1892–1922	NewsArch
Vorwärts!	1848–1849	Bavarica
Vorwärts. Organ der Gewerkschaft Druck und Papier.	1867–1877	ANNO
Vossische Zeitung	1928	CRL
Vossische Zeitung	1918–1934	DeGruy
Vossische Zeitung	1918–1934	ZEFYS
Wahrhafftige Newe Zeytung, Wie die Stadt Genff von der belägerung des Hertyogs von Sauoz entfledigt, vnd was sich nach derselben	1590	ANNO
Waldbröler Kreisblatt (Flamm)	1862–1866	NRW
Waldbröler Kreisblatt (Rosenkranz)	1850–1858	NRW
Waldeckisches Intelligenz-Blatt	1782	Hathi
Waldeckisches Intelligenz-Blatt	1776–1810	UKASL

Title	Dates	Key
Waldenburger Wochenblatt	1883	Euro
Waldenburger Wochenblatt	1858–1910	Jelenia
Walliser Bote	1869–2008	Switz
Walliser Wochenblatt	1861–1868	Switz
Warhafftige neue Zeitung des Sendtbrieffs	1527	ANNO
Warhafftige newe zeidtung wie die Türken dem Siebenbürger	1597	ANNO
Warhafftige Newe Zeitung. Welcher massen die Römische	1576	ANNO
Warhafftige und gründliche Zeitung	1620	DiLibri
Warnsdorfer Volkszeitung	1884	ANNO
Warschauer Zeitung	1859–1862	GooBook
Wartburg Herold	1896–1898	UJENA
Warte Jahrbuch	1943; 1944	Bethel
Wasserburger Anzeiger	1871; 1873	GooBook
Wasserburger Wochenblatt	1852–1864 6 y; gaps	GooBook
Weckruf	1919 March 19	DiFMOE
Wegweiser im Gebiete der Künste und Wissenschaften	1819–1832	SLUB
Weilheimer Tagblatt für Stadt und Land	1872	GooBook
Weilheim-Werdenfelser Wochenblatt	1865–1873	GooBook
Weimarer Zeitung	1856–1863	UJENA

Title	Dates	Key
Weimarische Volkszeitung	1906–1907; 1914–1916	UJENA
Weimarische wöchentliche Anzeigen	1755–1800	UJENA
Weimarische Zeitung	1832–1932	UJENA
Weimarisches Allerlei	1805	UJENA
Weimarisches Wochenblatt	1800–1832	UJENA
Weinheimer Anzeiger	1896	Baden
Wele-Neuigkeitsblatt	1881	ANNO
Weltbote	1793–1803	France
Werkzeitung Wien Staatsdruckerei	1939–1941	ANNO
Weser-Zeitung	1844–1845	GooBook
Weser-Zeitung	1886 Aug	UHEID
Westbote	1863–1895	Chron
Westfälische Lehrer-Zeitung	1872–1883	UMST
Westfälische Nachrichten	1946–2018	WN
Westfälisch-Schaumburgische Zeitung	1886 Aug	UHEID
Westliche Blätter	1865–1885	Chron
Westricher Tagblatt	1855	GooBook
Westricher Zeitung	1852–1856	GooBook
Wetzlarer Kreis- und Amtsblatt	1850–1866	UBONN

Title	Dates	Key
Wiener Allgemeine Zeitung	1886 Aug	UHEID
Wiener Allgemeine Zeitung	1917–1919	ANNO
Wiener Bilder	1896–1939	ANNO
Wiener Caricaturen	1881–1920; 1922–1925	ANNO
Wiener Diözesanblatt	1863–1941	ANNO
Wiener entomologische Zeitung	1883–1923	Bio
Wiener Feuerwehrzeitung	1871	ANNO
Wiener Film	1936–1938	ANNO
Wiener Gassen-Zeitung	1848	ANNO
Wiener Illistrierte Frauen-Zeitung	1897–1905	ANNO
Wiener illustrirte Garten-Zeitung	1887	Bio
Wiener Kirchenzeitung für Glauben, Wissen, Freiheit und Gesetz	1848–1849; 1853–1873	ANNO
Wiener Medizinische Wochenschrift	1851–1940; 1942–1944	ANNO
Wiener Montagsjournal	1911	ANNO
Wiener Morgenzeitung	1919–1927	CompMem
Wiener neueste Nachrichten	1934–1941	ANNO
Wiener Revue	1945–1947	ANNO
Wiener Theater-Chronik	1859; 1862–1889; 1891–1938	ANNO
Wiener Theaterzeitung	1806–1850 41 y; gaps	ANNO

Title	Dates	Key
Wiener Zeitschrift	1792–1793; 1816–1849	ANNO
Wiener Zeitung	1703–1940 gaps; 1945–1947	ANNO
Wienerische Kirchenzeitung	1784–1789	Euro
Wienerisches Diarium	1703–1779	CRL
Wiesbadener Badeblatt	1867–1933	Wiesbdn
Wiesbadener Tagblatt	1905–1914	RheinMain
Wilhelmshavener Tageblatt	1886 Aug	UHEID
Wimpfener Zeitung	1914	UDARM
Windausche Zeitung	1901–1931 17 y; gaps	Latvia
Wipperfürther Kreis-Intelligenz-Blatt	1843–1867; 1870; 1883	UBONN
Wirtschaftliche Rundschau	1925–1930	SLUB
Wissen und Kunst	1912	DiFMOE
Wissenschaftliche Zeitschrift für jüdische Theologie	1835–1847 6 y; gaps	CompMem
Wittenbergisches Wochenblatt	1768–1785	Euro
Wochen- und Amts-Blatt der königlichen Bezirks-Aemter Stadtamhof und Regensburg	1863–1867; 1869–1873	GooBook
Wochenbeilage der Darmstädter Zeitung	1906–1914; 1919–1920	UDARM
Wochenblatt	1854–1873	Hathi
Wochenblatt der Bauernschaft für Salzburg	1938–1942	ANNO
Wochenblatt der Frankfurter Zeitung	1914 Nov 17	Euro

Title	Dates	Key
Wochenblatt der Johanniter-Ordens-Balley Brandenburg	1873	GooBook
Wochenblatt der Stadt Amberg	1815; 1817–1818; 1835; 1841	GooBook
Wochenblatt der Stadt Dillingen	1819–1825; 1827–1827	Bavarica
Wochenblatt der Stadt Nördlingen	1842–1848	GooBook
Wochenblatt der Stadt Sulzbach	1852; 1865; 1872	Bavarica
Wochenblatt der Union	1866–1867	TX Hist
Wochenblatt des Bönnischen Bezirks	1808–1811	UBONN
Wochenblatt des Landwirtschartlichen Vereins in Bayern	1811–1840?	GooBook
Wochenblatt des Landwirtschartlichen Vereins in Bayern	1813–1818	Hathi
Wochenblatt des Westboten	1871–1872	Chron
Wochenblatt für das Fürstenthum Oettingen-Spielberg	1843	Bavarica
Wochenblatt für das Fürstenthum Oettingen-Spielberg und die Umgebung	1844–1847	Bavarica
Wochenblatt für das Fürstenthum Sigmaringen	1809	GooBook
Wochenblatt für den Kreis Adenau und Umgegend	1855–1862	UBONN
Wochenblatt für den Kreis Malmedy	1866	BelgArch
Wochenblatt für den Langensalzaer Kreis	1818–1823	UJENA
Wochenblatt für die königlich bayerischen Landgerichtsbezirke Pfaffenhofen und Schrobenhausen	1855–1856; 1859; 1862–1862	Bavarica
Wochenblatt für die Kreise St. Wendel und Ottweiler	1836–1861	ANNO

Title	Dates	Key
Wochenblatt für die Kreise St. Wendel und Ottweiler	1836–1867	NRW
Wochenblatt für die Provinz Fulda	1822–1867	UFULD
Wochen-Blatt für die Stadt und den Landgerichts-Bezirk Oettingen	1848–1853	Bavarica
Wochenblatt für die vier löblichen Kantone	1814–1849	Switz
Wochenblatt für Gößnitz und Umgebung	1879–1944 coming	CompMem
Wochenblatt für Land- und Hauswirthschaft, Gewerbe und Handel	1834	GooBook
Wochenblatt für Papierfabrikation	1915–1933 17 y; gaps	Hathi
Wochenblatt und Anzeiger für den Kreis Schleiden und Umgegend	1840–1866	NRW
Wochen-Post	1939	Euro
Wochenschrift der K.K. Gesellschaft der ärzte	1855–1856	GooBook
Wochenschrift des ö. Ingenieur- und Architektenvereins	1882	ANNO
Wochenschrift für das Fürstenthum Minden und die Grafschaft Ravensburg	1813–1814	NRW
Wöchentlich Oekonomisches Intelligenz-Blatt	1769–1772	UKASL
Wöchentliche Anzeigen für das Fürstenthum Ratzeburg	1833–1839; 1850–1894	Meck Lib
Wöchentliche Ostfriesische Anzeigen und Nachrichten	1747–1782	UGOT
Wöchentlicher Anzeiger	1930	Ancestry
Wöchentlicher Anzeiger für die katholische Geistlichkeit	1833–1839	Bavarica
Wöchentlicher Buffalo Volksfreund	1876	GB
Wöchentliches Kundschaftsblatt des Herzogthums Krain	1775	Slovenia

Title	Dates	Key
Wöchentliches Kundschaftsblatt des Herzogthums Krain	1775–1776	Hathi
Wöchentliches Unterhaltungs-Blatt für den Kanton Dürkheim	1836	BavLib
Wöchentliches Unterhaltungs-Blatt für den Land-Commissariats-Bezirk Germersheim	1833–1834	GooBook
Wochenzeitung für Kinder im Magdeburger Land	1928–1931	FES
Wohlstand für Alle	1907–1914	A-Bib
Wohlstand für Alle	1907–1914	Anarch
Wormser Sport=Zeitung	1926–1929	UDARM
Wormser Tageblatt	1893–1907	UDARM
Wormser Zeitung	1838–1851; 1853–1876	UDARM
Wormser Zeitung	1914–1918	Worms
Würzburger Abendblatt	1848–1873	GooBook
Würzburger Anzeiger	1862–1868	GooBook
Würzburger Diözesanblatt	1855–2006	BavLib
Würzburger Intelligenzblatt	1805–1806; 1810–1814	GooBook
Würzburger Regierungsblatt	1806; 1809	GooBook
Würzburger Stadt- und Landbote	1873	GooBook
Würzburger Tagblatt	1857	GooBook
Ybbser Zeitung	1912–1918; 1920–1937	ANNO
Ynnsbruckische Mittwochige Ordinari-Zeitung	1765	GooBook

Title	Dates	Key
Zabrzer (Hindenburger) Kreisblatt	1921–1922	ZEFYS
Zabrzer Kreis-Blatt	1907–1915	ZEFYS
Zeitbilder	1918–1934	ZEFYS
Zeitblatt für die Angelegenheiten der Lutherischen Kirche	1851	GooBook
Zeitschrift des Österreichischen Ingenieur-und Architekten-Vereins	1906–1915	UCOT
Zeitschrift des Österreichischen Ingenieur-Vereins	1900–1917	UCOT
Zeitschrift für Demographie und Statistik der Juden [Alte Folge]	1905–1923 15 y; gaps	CompMem
Zeitschrift für Demographie und Statistik der Juden [Neue Folge]	1924–1927; 1930–1931	CompMem
Zeitschrift für deutsche Mythologie und Sittenkunde	1853; 1855; 1859	Bethel
Zeitschrift für die Geschichte der Juden in der Tschechoslowakei	1930–1934; 1938	CompMem
Zeitschrift für die Geschichte der Juden in Deutschland	1887–1937 13 y; gaps	CompMem
Zeitschrift für die Wissenschaft der Juden	1823	CompMem
Zeitschrift für Schul-Geographie	1880–1911	ANNO
Zeitschriften-Musterung	1839–1843	SLUB
Zeitung … Im Jhaar einkommen und wöchentlich zusammen getragen worden = Frischmanns Berichte	1622	ZEFYS
Zeitung auß Deutschlandt, Welschlandt, Franckreich, Böhmen, Hungarn, Niederlandt und andern Orten = Frischmanns Berichte	1619–1620	ZEFYS
Zeitung auß Wormbs	1621	DiLibri
Zeitung der 10. Armee	1915–1918	UHEID

Title	Dates	Key
Zeitung der freien Stadt Frankfurt	1819–1831	UFFM
Zeitung des Großherzogthums Frankfurt	1811–1813	GooBook
Zeitung des Landsturm-Infanterie-Bataillon Zittau	1915	France
Zeitung des Vereins deutscher Eisenbahn-Verwaltungen	1900	GooBook
Zeitung deutscher Bergleute	1890–1892	FES
Zeitung für den deutschen Adel	1840–1844	GooBook
Zeitung für die Jugend	1806	UHEID
Zeitung für Einsiedler	1808	UHEID
Zeitung für Feuerlöschwesen	1868–1873	GooBook
Zeitung für Landwirtschaft	1877–1904	ANNO
Zeitung so im ... Jahr von Wochen zu Wochen colligirt und zusammen getragen worden = Frischmanns Berichte	1623–1625	ZEFYS
Zeitungszeugen	1933–1945	Zzgn
Zentral- und Bezirks Amtsblatt für Elsaß-Lothringen	1883–1918	BavLib
Zentral- und Bezirks Amtsblatt für Elsaß-Lothringen	1884–1904	GooBook
Zentral- und Bezirks Amtsblatt für Elsaß-Lothringen	1914–1918	France
Zentralblatt für Bauverwaltung	1930	ZLB
Zentralorgan der deutschen Brauer	1892–1893	FES
Zion	1929–1938	CompMem

Title	Dates	Key
Znaimer Tagblatt	1898–1919; 1939–1944	ANNO
Znaimer Wochenblatt	1858–1919	ANNO
Zniner Zeitung	1891–1920 20 y; gaps	Euro
Zollämter- und Finanzwacht-Zeitung	1888–1917	ANNO
Zuger Nachrichten	1886–1900	Switz
Zuger Volksblatt	1861–1900	Switz
Zugerisches Kantonsblatt	1849–1858	Switz
Zülpicher Anzeiger	1867–1868	UBONN
Zürcherisches Wochenblatt	1803–1842	GooBook
Zweibrücker Tagblatt	1869–1870	GooBook
Zweibrücker Zeitung	1832–1833; 1871–1872	GooBook
Zweybrückische Zeitung	1786	GooBook
Zweybrückisches Wochenblatt (and variants)	1767–1870 42 y; major gaps	GooBook
Zwischen Maas und Mosel	1916–1918	France
Zwischen-Akt	1859–1871	ANNO

CPSIA information can be obtained
at www.ICGtesting.com
Printed in the USA
FFHW012037111118
49326050-53593FF